D0850006

Mark Twain: Social Philosopher

Mark Twain:
Social Philosopher

Louis J. Budd

KENNIKAT PRESS
Port Washington, N. Y./London

MARK TWAIN: SOCIAL PHILOSOPHER

Copyright © 1962 by Indiana University Press
Published in 1973 by Kennikat Press by
arrangement with Indiana University Press
Library of Congress Catalog Card No.: 72-85286
ISBN 0-8046-1691-4

Manufactured by Taylor Publishing Company   Dallas, Texas

I've been a statesman without salary for many years, and I have accomplished great and widespread good.

Foreword

THIS BOOK points up the richness of Mark Twain's interest in politics, measures the aptness and force of his topical writings, and above all shows how directly his major books reflected many current questions.

To do so I have drawn heavily on his newspaper columns and personal letters. These day to day spot judgments often modified his generalities or revealed his unstated premises, which turn out to fit—with reasonable neatness—into the framework of nineteenth-century Liberalism. Therefore, from here on I use Liberal or Liberalism to mean only those political and economic ideas favored by the urban middle-class, which was still clearly distinct at least from the masses without a profession or investments in a small business, real estate, or corporation stock. Whatever its impact abroad, in later nineteenth-century America this movement of ideas fell short of what modern hindsight would consider a safely progressive pace. Still I hope I have showed that some of Twain's topical writing is still interesting even today and that his politics followed a coherent pattern that made solid sense to most of his contemporaries.

To put Twain fully in his context I have followed the order of his career. This is also the best way to avoid the common error of interweaving passages from widely separate periods and to show instead what was most on his mind as he wrote each of his major books. During his long life, society changed with at least average speed and his ideas made responsive shifts, some of them just as crucial as the plunges into pessimism that spoiled the serenity of his sunset years. Even in those years, though he never revised his map of society fast enough, his hunger for the truth could drive him to fresh insights that were brilliant rather than glowering. For entertainment it is sensible to prefer the younger Twain; for challenging bursts of vision it is better to take the older Twain—but in a perspective that reaches backward for both continuity and contrast.

To round out the perspective I have also taken up, now and then, the evolution of Twain's ideas about history and religion, which fell for him into an intricate and central triad with politics. Most critics tiptoe around the fact that only the lesser part of what he published qualifies as belles lettres by modern standards. Perhaps the San Francisco wits of the mid-1860's were right in tagging him a moralist; as he looked back over his life he indicated as much several times. But when he tested a moral principle he demanded that it work on political cases. Likewise, his interest in any segment of the past always included its political forms, which he restlessly compared with those of his own day. In other words Twain's politics united so deeply and widely with his other interests as to become an important avenue for exploring the whole range of his thought.

I hope that, in tracing the roots and branches of his politics, I have not made Twain sound untypically solemn. Both in his private and public life he could often be relaxed or even recklessly playful. But G. K. Chesterton made a shrewd distinction: "While irresponsibility was the energy in his writings, an almost excessive responsibility was the energy in his character." Sometimes the heaviest clowning sprang only from a fear that the public would think he took himself too seriously. When he said in 1901 that he had been a "statesman without salary for many years," he proclaimed a sober fact while apologizing lightly for being a gadfly; when he went on to claim that he had "accomplished great and widespread good," he coolly triggered the laugh because it might build up and explode in his face. Even when he was not using burlesque or irony as a cautious mask he could exploit their disguises almost too well. I have tried to remember that his hoax about the Empire City "massacre" was not the last pitfall he built for literal-minded readers.

However, Twain left plenty of evidence for an accurate map of his political mind at least. The cheerful scholars who screen his books for nuggets to enrich our democratic tradition have to brush aside much gritty skepticism, and the opposite school who expose him as a hypocritical profiteer on the Gilded Age could easily find that he never held the attitudes he is accused of betraying. And anybody who, without taking political sides, yet praises Twain as unshakably American must pass over much that will puzzle and irritate the star-spangled admirer who reads him with care.

The most popular picture of Twain puts him in pioneer swaddling clothes, even though Andrew Jackson did not get all the votes in the newest towns and John Marshall Clemens would have stiffly resented hearing his sons called wild horses from the canebrake. Actually, Orion Clemens became almost a parody of frontier virtues, and though brother Sam quickly showed some traits that the West is eager to claim—easygoing manners, hatred of silk-stocking pretense, and love for the racy vernacular—in the first chapter of *The Gilded Age* he drew backwoods folk who fall ridiculously short of epic vigor and especially sneered at their disdain for more cultured ways. In spite of Twain's trouble with the parlor mores of Hartford it is past time to stop sighing over him as a frontiersman caged by respectability.

His career as a tireless though amateur statesman for Liberalism weighs heavily against any theory that the real Twain was a repressed spirit or that he was weakly enmeshed in nostalgic dreams. Long before he tried his hand at fiction he was a livewire journalist, and his political writings, keyed to the latest headline, often aimed to shape the next event. And when he raised his personal goals he assumed that a major function of literature is to judge man's current social life in all its phases.

L. J. B.

Acknowledgments

The American Philosophical Society, with a grant from its Penrose Fund, made it possible for me to travel to Berkeley, California, and use the Mark Twain Papers. The Duke University Research Council has unfailingly supported my project with grants for travel and microfilm.

The librarians of Yale University and the University of California, Berkeley, were kind enough to let me use their facilities freely. I am also grateful for the help extended to me at home through the Duke University Library, which has bought Twain items I needed. I am grateful above all to Thomas G. Chamberlain who, acting for the trustees of the Mark Twain Estate, let me study the Mark Twain Papers, which were then made available by Professor Henry Nash Smith and Mr. Frederick Anderson, his assistant, more generously and helpfully than one could have hoped for.

My thanks are due to Samuel C. Webster and to the heirs of M. A. DeWolfe Howe for allowing me to quote from, respectively, *Mark Twain, Business Man* and *Memories of a Hostess*. For permission to quote from unpublished materials I am indebted to the librarians and trustees of the Henry W. and Albert A. Berg Collection of the New York Public Library, the Yale Collection of American Literature, and the manuscript collections at Harvard University, and—of course —the Mark Twain Papers. It should be clearly understood that the Mark Twain Company retains copyright over the passages that I use from previously unpublished letters or manuscripts by Twain.

Professor Arlin Turner of Duke University kindly offered to read my manuscript and made incisive, stimulating suggestions. Finally, I want to thank Isabelle M. Budd, my wife, for valuable counsel from first to last; without her self-sacrifice, patience, and ever-present sense of humor this book could not have been written.

L. J. B.

Contents

Illustrations

Oh, your Independent *is a consistent, harmless, non-committal sheet. I never saw a paper of that non-committal name that wasn't.*

ONE

Political Apprentice

HARDLY PAST BOYHOOD when he broke into the columns of his brother Orion's newspaper, Mark Twain was to write for almost sixty years and leave rich, full evidence as to what he thought about politics. But even his first scraps of print do not fit the notion that he was raised on a primitive frontier. If nothing else they are a reminder that many of the families who fanned out over Missouri brought along the patterns and ideas of the older sections. Besides the printing press Twain's boyhood town had schools, debating societies, and jails. There is little chance that his father bothered to carry a rifle or an axe across the Mississippi. There is proof, however, that an unabridged dictionary was part of their skimpy baggage when Sam and Orion Clemens bounced across the plains in a stagecoach in 1861.

Hannibal had quickly outgrown not only the cultural poverty but also the raw equality of the frontier. Both Tom

Sawyer and Huck Finn saw obvious social classes in their
village, even among the whites, and Twain's parents firmly
ranked themselves among the better families of Hannibal.
Though small slaveholders indeed, they had once dreamed
of becoming gentry—recent estimates put their holdings of
undeveloped land in Tennessee at close to 100,000 acres.
Local tradition there has it that the father was too much
of a would-be aristocrat for his neighbors and that the early
chapters of *The Gilded Age* reflect family memories of his
conflict with the backwoods community. When he prided
himself on his Virginia breeding he did not, however, claim
political kinship with Thomas Jefferson. Born in an age when,
as Twain said later, a man "called his children after his most
revered literary and historical idols," John Marshall Clemens
was named after the rigorously conservative chief justice and
would have been a Federalist himself if the party had not dis-
integrated in the early 1800's.

Without much sense of difference he became a stout Whig
instead: the year of his death he was not only the Whig candidate for clerk of the local circuit court but also a delegate
to the party's state convention. In spite of much resentment
toward a seemingly cold and rigid father, Twain never reacted against his political ideas. This simple fact has been
overlooked because most of our histories treat the Whig
party as incidental to the age of Jackson; but, rising to protect the rights of property and talent and to accuse the Democrats of appealing to poverty and the uneducated masses, the
Whigs figured as a major party for almost twenty years. Under their straddle on many issues and their sectional differences they agreed that property and political power must
continue to go together, that the majority can too easily vote
for the wrong side, and that the Constitution and the courts
are sacred, vital bulwarks against the gullible mob. For the
rest of his life Twain would keep echoing these axioms, sometimes varying their emphases but always true to their spirit.

Young Sam learned not only the principles but also the

facts of political life. Hannibal had its rich share of party barbecues and parades dogged by excited boys, affairs that were also natural fodder for the local press to which he became apprenticed around the age of thirteen. This newspaper training helps to explain his lifelong pull toward matters of current interest and his habit of choosing subjects most on the public's mind. But it should be realized fully that nineteenth-century journalism was intensely political in spirit. Editors were expected to be partisan; in turn they expected to win or lose readers as editorial policy shifted and to move higher in the councils of their party if circulation went up. When Orion Clemens bought the Hannibal *Journal* he knew very well that it was a Whig organ and faithfully kept it so with the glowing accounts of Whig doings or the standard sneers at Democratic chuckle-headedness that his readers were counting on.

If relevant at all, Sam's own fitful contributions to Orion's *Journal* were in keeping with its allegiances. On September 16, 1852, his "Blabbing Government Secrets" wildly satirized Missouri's Democratic governor and legislature for wasting time on bills that expensively did petty favors for friends. In the same issue, with an eye on the current presidential campaign, his "Editorial Agility" ridiculed the owner of the rival *Missouri Courier* as "this soft-soaper of Democratic rascality . . . this father of NOTHING." The next spring Sam helped carry on a quarrel with a neighboring newspaper over railroad routes and other matters that verged on partisan squabbling.[1] Though it is unrealistic to conclude that he took no time for girls and practical jokes and studied every letter by subscribers who signed as "Junius" or "Vox Populi," his term as Orion's unpaid assistant gave him an early glimpse of what goes on behind the façade of campaign oratory.

Between 1853 and 1857, as he wandered from city to city, Sam still wrote for Orion's newspapers. But he recorded no comment in the running debate about the limits for slave territory, perhaps because he heartily wished like most Whigs that it would quiet down. Clearly following their tactic of smoothing over the issue when they could not ignore it, he was especially vocal instead about the beauties of patriotism, and his travel letters from Philadelphia exclaimed over the places "dear to every American."[2] In Washington this note deepened into the Whigs' keening about a Götterdämmerung when he described a weakling Senate whose "halls no longer echo the words of Clay, or Webster or Calhoun." Still, revealingly, he paid greater respect to the more patrician Senate, which was not yet directly elective, than to the House of Representatives where "nearly every man seemed to have something weighing on his mind on which the Salvation of the Republic depended, and which he appeared very anxious to ease himself of."

Not yet twenty years of age, Sam was as willing as most to guide the public. Soon after gravitating to St. Louis in 1854 he issued the first of a long string of attacks on policemen, this time doubting "if the man is now living that ever caught one at a riot." He also dutifully reviewed the misdeeds of an Irish bookkeeper at the local Democratic office. Despite these bursts of righteous civic spirit it is a surprise to find Twain's comment, made twenty years afterward, that he had then been a "callow fool . . . imagining he is remolding the world and is entirely capable of doing it right."[3] This self-contempt was most likely due to his mature guilt over drifting toward the Know Nothings in the mid-1850's, a course followed by many Whigs as their party's collapse became obvious. Though he later jumbled the details confusingly, it is fair to say that he watched some nativist riots in St. Louis without disapproval.

Sam's nativist bile had shown up even in his Hannibal days with the play that his occasional editing gave to reports of brawls among the Irish immigrants, and his travel letters, by anti-Semitic asides and sneers at the polyglot tenement children of New York City, proved that his Americanism had become rather exclusive. He had also left home well-infected with the rabid hatred of Roman Catholicism that touched most Protestants but raged among the Presbyterians, the sect to which the Clemens family belonged. As elsewhere, Hannibal newspapers, by all means including Orion's *Journal*, often carried tense reminders about the horrors of the Inquisition, the sins of the European clergy, and the Romish drive for power. The deepest point of all this hubbub was tersely stated by the *Journal* on August 10, 1853: "We do not attack the *Religion* of the Church of Rome, but her *Politics*."[4] Sam could not help knowing that anti-Catholicism was one of Orion's few genuinely fixed ideas. In fact Sam could not help agreeing, and he wrote from St. Louis on February 28, 1855, "A new Catholic paper (bad luck to it) is . . . soon to be established, for the purpose of keeping the Know Nothing organ straight."

Twain's matured humanity makes an encouraging contrast with such crude prejudices. But its slow growth had not even started as yet. In his Snodgrass letters of 1856-57, which showed little growth of any kind, there was praise for the burghers of Cincinnati who "took a hoss whip and castigated" a profiteering Jew. The name of Thomas Jefferson Snodgrass that he invented for the brash and dully lecherous lout who was the comic relief in these letters should also puzzle anybody who believes that Sam was a frontier democrat from his birth onward. To oblige this pipedream the name should have been Alexander Hamilton Periwig or John Calhoun Ravenswood. Casting further doubt on his inbred love for natural rights, Sam next responded to the dream of a new slave empire in South America and started for the Amazon River country with the fuzzy hope of founding a coca plantation.

His service to expansionism was delayed by his stumbling into the pilot's trade on the Mississippi, which was so absorbing that from 1857 to 1861 he wrote almost nothing for print —a silence he would never match again. But his mind did not forget all the channels it learned in Hannibal. As he shut-

tled between St. Louis and New Orleans, Sam often heard
the case for the cotton kingdom expounded; if he had turned
out a flaming "secesh" it would not be surprising. However,
in the 1860 election he argued for the National Constitu-
tional Union party, composed mainly of former Whigs and
Know Nothings who straddled the slavery question by appealing to the symbols the new party label invoked. After
the election, by still honoring the Stars and Stripes in spite
of feeling drawn toward Jefferson Davis rather than Lincoln,
he was actually clinging to his old Whiggish devotion to
national unity while betraying how his choice would fall
when gunfire forced the issue.

Though Twain said much later that he joined the Confederate cause in 1861 out of social pressure, he may well
have felt a lift of enthusiasm at first, and the attitudes behind the Quintus Curtius Snodgrass letters could easily have
been his. Whatever his later vagueness and cheerful unreli-
ability about some of the details, it seems clear that he limped
through Missouri underbrush and swamps for a few weeks
in the belief that he was serving with Confederate guerrillas.
Then he deserted, probably reminding himself that he had
voted against sectional conflict in 1860. At least he did not
have to justify his desertion to Orion, who had moved toward the position that slavery was morally wrong and soon
found himself sent out as secretary to the governor of Nevada. In fleeing west with his brother, Sam had plenty of
company as, throughout the war years, many thousands of
able-bodied men crossed the plains in the same direction.
Some wanted to save their skins, some thought army pay
too small for their habits; others went because they had no
heart for shooting at either the blue or the gray. Sam, it can
be hoped, pretty much fits in this last group. Certainly it is
wrong to suspect he deserted his hollow lieutenancy because
he did not care what happened in the momentous struggle.
Before long he plunged willingly into much less vital affairs
of government. As more of an unconscious omen than a legal

fact the Nevada Directory for 1861-62 listed him as assistant secretary of state.

Arriving with even grander plans than helping to run the new territory, Sam first joined the hordes who were intent not on pleaching a sagebrush bower of democracy but on making a fortune and then heading home or building a mansion in San Francisco. They were as far from the legendary trailblazer as Sam was from raking in a bonanza on his own hook. Corporate money and methods had moved into Washoe after the first wave of lucky prospectors, and most of the men who ended up with a fortune made it by manipulating stocks or serving a company in some broad-angled or devious way. But, fresh from his climb into the aristocracy of the pilothouse, Sam naïvely expected to make good through luck and pluck in dime-novel fashion.

After a futile year he settled in Virginia City, which was already equipped—crudely but adequately—with hospitals, libraries, schools, and a refreshingly capable brand of journalism. It was this last tool of civilization that rescued him, at his own prompting, from the ragged edge of the mining frontier. By July of 1862 he was asking Orion to find him an outlet as a correspondent, and by September he was working on the *Territorial Enterprise*. The young elders of the *Enterprise* had liked his "Josh" letters, particularly one that satirized the oratory of the local chief justice. Quite possibly they also valued his link with Orion who could have swung much more weight in Nevada if he had known how to. Instead, when Sam's self-confidence bounced back on his *Enterprise* salary he appointed himself the political head of the family, a position he was never to resign.

His job on the *Enterprise* and his knowledge of Orion's problems made Sam an insider as, without a settled public to keep watch, most of the territory's officeholders exploited their powers over a boom economy. Later he described to his fiancée a " 'Committee of the Whole' in one of these one-horse State Legislatures, early in the Session when they keep sounding the lobby's financial pulse on certain bills, by 'reporting progress' and 'asking leave to sit again' till the lobby grows frantic & disgusted." Besides the flagrant bribery he learned all about the routine bartering of votes and the niceties of passing out jobs. A small plum that came his own way was the sinecure of recording secretary, at a salary of three hundred dollars, for the annual fair of the Washoe Agricultural, Mining, and Mechanical Association. For a while he gathered another windfall of seven dollars a day from the public orchard as legislative reporter.

He also saw shady vistas to his newspaper job and bragged that he had learned how to "levy black-mail" on the mining companies. Still his personal budget never indicated he was grabbing much extra money this way or any other. Instead, managing to make his position almost official at times, he enjoyed the sense of power and grandly claimed once that he could get the legislature to pass any bill he favored.[5] This sounds like sheer fantasy but he was deep in day to day realities because, soon after joining the *Enterprise*, he had been assigned to cover the capitol in Carson City. In old age he distorted the sober nature of this assignment by stressing the margin of irreverence with which he had carried it out and by reminiscing that he started using a short pen name to save time for a legislature "obstructed" with complaints against him from the floor. But, making his new name appropriate at once, he had sustained two roles. His weekly letter for the Sunday trade was often playful and sometimes irresponsible. Day by day however he ground out factual accounts that are too colorless for full reprinting even now when almost any Twain item can find a second life.

Far from feeling trapped in a dull job he took sides whenever possible, on both his plodding and his irreverent days. Because the Union party had come to dominate Nevada until the end of the Civil War, he said little about Republicans and Democrats for the time being. But, usually following the line marked out by the *Enterprise* editorials, he crisply judged the factional moves within the Union party. Bred to the tradition of partisan journalism, he sneered at the Carson City *Independent* as a "harmless" sheet with a telltale name: "Even the religious papers bearing it give a decided, whole-souled support to neither the Almighty nor the Devil."[6] Without strain he avoided being harmless himself, and his fellow reporters in Carson City gave him credit for it by making him "governor" of the Third House, a mock-legislature which let off the irritation built up from watching the sagebrush politicos stumble through their sessions.[7] So far as biting contempt for the demagogue was useful to membership in the Third House, Twain's Whig background came in handy. That he should be chosen its governor or chief satirist testified to his growing reputation for wit. The choice also suggests that he passed as a man of political savvy, capable of seeing what really went on behind the scene.

This rise to local prestige both marked and intensified a shift from routine partisanship to waspish criticism. Though most of the dispatches from Twain's first stint of legislative reporting are now unavailable, it seems they were favorable on the whole and their occasional bursts of humor were relatively impersonal, as in a burlesque on the overplus of toll-road charters. Then his sharpening talent for invective began to flash more and more recklessly, often even cutting across his factional loyalties. The Third House sketch ridiculed William M. Stewart, an imperious corporation lawyer, longer and more acidly than anybody else though he was close to the *Enterprise* editors. Nor did it pass beyond insult by obviously inverting reality, as when Twain later told friends about his wife's domineering harshness. His charges that Stewart had been giving the same "infernal speech for the last thirty days" and had wept too often and insincerely over the "poor miner" struck many Washoeites as mordantly accurate. Though it was well after Twain had started using his famous pen name, Stewart eventually rose to criticize the bumptious *Enterprise* reporter from the floor of the temporary capitol.

However, Twain was not ready to turn mugwump, as can

be seen from his changing stand on a constitution that was offered to Nevada voters. Since the *Enterprise* announced at first that it was favorable, he helped call for ratification and on December 30, 1863, published his least admirable Washoe columns, a grossly unfair attack on a meeting of bolters from the Union party and against the constitution. Deriding the audience as "noble human soda-bottles, so to speak effervescing with the holy gas of pure unselfish patriotism," his account reeked with its own partisan fumes. Yet he reversed himself within less than a week.[8] In a letter dated January 4, 1864, which covered "recent political movements" for a New York paper, he charged that the blueprint for statehood had "unfortunate defects which debarred it from assuming to be an immaculate conception," and he concluded, "Wherefore, when men say, 'Let our constitution slide for the present,' we say Amen." This was not simply another private desertion: Stewart had organized a drive to reject the constitution he helped write. The best guess as to his motives concerns a proposed tax on undeveloped mines and, significantly, Twain's reversed argument featured a criticism of that clause. Because the source materials for this period of Nevada history are surprisingly thin, the exact truth may never be known, but it looks as if a sardonic opinion of Stewart's character had not kept Twain from serving him—in 1867 Twain would jump at the chance to become his private secretary.

Of course Twain never enjoyed wearing somebody else's collar and must have felt more relieved than happy when this constitution went down to defeat on January 19. But he was soon reminded that politics can have rewarding moments. On January 27 he got a gold watch—inscribed to "Governor Mark Twain"—from Theodore Winters, a major stockholder in the Ophir Silver Mining Company, and Alexander M. Baldwin, Stewart's partner.[9] To call this a payoff would be unfair. The watch could mean merely that Winters and Baldwin had enjoyed his columns and amateur lectures. Whatever it meant concerning the past, it certainly suggested they wanted a friendly beam from the *Enterprise's* rising star in the future. So did Governor James W. Nye, it seems. The following March he gave Twain one of the "coveted notarial appointments" and—perhaps unknowingly—ended the chance that Twain would spruce up and print his speech burlesquing the governor's official style.

This was not a slim chance. During the third and last session of the territorial legislature Twain got recklessly personal, especially in backing up a campaign to move the capital of Nevada to Virginia City. This shift naturally involved rich spoils, and the raiding forces, who included Twain's employer, used every fair or foul maneuver while the other side fought back just as desperately. In the hardest slugging Twain leveled charges about the "stream of iniquitous private franchises" flowing from the Carson City gang and went on to name bills and expected rakeoffs so specifically that any half alert Washoeite knew exactly who was being accused. Three days after his sharpest barrage the enemy moved to abolish the *per diem* bonus to legislative reporters. Twain, who took this as a direct attack on his supply lines, clearly had become embroiled again in guerrilla warfare but fought with better heart than he had shown in Missouri swamps. A neat example of how he shifted tactics as strategy demanded lies in his comments on a bill to grant twenty thousand dollars to the Sierra Seminary, a private school in Carson City with about forty students.[10] On January 14, 1864, he held that the "money could not be more judiciously expended"; on February 16 he called the school "a private affair," hinted at boodling, and suggested support for a public mining college instead; on April 25 he had the gall to refer to the Sierra Seminary bill as a "really worthy measure."

Though there was some good humor evident when the session closed, his final tour of duty in Carson City killed any hope that observing Washoe's lawmakers might ease his doubts about the kind of men the majority is likely to pick. After this his opinion of elective bodies was irredeemably low and, Twainlike, he only watched for better ways to insult them. Perhaps the wittiest was: "It could probably be shown by facts and figures that there is no distinctly native criminal class except Congressmen." The most sweeping was to call them the "smallest minds and the selfishest souls and the cowardliest hearts that God makes." The era of Grantism solidified this contempt but its first full vehemence must be listed among the effects of his westward swing.

As *The Gilded Age* proved later, his criticism of venal legislators did not push on to emphasize that men of property often suggested the payoff and made a fat profit on the deal. He saw the bribetaker as a cause rather than a symptom, as a seedy predator who searched out victims rather than—many times at least—merely saying yes to an offered price. Twain's assumption that Washoe citizens "whose pecuniary condition is comfortable" would not stoop to graft pointed clearly toward his faith both in the political morals of the wealthy and in the broader notion that money is probably a mark of sterling virtues. He could not help admiring or deferring to those who amassed it and he showed a revealing humility in the debate over the first constitution: "I listened as one having no taxable property and never likely to have . . . as one having no tangible right to take an interest."[11] Like his Whig and Federalist forebears he would always assume that a man's economic stake in society was an important measure of his political rights.

Except for a blast at the telegraph monopoly that overcharged everybody in Washoe, Twain had no harsh words for the big companies either. His restlessness under mouthings about the "poor miner" came from a dislike of Stewart's hypocrisy, not from a sense that the corporations were encircling the lone prospector. Several times he squarely served their needs by praising that open sesame for high-riding methods, the principle that individuals should not be held financially responsible for corporate fiascos. Badly misread to begin with, his famous hoax about the Empire City massacre, which has later been said to indict the speculator, aimed only to spike the claims of San Francisco newspapers that investors were much less likely to be swindled on California than Washoe mining stocks.[12]

It is known that Twain himself took away no fortune, honest or dishonest, from Nevada. But he left with unshaken faith in a simple profit system and its leaders and was worried instead that its horny-handed followers might use their vote to penalize the successful few. The argument that mining firms were threatened with heavy taxes weighed heavily with him against the first constitution. Ignoring the facts as well as his private reasons, in *Roughing It* he went so far as to claim he left the Comstock because he thought the revised constitution that was actually adopted would "destroy the 'flush times'" after carrying against the wish of the property owners and by the votes of the "folks who had nothing to lose." Economic democracy was never one of Twain's emphases. And all his life he schemed hard to become somebody who had plenty to lose.

The actual causes behind his exit furnish a still better example of how politics affected his personal life. That he found himself hotly beleaguered almost overnight indicates smoldering fires; some influential people had been waiting for the brash reporter to make a vulnerable move. It is surely relevant that the committee of indignant ladies who helped to hound him out of the territory was headed by Mrs. W. K. Cutler, whose Sierra Seminary had suffered from his opinions only weeks before. It is also relevant that the climactic duel of insulting notes was fought with the staff of the Virginia City *Daily Union*, which more and more opposed the *Enterprise* as Nevadans started drifting away from Union party harmony and toward the Democratic and Republican poles.[13] It is both relevant and appropriate that his exit was connected with the Sanitary Fund—the Unionist forerunner of the Red Cross.

During his first year or two of Nevada life Twain had

lingering Confederate sympathies, which he could nurse without feeling lonesome. When Northern armies started to do better and local opinion turned in their favor, he followed along, but seemingly he did not put himself above suspicion like Orion Clemens, who had emerged strongly loyal to the government under which he held office. Never confessing he had once shouldered a rifle, he kept essentially quiet on sectional issues and in the spring of 1864 told his sister, "I stipulated [recently] . . . that I should never be expected to write editorials about politics or eastern news. I take no sort of interest in those matters."[14] Of course he took interest in them and his job demanded it. He meant that, soured by his experiences in Carson City, he would write no more party-line squibs and still did not care to comment suitably on the war. About the same time however he published a burlesque on Unionist anger at the idea that the Negro was not potentially the white's equal.[15] This latent Southern racism made possible his fatally clumsy wisecrack that local money for the Sanitary Fund would go to a "miscegenation society."

The cheering at his sudden exit from Washoe was mostly raucous but he landed lightly because he rated high in San Francisco, where the magazines had already used some of his essay-skits like "The Great Prize Fight." Though this piece is brushed aside today as an empty farce, it took its point from a recent struggle between two contenders for governor of California; its fantasy about a "fight which had never occurred, and was never likely to occur" poked fun at the fierce namecalling before the undercover deal that cozily settled the matter. Increasingly alert to the hollowness of much political invective, Twain soon devised—with touches worthy of his later skill—a similar sketch about a Calaveras election in which the gullible populace seethes over the merits of rival sewing machines while the leading orators for the "machines" coolly fraternize behind the excitement.[16]

Unfortunately, Twain could not yet earn a living from the

magazines, so he tried to take up the routine of a city reporter. Both his rising habit of unbridled satire and his convictions made this an unhappy move. In old age he still detested the San Francisco *Call* for having refused to let him criticize anti-Chinese brutality because its Irish subscribers would be offended. To this muzzling of honest anger he traced his lackadaisical work for the *Call*, claiming that he had felt a "deep shame" over his predicament and soon lost interest in this "paper of the poor." Though he elsewhere gave a droller reason for quitting, he obliquely reinforced the sober account by sneering in 1866 that "the *Call* circulates chiefly among a class who don't own much city property and don't pay any taxes."[17] Obviously its readers were not his favorite audience. He had fully kept his liking for the popular catch-phrase, "No Irish need apply," and had also kept his related contempt for the city masses and their "trundle-bed trash." Studiedly anti-sentimental, his harsh portrait of "Uncle Lige" in 1865 wasted no sympathy on the poor.

Twain managed before long to establish himself on a wider basis than that of city reporter. The range of this freelancing was great, its tone exuberantly uneven. However, patient analysis has been revealing more and more social point behind more and more of his wild sketches. And at times he gave straight advice, especially after he began writing regularly to the *Territorial Enterprise* as its Pacific Coast correspondent. Two letters—again among those passed over for reprinting even today—pleaded the case for greenback money as a way to ease the credit pinch, and he was even more emphatic against a proposed law forcing any company that owned mines in Nevada to set up its home office there:

It is an important affair to have the control of one's own house, or one's own family affairs, or one's own mine, and when you pass that law you roll back the tide of eastern capital which is now setting so steadily toward Nevada. . . . You can make those mines flourish and you can make money like smoke out of them, and open up a vast field for well-paid labor and a profitable commerce if you take pains to make the road straight and the passage easy for eastern capital.[18]

Equating a man's house, however small, with a corporation's mine, however large, belonged to the axioms that tolerated the robber barons, and eagerness to clear the road for capital would bring the west many problems and finally the Populists.

Having formed the habit of working close to home, wherever that might be, Twain also had advice for San Franciscans wrestling with the problem of organizing a large city. Too free with his superlatives but dead serious he even went out of his way to defend a paid fire department as the "biggest thing that was ever done for San Francisco and the best thing for her finances, her character and her good morals." This quaint enthusiasm made sense at the moment to businessmen who had disliked the expensive volunteer system because it pumped more political gravy than water; in spite of his sprees at the Cliff House, Twain faithfully pulled with the "taxpayer's party" that wanted the city run honestly.[19] To this end he intensified the grumbling he had started in St. Louis and Virginia City about the paid guardians of law and order.

His campaign of abuse, which continued into the 1880's, was not so eccentric as it seems today. Nor did it depend only on his humane outrage because patrolmen winked at the crowds stoning Chinese laundrymen. More basically it reflected the practical-minded complaint that the police had failed to protect the profits of honest initiative from the riff-raff spawned by urban life. Too often, as in San Francisco during the 1860's, the chief of police was still an elective stalwart of the city hall ring and chose assistants better at ward-heeling than their salaried job. Too often the police had ties with the underworld or else stole on their own. Because Chief Martin G. Burke and many of his minions were both Irish and Democrats, Twain ran the gamut of charges with heightened pleasure and worked harder to find fresh variations, which could get farfetched. Except for his note in a scrapbook it would not be clear any more that "A Remarkable Dream," a wild flight of comedy, was another "shameful satire" on Burke's gray-coated retinue.[20]

Twain's savage abuse of the police has overshadowed his arguments for greenbacks or laws favorable to corporations, partly because it gave wide play to his talent for invective and is therefore more readable today. In his day it was so readable and aroused so much comment that he suddenly found he had overreached himself again. There is a theory that Chief Burke's hostility forced him to hide out for a while at Jackass Hill.[21] Considering the dates of the newly recovered letters to the *Enterprise*, it is likely instead that any pressure from Burke helped to hurry Twain toward the Sandwich Islands early in 1866.

In leaving for new horizons Twain could look back over a long, rich trail already proving his concern with public affairs. About a fourth of what he published before 1866 treated such matters. Though the jumping frog story has emerged as the peak of his writing in the West, he did not feel that a "villainous backwoods sketch" showed what he was really capable of doing. This complaint was not simply a sign of his still vague ambition to write literature; he took himself seriously as an overseer of the public conscience and yearned to set it straight. When he talked about being "interested" in something besides journalism he did not mean to slur his topical writing. And in spite of his obvious tendency to get out of hand, editors apparently thought him well suited to cover the large segment of the nineteenth-century newspaper world that politics pre-empted.

His breezy way of covering it should not be misread as indifference or naïveté. The clowning with which "Concerning Notaries" handled the scramble for petty office is balanced by the fact that he landed an appointment as notary

public for himself a few days later—without needing to collect signatures on a petition—and his Carson City letters
nimbly played the statehouse game of give and take in both
senses of the phrase. This does not mean he lacked principles
either, though, feeling vaguely that the issues agitated after
1861 were not the major ones, he held back from supporting
any party on national questions. Still clinging to the Whigs'
distrust of unstable majorities, he was looking for another
party that would stress the authority of the property owner.
If he had read it he did not disagree seriously with James
Madison's economic and social analysis in the Federalist Papers. If the frontier pulsed a leveling democracy into the
dusty air of Washoe, he avoided full contagion. Instead,
ironically, the crude and venal ways of the territorial government confirmed his suspicions about the results of our elective process. He had found mostly alkali beneath the sparse
grassroots of Nevada.

The discovery further soured his patriotism, already tainted by the confusing bitterness of the Civil War. Like many
of his friends Twain learned the trick of admiring the United
States from a global perspective while taking it much less
rhapsodically from the inside. When he matched it against
the royalist Old World, he glowed with pride, but in arguments limited to this country he could sneer at the flaws of
democracy almost as coldly as Alexander Hamilton. This
seeming inconsistency had a center his age saw easily. Firmly
poised between monarchy and absolute equality, he was republican rather than democratic in politics and—later—Liberal rather than liberal.

To some extent these formulas are too simple. Everybody
has a sweep of relationships—personal, social, and economic
—and seldom integrates them completely. One of Twain's
finest qualities was his unpretentious, open-hearted way of
mixing with all sorts of people he happened to meet. This
quality, apparent from the first, grew stronger in the restless
melting pot of Nevada and even earlier, to our eternal profit,

made him start to savor the vernacular tradition. But, like the antebellum humorists of the Southwest, he could still betray more contempt than warmth in his portraits of common folk such as the stupid witnesses who confused the court with "The Evidence in the Case of Smith *vs*. Jones." In a casual situation Twain was for the gallused squatter when the other choice was the dandy. In a courtroom or legislature he was already anxious for sobriety and informed, responsible behavior.

Still, more than most men, Twain eludes any rigid judgment of even his political and economic attitudes alone. The ugly extremes of the opinions he started out with were offset by signs of his maturing integrity and by fine examples of his hatred for fat-cat pretense or brutality toward the friendless. It is finally to his credit that he was not enough of an organization man to last in Nevada or San Francisco when he discussed public affairs. It is to our gain that he was nevertheless thought serious and concerned enough for an assignment to "write up the sugar interests" in the Sandwich Islands.

*I wrote to Bill Stewart today accepting his private secretaryship.
. . . When I come to think of it, I believe it can be made one of
the best paying berths in Washington.*

TWO

Acquiring Reporter

HINDSIGHT CAN SEE CLEARLY that Twain was climbing toward
success when he boarded the steamer to the Sandwich Islands
in March of 1866. Though he joined the card-playing clique
who made the best of a rough passage and though he had a
merry and perhaps rowdy time in Hawaii, he kept aware that
his assignment had a serious side. His notebooks show he arrived full of ideas on the fight that was raging over the control of trade with the natives. Far from turning lackadaisical
even in the tropics, he followed through with some letters
that were carefully discussed by the San Francisco Chamber
of Commerce.

Still unplagued by tourists, the exotic islands fascinated
Twain. His letters covered everything from volcanoes to
the hula-hula girls who swayed in perfect time. But, after
seeing how profitably the sugar planters brought in coolies
as the Hawaiian natives died off, he also discussed the beau-

ties of importing the Chinese to work the submarginal mines of the Pacific slope for five dollars a month where the whites got from eighty to a hundred; and he noted persuasively that the Central Pacific Railroad smiled on coolies as "the cheapest, the best, and most quiet, peaceable and faithful" workers to be had. He made it sound inviting for almost everybody including the displaced whites, who would graduate to better jobs. Though the unemployed who had not become timekeepers or foremen would riot within ten years against the pigtailed drudges, he was trusting to the naïve axiom that an increased labor force naturally makes for more prosperity all around.

Never likely to overlook the fight at hand, Twain quickly moved into the politics of the islands, where American planters and businessmen were increasingly nervous about their foreign rivals. He was hardly off the ship when his letters started ringing an alarm with the emphasis he could muster so easily. In another typical tactic he turned to personalities and fired heavily at Charles C. Harris, a former New Englander who had become a Hawaiian subject and ran with the pro-British faction behind the throne.[1] As a renegade from American interests and the republican tradition, Harris drew a barrage of abuse that surpassed the mark set by Twain's campaign against the chief of San Francisco police.

Showing that Twain could act responsibly even when he seemed to be cavorting beyond restraint, his columns for the Sacramento *Union* that smeared Harris still treated Hawaiian royalty with ambassadorial tact. Besides, he felt that Kamehameha V had now and then used his power wisely, especially in a decree that cut off voting rights for the unpropertied. The languorous air had not soothed Twain's irritations about full-throttle democracy. Visiting the local legislature provoked a bilious comment on all such bodies and their typical members, like the "solemn ass from the cow counties" who sleeps while the "one-horse village" lawyers gabble their "threadbare platitudes and 'give-me-liberty-or-give-me-death' buncombe." This bitterness looked back of course to what he had seen in Carson City. He was already beginning to refer to his Nevada days with hearty nostalgia but he never glossed over the failings of its politics.

Though his look at the islands often noticed only what confirmed his prejudices, the four-months jaunt was still a broadening experience. Above all it started him toward cosmopolitan balance, toward the wisdom of his final years when he measured strange customs or ideas freshly and when he brushed aside the smoky clichés of expansionism. Even in 1866, in spite of hoping for more visits by American warships to intimidate the natives, he learned that their culture had its own comfortable values, superior in some ways to the results of western progress. But his leaning toward primitivism —which later gave vitality to the rafting passages of *Huckleberry Finn*—was held back by his principled dislike for the feudal patterns beneath the surface of the natives' easygoing life. It was this dislike that decided him in favor of the Protestant missionaries; while cynical about their secondary motives, he approved their proselyting as an inroad on rigid, benighted superstitions. For the present any distrust of imperialist mechanics was overridden by his hope that American influence of every kind would stretch out toward Hawaii.

All the talk about who ought to acquire what sharpened Twain's own ambitions. Later he recalled that he got crucial advice in the islands from Anson Burlingame, who was en route to broad-gauged labors as our minister to China; at best this advice, which impressed him only because he was ripe for it, reworked the most prudential vein of Benjamin Franklin into the motto of "Never affiliate with inferiors; always climb." Though he could in time describe the islands as a refuge from modern tension, he left them with a freshened urge to rise in the world and a matching worry that he was not making the grade. Happily, he was more welcome than ever on the Pacific slopes, so he stormed over them as a lecturer and at last made enough money to go home in style.

More hopeful now about his own prospects, he rounded off his farewell lecture with a whoop of encouragement to California, luckily placed "midway between the Old World and the New" and destined to collect "tribute" from both.[2] Swelling the prophetic note to describe the uses of this tribute, he envisioned a new reign of industry rather than purple luxury:

. . . this sparsely populated land shall become a crowded hive of busy men . . . railroads shall be spread hither and thither and carry the invigorating blood of commerce to regions that are languishing now; mills and workshops, yea, and *factories* shall spring up everywhere.

It is reasonable to suspect burlesque here but none was intended.

Flourishes like this convinced the editors of the *Alta California* that, along with his increasingly skillful humor, Twain could keep western interests in mind. So he was able to make money on his trip home with the letters now collected in *Mark Twain's Travels with Mr. Brown*. But he started to turn as usual toward matters right at hand and, while triumphantly visiting his family, made copy from the drive of Missouri women to vote "along with us and the nigs."[3] His first newspaper letter (from a "husband and father") predicted a vicious campaign someday for state milliner and clowned even more broadly about the prospect of husbands ending up as wetnurses for their neglected children. Using a routine he had perfected as the wild humorist of the Pacific slopes, the next day he followed up with a barrage of fake replies from harridans who threatened varied kinds of violence before signing themselves as officers in benevolent societies of immense or minute sweep.

So far he had only been churning out salable copy. When it provoked serious answers, especially from a "Cousin Jenny" who accused men of blindly holding on to selfish prerogatives, he promised to "speak with the gravity the occasion demands." Soberly and meekly, he conceded at once that capable women could do better in many public posts then "held by third-rate ability because first-rate ability can only afford to hold offices of great emolument" and also conceded that an educated American woman would vote with "fifty times the judgment and independence exercised by stupid, illiterate newcomers from foreign lands." Though this last touch was a bad omen for his next trip abroad, such lines of argument must have reassured old friends that he had not changed completely during his five years in the far west.

His Whig and Know-Nothing suspicions undercut even the slender comfort he had given Cousin Jenny. He went on to predict that while the "good" women would second the wise males, the "ignorant foreign women would vote with the ignorant foreign men" and so the same level of candidates would win as before the suffragist dawn. Not very logically he next shifted to arguing that since the "best and wisest" women would always cling to the holy ground of the home, then the ballot would have no result—except degrading them "to a level with negroes and men." This wild stab at wit having broken his promise to talk seriously, he roared on to visions of women who would hide their right age at the polls or pass antisaloon and even anticigar laws. Then he closed:

Content yourself with your little feminine trifles—your babies, your benevolent societies and your knitting—and let your natural bosses do the voting. . . . We will let you teach school as much as you want to, and we will pay you half wages for it, too, but beware! We don't want you to crowd us too much.

Such a hash of male superiority, concession, and erratic irony most likely pleased nobody, including Twain.

Of his other freelancing during these weeks the biggest share went to a New York sporting journal, for which he whipped up some even more tasteless material. He knew he was floundering and privately shrugged off his *Alta* letters as the "stupidest" that were ever written from New York City. Its subcurrent of strange accents and languages irritated him, its tenement swarms too often struck him as "*canaille*." Only when he heard that "respectable" people escaped the grip of cholera did he relent, exclaiming:

It seems hard, but truly humiliation, hunger, persecution and death are the wages of poverty in the mighty cities of the land. . . . Honest poverty is a gem that even a King might feel proud to call his own, but I wish to sell out. . . . I wish to become rich, so that I can instruct the people and glorify honest poverty a little, like those good, kind-hearted, fat benevolent people do.

Though the ironies again interlace confusingly here and Walt Whitman would not have joked about the matter, this passage held out a false hope that Twain might see Europe humanely during the *Quaker City* tour.

The newspaper letters he wrote, which are better than *The Innocents Abroad* for telling how he reacted on the spot, make it clearer than ever that he did not measure the Old World by frontier rules of thumb.[4] Irreverent he was, particularly when some of the touted wonders fell short of their billing. But he usually respected the storied shrines—respected them so copiously that most readers today will skim on to the next zany flight, perhaps missing his typical homage to the Crusaders as the "most gallant knights that ever wielded sword." This reverence toward the past was continually jostled, however, by highly topical attitudes and interests. Furthermore, he had carried abroad his live qualms about the gallantry and good sense of mass man.

Before his quizzical scrutiny of the Holy Land crowded out other subjects, Twain's travel letters emphasized the dirt, poverty, begging, and endemic disease that showed up at the Azores and reappeared often during the rest of the trip. The key fact is that he judged all this by the current gospel of success, blaming it either on laziness or a lack of gusto for applied science.[5] Besides believing like William Graham Sumner that poverty continues to haunt only those who deserve it, he also soothed himself with the delusion that the starving masses were dully content, that they only cared for "enough to exist on;" he felt more resentment than sorrow in Palestine when the "usual assemblage of squalid humanity" hovered around the breakfasting pilgrims and doggedly watched every swallow while waiting for the scraps. It would be a relief to explain away this hardness as masking his despair over misery too widespread for the syrup of personal charity to cure. But he cheerfully reported how he pretended to believe that an "unspeakably homely old hag" who beseechingly "curtsied over and over again" was in love with him and how he offered to repay the compliment by reading his "poetic paraphrase" of the Declaration of Independence.[6]

He came painfully close to inverting all the reactions to be expected from a backwoods democrat. The bottom swarms of Paris got no more sympathy than those of Italy, Greece, or Palestine, and he said of the blighted Faubourg St. Antoine: "Here live the people who start revolutions. . . . They take as much genuine pleasure in building a barricade as they do in cutting a throat or shoving a friend into the Seine." In contrast he solemnly called Napoleon III the "greatest man in the world today" because he had revved up the "commercial prosperity" of France and "rebuilt every city . . . at no expense to commonwealth or city." Though any property Twain had acquired as yet was not worth taxing, such business-like ways impressed him into justifying the new Napoleon's dictatorial grip:

. . . he has taken the sole control of the Empire of France into his hands, and made it the freest country in the world—perhaps—for people who will not attempt to go too far in meddling with government affairs. No country offers greater security to life and property than France does, and one has all the freedom he wants, but no license.

Instead of rattling the chains protestingly, this distinction gilded them with dollar signs.

Even before the trip was over Twain got more thoughtful about freedom under Napoleon III, but he let other European kings off easy too and could believe anything favorable to Czar Alexander II, who was undeservedly popular with the *Quaker City* pilgrims because of Russia's pro-Union diplomacy during the Civil War. Twain's only fighting criticism of Europe sprang from his anti-Catholic prejudices. Though it had been a crowded and exciting period, hardly more than ten years separated him from the sometimes murky outlook of Hannibal; his first letter, describing the Azores, was quick to slash at "Jesuit humbuggery" and the letters from Italy grew eloquent about that "priestridden" land which had "groped in the midnight of priestly superstition for sixteen hundred years!" The revoltingly low standard of living seemed to prove that the Roman Catholic Church also had a depressing, if not downright hostile, influence on social progress. Not just a village printer turned traveling correspondent thought so; fresh from Yale, the future historian and college president Andrew D. White had his worst fears confirmed by a visit to Italy about the same time. Twain only put the Protestant case more memorably and sweepingly as he even belittled Renaissance masters who had painted saints and sacred anecdotes for princes ruling city-states in dark harmony with the Vatican.

If he just barely indicated how the backward countries might wake up to better ways, this was because the remedy seemed obvious: inventive energy was ready to start its brightening wonders anyplace where the bishop or autocrat did not block practical reason. To save the hurried tourist from grubbing in factories or statistics, Twain suggested that "one can tell what a nation is if he can only see its roads." By this standard Napoleon III was proving himself with macadamized turnpikes, and Alexander II proved he was a "genuinely great man" by planning a mammoth railroad network and appointing as his builder a "man of progress and enterprise—and representative man of the age—what is called 'rustler' in California." Twain's only other evident criterion was how high the taxes ran. Posterity lost very little when he threw in with the tour to the Holy Land instead of following an urge to take off for China and observe Burlingame's operations there. For the present he had traveled farther than his mind could reach.

Its limits were set by Manchester Liberalism rather than starspangled smugness. Other than the passage that told how wildly the *Quaker City* wanderers saluted a ship flying their country's flag, his steady parade of newspaper letters were surprisingly mild in their nationalism. While there were touches of official gravity such as advising Washington to send more than a "contemptible trap of a gun-boat" to awe the Moors or warning the home front that the Turks resented our sympathy with the revolt in Crete against their regime, this seriousness as a self-appointed diplomat made Twain more critical of his companions because he worried about the impression they were making. Sometimes back to back with the famous episodes where he played the anti-genteel clown, he just as often fretted about his traveling party as New World "Vandals." The self-righteous mood was the one that dominated his summary comment for the New York *Herald:* "Many and many a simple community in the Eastern hemisphere will remember for years the incursion of the strange horde in the year of our Lord 1867, that called themselves Americans, and seemed to imagine in some unaccountable way that they had a right to be proud of it." Though he was also working off private grudges here, he could have masked them in other terms. He had been hard on Europe at times, but he had been almost as hard on his countrymen—and would be again.

An inside look at Washington did nothing to rebuild his national pride. From Italy he had accepted the job of private secretary to William Stewart—now a senator from Nevada —and he took it over within a week after his ship docked, becoming also a committee clerk with a voting proxy but not a "devilish thing to do, & six dollars a day."[7] The two ex-Washoeites surely thought they understood each other. Twain could not help knowing that his employer had become a Republican wheelhorse as well as a millionaire on legal fees from the mining companies while, on the basis of past dealings, Stewart had reason to believe that he would also play the game of politics for all it was worth instead of letting disgust drive him away from our capital after a while. If nothing else, Stewart meant to hire a good publicity man, and during the next three months Twain worked many plugs into his letters for western newspapers, even declaring once that he "wouldn't want anything better than to take the stump for Stewart" in Nevada.[8]

As yet nobody knows exactly when they fell out. Stewart's later account was obviously vulnerable as well as spiteful; Twain's recollection in 1884 that he endured two sessions of Congress as a private secretary seems wrong unless the tie was very elastic.[9] In any event it is clear that from early December until the following March of 1868, when Twain rushed off to California on personal business, they worked together loosely yet profitably. After that he no longer had to endure the discomforts of errand boy to "bullyragging Bill" Stewart. His contacts with other influential people had expanded as quickly as he had hoped when, hardly settled in Washington, he wrote to his mother, "Am well known, now —intend to be better known. Am hob-nobbing with these old Generals & Senators for no good purpose."

One not too evil purpose was to find a suitable niche for brother Orion, preferably in the patent office, and he got Stewart and others to help—futilely. He also worked on toeholds for friends trying to climb above the hordes of office-seekers and even toyed with a bigger deal for himself. Eventually he fought rather hard to become postmaster of San Francisco, a job which he described as the "heaviest concentration of political power on the coast" with "perquisites" double the legal salary.[10] Depending on the audience, he gave different reasons for avoiding this control center of patronage after he had the nomination clinched: he was rushing to revise his *Quaker City* letters; he was dubious about the timing because he might instead "want such a thing under the next administration"; he discovered (he told his fiancée in 1869) that the job did not pay enough if "handled honestly."

There is no doubt at least that he had grown welcome in important Washington circles. Senator John Conness of California, who was behind him for the postmastership, offered next to make him Burlingame's successor in China.[11] He had different reasons again for saying no: he wanted to settle down, did not feel qualified, knew he could get along as a freelance columnist, or thought the salary too small. But he kept this line baited for the future, genially reminding Burlingame to save a "gorgeous secretaryship or a high interpretership" for him; later in 1868 he would think about landing a "nice sinecure" under the new minister to China. It was easier to picture himself smoothing the way for American exports than collecting graft and dealing out jobs in San Francisco.

His official biographer suggests that the politicians who looked out for Twain were merely helping a needy artist. But even Bret Harte, who was busier in party warfare than anybody has bothered to prove, got much less coveted plums while showing higher literary promise. Whatever their taste in art or humor, the senators, congressmen, and Supreme Court justice who pushed Twain for wide berths worked by habit in a pattern of quid pro quo. At the time Justice Stephen J. Field was recommending him here and there, Twain was helping to boom Field as the best Democratic choice for president in 1868. A few weeks later he slashed heavily at a rumor that Field, to curry political favor, was swaying his fellow justices against the Reconstruction Acts; when the House of Representatives formed a committee to probe charges about Field's pro-Southern bias, Twain published arguments that came from the dark horse's mouth. Though Field was destined to stay on the court (and become its surest vote for unrestrained laissez faire), Twain obviously could be energetic about paying back favors.

He was just as nimbly useful in the push for a reciprocity treaty with Hawaii. When sugar planters and California refiners agreed on the details with Harris, who negotiated for the king, Twain proclaimed that they had built a "perfect monument of mathematics and virtue"; though critical of Harris's request that our warships leave Hawaiian waters, he even professed to like that pariah a little better. After a while he could sigh to a friend that he felt a "personal interest in its ratification" because he had "bothered so much with that treaty."[12] But it failed to pass because too many senators suspected that reciprocity was meant as a step toward annexation. Regarding Twain, as well as his clique, the suspicion was correct; his visit to Hawaii had led him to ask in 1866, "The property has got to fall to some heir, and why not the United States?"

Another west coast drive had better luck in 1868 when the Burlingame Treaty with China was signed, assuring a continued flow of coolies while promising to curb their mistreatment. Twain quickly greeted it in the New York *Tribune* with "The Chinese Mission: What Mr. Burlingame Has Accomplished," which climaxed with the cry that the "vast commerce of 400,000,000 of industrious people must soon pass to us—and to us alone, almost." This grandiose vision was buttressed with more workaday prospects such as satisfying the middle-class demand for cheap servants, a demand he also tried to marshal in several other briefs for importing coolies. When the Senate ratified the treaty he rushed into the *Tribune* of August 4, 1868, with explanatory facts that came patently from Burlingame or his office. Still, Twain apparently put his own heart into the platitudes that completely gilded the treaty before ending, "It acquires a grand field for capital, labor, research, enterprise—it confers science, mechanics, social and political advancement, Christianity."

His effusions were no more ingenuously hopeful than most support for the Burlingame Treaty. However, opinions clashed within a year to fire a debate that turned basically on white labor's complaints about the growing preference for coolies shown by California and also some New England companies. Significantly, Twain's recent western outlet, the *Alta California*, put more emphasis on the needs of employers than the idea of a New World refuge, and his next major comment was frankly practical:

It was found just about impossible to build the California end of the Pacific Railroad with white men at $3 per day and take care of all the broils and fights and strikes; but they put on Chinamen at a dollar a day and "find" themselves, and *they* built it without fights or strikes or anything, and saved the bulk of their wages too.[13]

Toward the displaced whites who were making an increasingly loud protest against such economies, he was just as frankly contemptuous: "To swing a pick or shoulder a hod comes as natural to them as anxiety in the presence of a jug." This contempt came all the easier because the anti-Chinese rioting was sparked mainly by their Irish competitors. As sketches from this period like "A Visit to Niagara" or "John Chinaman in New York" prove, he had not learned to take the swarms of uneducated Irish immigrants tolerantly.

His final comment about the coolies had belletristic overtones. The literary circle in San Francisco had championed fair play from the start, and he had already written in the same vein against streetcorner brutality, more than once. When Harte's poem "The Heathen Chinee" made a sensation in the fall of 1870—partly because its irony could be misread for the wrong side—Twain got in the swim with

"Goldsmith's Friend Abroad Again." Imitating the *Citizen of the World* letters he planned to detail a coolie's reaction toward his experiences and treatment here. But Twain never allowed his Ah Song Hi the quiet sagacity of Goldsmith's figure; also, after trying at first to stress the American tradition of justice for all, in later instalments he moved over into muckraking the brutal venality of San Francisco policemen, especially Irish ones. This shift of direction, as well as failure to finish the series, indicates that his sympathy had narrow limits—a verdict the Chinatown passages in *Roughing It* do not shake.

That Twain mostly subserved Pacific coast businessmen when he discussed China and Hawaii is also suggested by his anti-expansionism in other cases. From the first mention of buying Alaska in 1867, he echoed hostile epithets such as Walrussia and devised hostile farces such as one about an Alaskan iceberg that, before melting away, floated in and out of the jurisdiction of several countries.[14] The chance we might buy the Virgin Islands evoked "Information Wanted" —a wild routine about the difficulties of living on volcanic St. Thomas—and talk about taking over Cuba moved him to pure savagery. Though willing to make exceptions for his friends he basically agreed with the "little America" position that foreign real estate, unlike foreign trade, dangerously built up federal over state government at home and gave the politicians more patronage to misuse.

Meanwhile, he had been slowly making himself independent of patronage or—as he called it loftily—"government pap." He tried without success to set up a syndicated newsletter but kept earning so many new offers from the leading dailies for exclusive material that he soon felt swamped. Later he could claim to have covered a session of Congress in 1868 as a reporter. Because his copy appeared in so many places during a jumbled period of his life, not all of it has even been identified. Yet it was substantial in bulk and also in meaning.

While he was still working faithfully for Stewart, the light side of his reporting stopped at innocuous comedy. In the stance of court jester he used safe targets like George Francis Train—the "great Fenian Female Suffrage Ass"—or if he used important people, as when "Concerning General Grant's Intentions" spoofed that budding candidate's taciturnity, he felt his way with caution. Still, he could not be too timid about whom he criticized if he wanted to keep up the demand for his material. Much less jovial than it seems now, "My Late Senatorial Secretaryship" paid off an old score by ridiculing the hollow double talk of Senator James W. Nye, the former governor of the Nevada Territory. Inevitably, he also edged into broader criticism though "The Facts Concerning the Recent Resignation" clowned so broadly about a government clerk with nothing to do that few readers would notice its complaint against creating jobs merely to pay off political debts. In spite of a similar title "The Facts Concerning the Recent Important Resignation" soon drove more clearly at showing that congressmen degrade their office by "uttering offensive personalities—slang—inferior wit—unnecessary and procrastinating speeches upon unimportant matters."[15] For his own relief, after seeing whiskey drunk in committee sessions he polished up the pun: ". . . carry it [in] in demijohns and carry it out in demagogues."

Most revolting of all, but unmistakable, was the trail of graft that, he quickly discovered, ran deep into Congress. Without intending a defense of Republicans he compared their Democratic critics to the wolf who whined at shepherds eating mutton, ". . . there'd be hell to pay if I was to do that." For the present, however, he avoided making specific charges against the kingpins of million-dollar hauls. Instead his "General Spinner as a Religious Enthusiast" praised the treasurer of the United States for profanely refusing to cash a dishonest but small voucher, and "The Case of George Fisher" studied the course of a very minor fraud against the government.[16] He was not ready to write *The Gilded Age* though the necessary knowledge and anger were building up fast. His letter to the *Territorial Enterprise* of March 7, 1868 sardonically described an obscure federal clerk who had "no rules of action for his guidance except some effete maxims of integrity picked up in Sunday school" and therefore struck everybody as queer because he refused to live by the truth that the "whole city was polluted with peculation and all other forms of rascality—debauched and demoralized by the wholesale dishonesty that prevails in every single department of the Washington Government, great and small."

Such insights delayed his taking on a party label. Besides, he still felt an instinct to hedge until the political future looked clearer; during the months when there was no obvious successor to the dying Johnson regime, he seemed to follow the maxim that "first-rate Washington policy" was to "carry water on both shoulders."[17] This balancing act was prolonged by his lingering Southern heritage. Though he could soon roast a violent Colonel Jay Hawker who "lost very heavily by the war . . . an uncle, a nigger, a watch, and thirty dollars in Confederate money," one word in this gibe underscores the larger fact that he felt the idea of making the freed slaves into fellow citizens was "startling and disagreeable." It is obvious that he sacrificed little if any principle by defending Justice Field when the Republican Radicals accused him of softness toward the ex-Rebels. When the Radicals made their all-out attack on President Johnson, however, Twain vacillated.[18] Having already joined the fun of stoning a scapegoat caught in a trackless swamp, he first responded to the impeachment move by satirizing Johnson's defenders through "Mr. Welles and His Marines"—a sketch about the Secretary of the Navy leading a rescue force armed, like true Democrats, with whiskey jugs. But his reports on the trial gave Johnson a cautiously favorable press. Pulled away from Washington right after the trial by personal business, he must have been relieved at cutting short his commentary on issues puzzling to much more dogged minds.

During the fall election he was busy courting, rewriting

The Innocents Abroad, and establishing himself as a lecturer. This left no time for judging the successful candidacy of Grant. But on March 4, 1869, he libeled the outgoing administration with a searing piece for the New York *Tribune* titled "The White House Funeral"; alert to the complicated swirlings of the past few years and keyed to the personalities involved, it is full proof in itself that he followed politics closely. After a rundown on recent scandals it imagined a farewell cabinet meeting at which Johnson, who lamely denied he had been drunk for his inauguration, bragged fuzzily about "nursing anarchy and rebellion" and stupidly described his moves in Radical phrasing while his secretary of state bragged about buying "all the icebergs and volcanoes that were for sale on earth." The less prominent members of the cabinet Twain roasted more quickly while having them play seven-up for the White House furniture. If he had set out to prove he had finally hoisted a party banner, he could not have written more to the purpose.

His most faithful readers had no cause for surprise. As he increased his newspaper outlets, he had more and more picked or accepted them in the range from moderate to shrill Republicanism, knitting his strongest tie with Horace Greeley's *Tribune*. With the encouragement of its managing editor he considered buying into it when he began looking for a settled career in late 1868. Commenting that its Republican policy was "suitable," he next sized up the Cleveland *Herald* as an "anchorage." He also dickered with three other newspapers that lined up the same way though his prime choice was the "high-principled" Hartford *Courant* run by Joseph R. Hawley, president of the latest Republican National Convention; before the *Courant* seers could decide Twain was a rising star he bought into the Buffalo *Express*, another solidly partisan sheet. Indeed, the owners of the Cleveland *Herald* had planned to use him as their political editor, and his answer that he "always did hate politics" must be read against a remark to his fiancée that the "trimming, time-serving" *Herald* "would change its politics in a minute, in order to be on the popular side." By politics he meant, in 1869 and always, a slimy mixture of graft, demagoguery, and nimble-footed service to party bosses. As the game was played in his day, he was not finicky in having no real stomach for it and announcing with his "Salutatory" on the *Express*, "I shall not often meddle with politics, because we have a political Editor who is already excellent and only needs to serve a term or two in the penitentiary to be perfect." Nevertheless, anybody in Buffalo who believed that Twain took no interest in elections would soon know better.

As Twain was getting his bearings in Buffalo, *The Innocents Abroad* started its sale with a success that eventually freed him from holding a regular job. He had expanded his travel letters, especially widening their margin of humor and projecting a complex yet engaging personality that ranged from buffoonery to purple rhapsodies over landscape. Though the social commentary was made somewhat more kindly toward European squalor, there had not been time for a real growth in humanity or a major decline in his gusto for the firmness with which Napoleon III held down the "starving, discontented revolution breeders." He had added, however, a thicker sprinkling of republican sentiments—like the aside that praised the "nobler" royalty of "heart and brain" —and his only detailed statement of the American dream in his first fifteen years of writing. As a reproach to servile Italians, he described a land without an "overshadowing Mother Church" or a large standing army or ruinous taxes and extolled our public schools, economic freedom, and knack for inventions; emphatically professing a respect for the "common people" and their right to "take hold and help conduct the government," he went on to tout our social equality and our devotion to tolerance. But, for the good of smug Americans, *The Innocents Abroad* kept the less patriotic touches of his original letters and added his flip account of an Independence Day ceremony at sea that climaxed with

the "same old speech about our national greatness which we
so religiously believe and so fervently applaud."

Whatever the complex balance of his entries on the ideo-
logical trade between the Old World and the New, they did
not reveal the instinctive democrat-patriot some suppose or
the patient cosmopolite he actually became. But Twain himself was not worrying much about the over-all picture. He
had been earning most of his living as a topical columnist who
served up the news with a humorous sauce and met his dead-
lines without agonizing over consistency. This slapdash pattern was complicated by a personal confusion. Some of the
Whig ideas learned in his boyhood held on with grim
tenacity, and until the time when he moved to Buffalo the
key phrase of "lower classes" flowed easily from his pen; on
the other hand, the American atmosphere was radiating with
the slogans of romantic democracy, and he could not escape
their influence—he could even add to the fallout if his mood
was hopeful. So far the most progressive influence on him
had come, surprisingly, from the friends he was making in
New England while, sad to say, his experiences in our capital had only stepped up his qualms about political equality
and its spokesmen.

When he inspected the economic framework, he continued to be guided even more heavily by his early training,
which owed far more to the school of Hamilton than Jefferson. Accepting laissez faire in business without a second
thought, he criticized any prospect of "consolidated and all-
embracing government" as vehemently as a railroad or steel
magnate:

. . . the mania for giving the Government power to meddle with
the private affairs of cities or citizens is likely to cause endless
trouble . . . and there is great danger that our people will lose that
independence of thought and action which is the cause of much
of our greatness, and sink into the helplessness of the Frenchman
or German who expects his government to feed him when hun-

gry, clothe him when naked . . . and, in fine, to regulate every act of humanity from the cradle to the tomb, including the manner in which he may seek future admission to paradise.[19]

Such fustian was woven of simple fibers—the devotee of pioneer handicrafts might call it linsey-woolsey. But it consisted primarily of a belief that the acquisitive instinct and technical skills would combine to sweep away poverty if allowed full play.

This belief cramped the kindness needed when the march toward universal prosperity faltered for a while. After sighing over the many thousands jobless in New York City, Twain said resignedly that a move to appropriate half a million dollars for relief was "of course . . . cried down by everybody—the money would never get further than the pockets of a gang of thieving politicians."[20] Coming revelations about the Tweed ring would show he was partly right in this case. But his faith in the social magic of a profit system harnessed to technology made it too easy to oppose state relief anywhere. In its less cheerful form his sense of the profit motive was just as hostile to private charity and held him back from "confidence in people who walk a thousand miles for the benefit of widows and orphans and don't get a cent for it."

His remarks on economic man were essentially casual, as if supply and demand was a fixed law rather than a debatable theory, and he usually stuck to narrower day-to-day themes. A typical example is "The Great Beef Contract," inspired by Senator Stewart's anger at federal clerks who would not quickly tell him something he wanted to know; beginning obliquely about an inflated claim against the army for beef that was never delivered, it awkwardly switched emphasis near the end to lampoon petty bureaucrats and the windings of official procedure.[21] Today it seems almost worthless. However, George Washington Cable, then an obscure reviewer for the New Orleans *Picayune*, declared that its "sword of sarcasm flashes like fire as it falls upon the trick-eries of the Government." Rating "The Great Beef Con-tract" superior to the Jumping Frog yarn, he also found in it Twain's "true genius"—the serious purpose that set him above the class of a Josh Billings.

Like any substantial person Twain took himself seriously from the start—and ended by taking himself too seriously ever to find full serenity for long. A sense of integrity not only kept him from becoming a spoilsman in 1868 but also prodded him into bursts of muckraking. Though ethics inter-ested him even more than politics, he weighed moral values too closely to ignore their working in public affairs. Of course his readers expected him to be amusing, and some-times, as when he felt exposed to a possible crossfire, he took evasive action with humor where it was not called for. Still, he was more and more getting into the habit of having and expressing serious opinions on how to run the country.

THE UNPREJUDICED JURY.

"It was a jury composed of two desperadoes, two low beerhouse politicians, three bar-keepers, two ranchmen who could not read, and three dull, stupid human donkeys!"—*Roughing It*

I am a candidate for the legislature. I desire to tamper with the jury law. I wish to so alter it as to put a premium on intelligence and character.—Roughing It

THREE

A Curious Republican

By moving to Buffalo, in mid-August of 1869, Twain put himself well within the orbit of the Langdon family and what he described to his future father-in-law as a "high eastern civilization." There is no sign he was reluctant to raise his social level, however apologetic he may have felt about his rough edges. Though he did not court Olivia Langdon for her money, it impressed him almost as much as her breeding and posed another challenge. Instead of gloating like a prospector who had made a lucky haul, he took the proper Victorian attitude that he had to justify her father's faith in him by working harder than ever.

The respect with which he met Jervis Langdon can be seen indirectly through his "Open Letter to Commodore Vanderbilt," attacking a notorious Wall Street pirate for his personal crudities and "lawless violations of commercial honor."[1] When this drew a defense of Vanderbilt for creating more wealth and new jobs, Twain accepted it as "able bosh"—bosh because it nicked him as well as claiming too much for a ruthless profiteer but able because it persuasively stated the case for capitalists in general. His taunts had not meant to criticize solid businessmen, who in fact resented the disruptive forays by the robber barons as much as anybody, and he felt no impulse to bait Langdon or ridicule him behind his back. Soon after pushing into the family circle Twain gladly tried to help him collect a half-million dollars from the city of Memphis for wooden pavement.[2] There must have been backslapping around the fireside when Twain's influence produced a scolding editorial in the New York *Tribune* that did some good.

Langdon's main energy went into a network of mines and retail outlets for coal. When some voices around Buffalo accused the big companies of price-fixing, Twain answered them firmly in his own newspaper with "The 'Monopoly' Speaks," which complained that the public was listening too naïvely to the consumers' side and argued that legitimate market pressures were driving up the price of coal as winter came on.[3] Though Langdon put up the $25,000 with which he bought into the *Express*, Twain would not have gone so far and so openly if he agreed with the other side or cared little about the economic principles involved. Even where his loyalties were not aroused, he took up serious issues as soon as he got oriented in his new job, vaguely hoping to lift the *Express* into the class of often quoted newspapers like the Springfield *Republican* or the Toledo *Blade*. This meant he could not ignore politics. Property holders, large or small, had their stake in the state and expected to be kept informed about it. Furthermore, while they looked down on the city boss and ward-heeler, most educated or well-to-do northerners already felt a proprietary concern in the future of the Republican party.

Having finally committed himself, Twain harried the Democrats with original material in the *Express*. A typical

This is the Priest (not) shaven and shorn, that married the man all tattered and torn unto the maiden all forlorn that milked the cow with the crumpled horn that tossed the dog that worried the cat that caught the rat that ate the malt that lay in the House that Jack built.

From *Mark Twain's (Burlesque) Autobiography and First Romance*. The priest is Boss Tweed; Cornelius Vanderbilt is next to him; the trio being wedded with the Erie "ring" are Jay Gould, Jim Fisk, and Daniel Drew.

piece, "Inspired Humor," professed to see comedy in their latest call for an honest legislature in New York and derided them as hypocrites "whose religion is to war against all moral and material progress, and who never were known to divert to the erection of a school house moneys that would suffice to build a distillery."[4] His frontal attacks were reinforced by a then standard maneuver of pointing up news items the way he did with "A pig with a human head is astonishing South Carolina. Are they rare, there?" But it so happened in the fall of 1869 that baiting the Democrats was easier than praising the Republicans, at least in New York where the spoilsmen had taken over both sides and even worked together across party lines. Letting other hands keep the *Express* filled with partisan cheers, Twain used his positive moods on more basic Republican planks like the need to recall the greenbacks issued during the war—the point of his "Adventures in Hayti," another sketch that looks weightless today as it clowns about ridiculously high prices for everyday items.

After his furious debut as an editor Twain made the lecture rounds again and then put all his thoughts into getting married. When he got back to writing for the *Express* he was more impartial and relaxed but not aimless. Unfortunately, to know that "A Curious Dream"—about corpses that move their coffins to a better neighborhood—was lampooning the rundown state of a Buffalo cemetery does not make this grisly sketch any funnier. However, such insight builds alertness to worthwhile content behind the slapstick of pieces like "A Mysterious Visit," an account of his dealings with a tax assessor which finally criticized the wealthy sharpers who falsify their returns. This restless dislike of hypocrisy soon killed his dream of being an editor. After openly complaining that "Cain is branded a murderer so heartily and unanimously in America, only because he was neither a Democrat or Republican," he acted out his disgust in "Running for Governor," a parody on a state election in New York that saw two corrupt machines splatter each other with muck. Ominously, this parody attacked the press of both parties without favor.

For the rest of his life after leaving the *Express* Twain thought of most newspaper editors as noisy puppets, and in 1871 he willingly took a big loss to set himself free. Even before then he branched out in monthly "Memoranda" for the *Galaxy*, but not as an escape from writing about current affairs. Along with frothier humor he kept turning out items like "The Coming Man," a superbly witty warning against making some ward-heeler our new minister to England. Put together while the "Memoranda" were appearing, *Mark Twain's (Burlesque) Autobiography and First Romance* had about the same mixture of ingredients. It extended his campaign to project a colorful front and gave further sign of his literary instincts, but its third facet, a sequence of cartoons on the Erie Railroad scandal, showed he had not deserted from guarding the public conscience.

Though Cornelius Vanderbilt was the best-known villain in the Erie scandal it also established Jay Gould's lurid fame, and much later Twain would pick Gould as the prime corrupter of our "commercial morals." Even in 1870 there was widespread comment in this vein—especially by conservatives like brahmin Charles Francis Adams, Jr., who also protested at length that such doings sapped the health of sound business. Keyed by apt variations on the nursery jingle about the house that Jack built, the cartoons in the *Burlesque Autobiography* proved that Twain had gathered every whisper about Jim Fisk's sex life and the payoffs to judges and editors.[5] In fact he capitalized on popular reaction instead of saying anything new; cartoons like those in his book were common and the parody on the nursery rime belonged to current folksay. But he was revolted rather than amused by the Erie tragi-comedy, which attuned him to the looming furor about Tweed's burglaries and other scandals that led to *The Gilded Age*.

In the meantime, this mounting disgust was allowed to

have only a side-effect on *Roughing It* (1872). His appetite
was whetted by a steady sale for *The Innocents Abroad*, and
he worked hard at spinning another best-seller. More fiction
than history wherever the change might please the reader,
Roughing It is his sunniest book. If it offended Senator Stewart, he was being too touchy. If its passing sarcasms really
belittled the old territorial legislature, Twain's experiences
could have inspired a much more trenchant critique. Indeed,
when he refreshed his mind in 1871 by going over some clippings of his feisty columns for the *Territorial Enterprise* he
scribbled a comment about the resemblance between Carson
City graft and the national scandals that were building up. A
few years later he made promising notes for a book about a
Senator Bonanza, who routinely bought off state legislatures.
Much later he jotted down ideas for a social history from
1850 that would include the effects of the "California sudden-
riches disease."[6] Still, though it gave edge to *The Gilded Age*,
little of this insight showed up in *Roughing It*, least of all in
the now ignored Appendix C—which jeered at an alkali
populist who was resisting the push of the mining companies
for cozier tax laws.

Roughing It also gave darker signs of misdirected bias from
Twain's western years, especially when the Indians slouched
across its pages. From the time he crossed the plains he felt
only contempt for the red men, and loudly and often said so.
In *The Innocents Abroad*, his celebrated ear failing him, he
orated against Tahoe as a primitive name not good enough
for the famous lake—where he had carelessly burned a stand
of trees while toying with the notion of staking out a rich
timber claim. In the *Galaxy* he derided the Indian with a
white settler's passion as a "filthy, naked scurvy vagabond"
whose extinction by the army should continue in spite of the
"wail of humanitarian sympathy" from the older sections of
the country.[7] There is no good reason why he reacted so
violently. Dan De Quille, his crony in Nevada, took a much
kinder, more relaxed attitude, and Bret Harte could bur-

lesque James Fenimore Cooper's stagy figures without wink-
ing at mistreatment of their flesh and blood counterparts.
The ugly truth is that Twain as yet had little respect for any
peoples who were outside the pattern of an industrial society.
Though he managed to see more humor in tropical languor
than in the Digger Indians' struggle to subsist, he also came
down harder on the Hawaiian natives than he had in the letters he revised to swell his book to subscription size.

The circle of his sympathy was still actually too small to
include even all classes of white Americans. In spite of his
eloquent if incidental tribute to the forty-niners as "stalwart,
muscular, dauntless young braves," he grimaced at the heavy
"scum" on the western surge and, damning politicians as their
"dust-licking pimps and slaves," fumed about the absurdity
of letting this scum serve on juries. With a steadier eye on his
intentions than usual, he gave an exotic picture of the mining
frontier; but his colors were occasionally somber or clashing.
The continual references in *Roughing It* to the "flush times"
suggest that he had a secondary motif in mind and, like
another old Whig, meant to highlight the ludicrous yet
deplorable crumbling of order before the speculative flood.
Somewhat lamely he rang the same note as Joseph G. Baldwin's *The Flush Times of Alabama and Mississippi* in his final
"moral": "If you are of any account, stay home and make
your way by sober diligence."

Roughing It was western and democratic in the finest sense
of these terms only when Twain described himself as a ten-
derfoot who fraternized with seedy prospectors and shared
their sourdough dreams, when readers were asked to take
Scotty Briggs as a man of sterling character under his rough-
ness and profanity or were assured that though Dick Baker
was "slenderly educated, slouchily dressed and clay-soiled"
his heart was "finer metal than any gold his shovel ever
brought to light." Scotty's slang and Dick's muscular idiom
belong to the supreme achievement of Twain's personal
democracy—the sinewy vernacular that controls the choicest

MALE LOBBYIST $3,000.

FEMALE LOBBYIST $3,000.

From *The Gilded Age*. Amounts of money under the pictures were meant to represent the standard payoffs that it took to get a bill through Congress.

HIGH MORAL SENATOR $3,000.

CHAIRMAN OF COMMITTEE, $10,000.

A NEW CRIME.

LEGISLATION NEEDED.

THIS country, during the last thirty or forty years, has produced some of the most remarkable cases of insanity of which there is any mention in history. For instance, there was the Baldwin case, in Ohio, twenty-two years ago. Baldwin, from his boyhood up, had been of a vindictive, malignant, quarrelsome nature. He put a boy's eye out once, and never was heard upon any occasion to utter a regret for it. He did many such things. But at last he did something that was serious. He called at a house just after dark, one evening, knocked, and when the occupant came to the door, shot him dead, and then tried to escape,

187

From *Mark Twain's Sketches, New and Old* (1875), when Twain was angry about the use of temporary insanity as a legal defense.

passages of *Roughing It.* To adapt a figure he once exploited, he was better at the tune than the words in 1871—his political attitudes needed reshaping but he rose to magnificent cadences when he chanted the virtues of his motley friends. Later, in *Huckleberry Finn* and *A Connecticut Yankee,* the vernacular style would support themes greater than robust camaraderie, and the result would be even more satisfying.

Appropriately, Twain dedicated *Roughing It* to Calvin Higbie, another "Genial Comrade" of his Washoe days. But he had first planned instead on honoring Cain as a consolation for "his misfortune to live in a dark age that knew not the beneficent Insanity Plea" to excuse his murder of Abel. This uninspired idea at least proves that Twain was not lost in a haze of Washoe memories. When a trial in 1870 set the precedent for pleading mental illness as a defense, he had reacted quickly with two protests in the Buffalo *Express* and another in the *Galaxy*, opposing what he took to be merely a legal dodge that interfered with the state's main job—the punishment of thieves and murderers.[8] It is only fair to realize that he was staggered by the first impact of questions that are still troublesome to modern minds when the defense rushes to plead temporary insanity, and that many of his contemporaries were just as afraid of encouraging crime through softness. Before he started coming around to a more humane stand, he also got excited about juries that helped to pamper the sinners against property rights and personal safety. *Roughing It* erupted with criticism of our jury system as the "most ingenious and infallible agency for *defeating* justice that human wisdom could contrive"; and, just as *The Gilded Age* was being finished, he raged openly at the stalling and soft-soaping of the defense in a highly publicized case of wanton murder.

The friends Twain was finding in New England had no reason to mistrust him as a brash westerner who undervalued law and order, even if he wore a sealskin overcoat or was likely to veer suddenly into clowning. Indeed it soon became evident that the clowning could be harnessed to their solemn purposes, as when he dashed off a long and madly punning "ballotd" in 1871 about how the Democrats had tried to steal the last election for governor of Connecticut. Somebody, perhaps in the Hartford *Courant* office, saw fit to print it as a broadside.[9] As always, making himself at home had included mixing in local politics; in old age he recalled guiltily that once he even gave twenty-five dollars to buy votes after being assured the Democrats had started playing dirty first.[10] Such close partisanship demanded of course that he do his special bit in national elections too. On the day the 1872 campaign formally began he sent the Hartford *Courant* an unsigned skit titled "The Secret of Dr. Livingstone's Continued Voluntary Exile," which claimed that the missionary, recently contacted in the heart of Africa, had decided to unpack his trunks and "unlearn" his "civilization" because of disgust at the news of Horace Greeley's accepting the Democrats' support for the presidency.[11] Committed at least as much to the Republican party as to its general, Twain hailed the results of the election as a "prodigious victory for Grant —I mean, rather, for civilization and progress."

In spite of deserting his post on the Buffalo *Express*, he had obviously remained an active citizen who studied his daily newspaper, and not just any newspaper either. Around 1870 he toyed with "Interviewing the Interviewer," which would have scolded the New York *Sun* for aiming to "achieve the applause of the bone and sinew of the backstreets and the cellars."[12] He had especially come to admire the New York *Tribune;* and, when there was a fight in 1872 over its future, he showed inside knowledge of the men and issues involved.[13] After Whitelaw Reid came out on top against the odds, Twain congratulated him, "I grieved to see the old Tribune wavering & ready to tumble into the common slough of journalism & God knows I am truly glad you saved it." At this time Reid was prominent for imploring the better classes to counteract the tyrannical, gullible majority as well as the party boss.

Less than a week after he took over the top *Tribune* slot, Reid asked Twain for "something, no matter what" and soon arranged for two long letters on Hawaii, which was again in the headlines because American planters there were again pushing for a closer link with the United States. In these letters Twain deployed his humor with a politician's touch, genially approving the royal claims of the planters' choice but echoing the *Tribune's* distaste for the expansionist clique here and making the Kanakas look undesirable as fellow Americans.[14] Feeling secure as a valuable spot player on the new *Tribune* team, he also sent in several unsolicited letters, which were published promptly, and a telegram (signed "Public Virtue") protesting against the raise in salary that Congress had given itself. With obvious self-satisfaction he chortled to Reid: "God knows I was intended for a statesman. I can solve any political problem that ever was invented."[15] He saw no difficulty either in expecting the *Tribune* to help the advance buildup for *The Gilded Age*. Before he suddenly decided that Reid was a "contemptible cur" and the *Tribune* must not get a review copy, there was even an editorial on the forthcoming feast of humor and wisdom. Seemingly the break came because Twain expected still more and flashier free advertising. In any event, though he added broader reasons for hating Reid as time went by, the split was personal rather than political at first. Unfortunately, it ended the flow of his squibs and letters for the *Tribune*. Reacting with his usual vehemence, he stopped buying it, much less writing for it; the dignified New York *Evening Post* became his supplement to the Republican fare of the local *Courant*. However, he had read the *Tribune* carefully between 1871 and 1873, and skimming any week's run from that period will supply at least one clue to the reference in some passage of *The Gilded Age*.

Of course *The Gilded Age* also had deeper roots drawing on Twain's basic attitudes and past experience. His Nevada days had left a suspicious contempt for men like James W. Nye, tagged by several reviewers as the senator who mails seven crates of personal odds and ends as official matter; and serving as a private secretary and a reporter in Washington had broadened his insight. Without really needing it he got a quick review by going back in July, 1870 to lobby for a bill favored by "our Tennesseans."[16] This bill probably involved the famous Clemens tract of land though the tie-up was fittingly so devious that nobody has figured it out. Exploiting old friendships he bustled around the capital for several days and, whether for business or curiosity's sake, had lunch with venal Senator Samuel C. Pomeroy. More out of disgust than prophecy, he grimly wrote to his wife: "Oh, I have gathered material enough for a whole book! This is a perfect gold mine." When the chance to collaborate on a novel with Charles Dudley Warner did come along, he was fully primed.

The fact that Warner co-authored *The Gilded Age* (1874) poses no serious problem. Twain wrote almost all the political chapters, though Warner's daily routine as editor of the Hartford *Courant* led him into the latest tunnels under public affairs. Whatever the reason for this sharing of the work, they agreed easily on the line to follow; if any minor snarls did develop, Twain was mostly the one pulling to the right. In an essay published the same year as their novel, Warner darkly preached against "loose commercial and political morality," but he also showed himself stoutly hopeful about the democratic way and nettled rather than dismayed by the growing sores of corruption.[17] Anybody who sees Hartford life as a reactionary pressure on Twain should compare Warner's ideas with his: seldom will Warner be found the more conservative, even in the 1880's.

Above all, Twain and Warner could work together smoothly because neither wanted to change anything more basic than manners and public morals. Accepting the framework of their society, they flayed minor evils like steamboat racing, religious journals that took dishonest advertising, or the rudeness of clerks and railroad conductors. In spirit, this last, recurring note harmonized with the heavy satire on parvenus who ape the ways of their betters and with the key epithet of "gilded," which appeals to owners of the real thing. Righteous gentility also guided the approach to a more serious matter, the health of our system for punishing criminals. Besides raising angry eyebrows at allowing temporary insanity as a defense, the handling of Laura's trial—spotted in New York City for this purpose—sneered at the fiasco of Boss Tweed's first trip to court. Braham, Laura's crafty lawyer, openly parodied the John Graham who protected Tweed with foxy calm but broke into sobs over his own pleadings for mercy to his client.[18] Furthermore, *The Gilded Age* stressed the Irish background of the jury and judge so heavily that anybody who had heard of Tammany Hall got the point.

The references to affairs in Washington were just as obvious for the informed. Laura's career there fitted in with a buzzing about woman lobbyists of uncertain virtue; more specifically, in the description of Lincoln's statue, alert readers found a direct criticism of a sculptress who had lately inveigled a commission through her youthful charm rather than proved ability.[19] Yet in good Victorian fashion the Lauras turned out much less blamable than men, and especially congressmen, whose trading of legislative favors for everything from railroad passes to stock in shady corporations was typified in *The Gilded Age* by giving one busy lawmaker the name of Trollop. There were also plenty of damning allusions to specific solons; and Dilworthy matched his real life model, Senator Pomeroy, with daring closeness both in mannerisms and the brazenly venal dealings that an ignominious Senate committee refused to censure. For once Twain was not exaggerating: the truth about "Old Subsidy" Pomeroy or his henchmen was extreme enough and too obvious; and when even Colonel Sellers took insult at the idea of becoming a congressman, he merely capped a standard joke of the day.

Nobody had trouble seeing also that Twain and Warner's immediate lesson was, as one magazine put it, "PURIFY THE SUFFRAGE." Yet *The Gilded Age* said little to prevent future Dilworthys from refining platitudes into bullion when it called for a return to the "old-style" congressman—the founding fathers can easily be used for a smokescreen too. It was more sensible when it scolded "good and worthy" citizens for continuing to "sit comfortably at home and leave the true source of our political power (the 'primaries') in the hands of saloon-keepers, dog-fanciers and hod-carriers," though this slur on the hod-carriers, added to numerous other slurs on voters who had a brogue or whose mouths were shaped for living on potatoes, put far too much blame on Irish immigrants. In its economics *The Gilded Age* was just as clearly genteel, preaching against the hunger "to get on in the world by the omission of some of the regular processes which have been appointed from of old." This has Warner's ring and like other, often stuffier passages in *The Gilded Age* is a happy reminder that Twain was at least not given to buttering the gospel of hard work with Christianity. But his basic attitude was just as narrow. In 1867, deploring the post-war boom, he had predicted a crash and growled like a bond-holder that "the sooner it comes in its might and restores the old, sure, plodding prosperity, the better."

The Gilded Age carried over this suspicion of the boom but did not ask if the profit motive was dangerous in other ways. In fact Twain's preface for the British edition hedged strongly about "speculativeness":

It is a characteristic which is both bad and good for both the individual and the nation. Good, because it allows neither to stand still, but drives both forever on, toward some point or another which is ahead, not behind nor at one side. Bad, because the chosen point is often badly chosen.

He went on to tip the balance cleanly, "Still, it is a trait which it is of course better for a people to have and sometimes suffer from than to be without." To forestall charges of hypocrisy from critics in the 1920's, he should also have added that he still drew a sharp line between the piratical raids by Gould or the will of the wisp chases by a Sellers and the healthy, shrewd business gambles by Jervis Langdon or Andrew Carnegie. His own gambles almost always backed some invention—from the adjustable vest-strap to the type-setter—that was supposed to increase human comfort or productivity.

The closing chapters of *The Gilded Age* solemnly totted up the rewards for the different kinds of enterprise. Named for his true mettle, Philip Sterling made good after toiling hard and long and enduring a penance of discouragement for his passing interest in wildcat ventures. His success was a practical reprimand to Harry Brierly and Mr. Bolton, among others, for drifting into the clutch of promoters who angled for favors from legislatures. Digging on his own, he found a coal mine while the lobbyists went bankrupt or, like Colonel Sellers, retreated from Washington nursing a worthless old trunk. To pull off this contrast it was necessary to glide over the Union Pacific clique and play up tinhorn operators, brokers of mudflat real-estate, and the idle apprentice who sank toward the fleshpot of federal subsidies—small fry who could not have got past Gould's secretary.

Modern critics of the robber barons have found ammunition in *The Gilded Age*, and some Wall Street entrepreneurs of 1874 must have hoped it would flop. Yet Twain and Warner were only asking for a chaste retreat. As they were getting their book into shape, E. L. Godkin, who rallied the middleclass with his new weekly *Nation*, argued that corruption mainly came from the power of Congress to make grants, and he concluded: "The remedy is simple. The Government must get out of the 'protective' business and the 'subsidy' business and the 'improvement' and 'development' business. It must let trade, and commerce, and manufactures, and steamboats, and railroads, and telegraphs alone." *The*

Gilded Age fully backed up this demand for pure laissez faire instead of legislative planning, and its main case of boodle hit the reformer as hard as the fixer. With no harm to what was a thin part of the plot anyway, it might have used the Tennessee land for satirizing the prodigal right-of-way grants to railroads or the windfalls from the protective tariff rather than the relatively minor larceny in a bill to found a university open to any race, creed, or sex. In fact, *The Gilded Age* showed no sympathy for the common man economically or otherwise. Angrily, it implied that he deserved none since he let jackals like Tweed or Pomeroy into the public larder and was too ready to share the spoils, and one British reviewer actually took it as a terrifying picture of mob rule. Though this was too strong it did sneer at the coarser varieties in the democratic garden, saying of the jury at the Hawkins trial: "Low foreheads and heavy faces they all had; some had a look of animal cunning, while the most were only stupid. The entire panel formed that boasted heritage commonly described as the 'bulwark of our liberties.'" *The Gilded Age* was the first serious outbreak of Twain's lifelong suspicion that the mass of mankind is venal, doltish, feckless, and tyrannical, that the damn fools make up a majority anywhere.

Distinctly less penetrating than John W. De Forest's *Honest John Vane* (1875), which covered similar ground, the scolding of speculators and grafters in *The Gilded Age* only pleaded for a middle-class code of doing business. Its readers had not bought a Trojan horse in a book that fleshed out the longing of its preface for a happy hunting ground "where there is no fever of speculation, no inflamed desire for sudden wealth, where the poor are all simple-minded and contented, and the rich are all honest and generous, where society is in a condition of primitive purity and politics is the occupation of only the capable and the patriotic." There was a limit to how much of this line Twain himself could swallow, and "Life As I Find It," dashed off around the same time, parodied the homily about the boy who got his big break because his elders saw him thriftily picking up stray pins. Still *The Gilded Age* did not even side with the discontented farmers in the current debate, unheretical as their "granges" were. If the conservative side can be defined as putting fear of "paternalism" above corrective federal or state action and elitism above majority rule, then Twain's alignment was clear beneath the American habit of mixing ideas loosely.

Elsewhere he expanded on two matters handled too loosely in *The Gilded Age* for firm sense. His diatribe on "The License of the Press" indicates he had meant the novel to attack the standards of American journalism—and with just cause, seeing the way most newspapers served political and corporate masters. Yet, at least partly out of character, he merely charged that the press too often made fun of religion as well as purveying cheap sensation that further confused the "stupid" majority. Ironically, this hauteur had one happy influence. As late as 1871 he had planned to amuse the lyceums with "An Appeal in Behalf of Extended Suffrage to Boys"—a satire on the "general tendency of the times," meaning especially the rise of the suffragettes—[20] but in 1873 his essay on "The Temperance Crusade and Woman's Rights" argued that it was unreasonable to keep educated ladies from voting "while every ignorant whisky-drinking foreign-born savage in the land may hold office, help to make the laws, degrade the dignity of the former and break the latter at his own sweet will"—a position still short of Nook Farm's ideas on the subject.

These two essays, it should be noted, were done for the sake of progress. For his next bread and butter work after *The Gilded Age* Twain planned a book about England and negotiated with Thomas Nast to illustrate it. They had tried to lay out a joint project several times before, as when Nast proposed to do cartoons for a pamphlet of items that would include "The Great Beef Contract." When Twain approached him in 1873, "Nasty" Nast—as his enemies called him—was the leading political cartoonist of a hard-hitting period: this was exactly his chief lure for Twain, who assured his publisher that his text would fit Nast's genius at caricature. Their dealings fell through again, but Twain's offer is a good sign of the mixed purposes that kept his book from ever getting written.

Though he could straddle as nimbly as a circus rider, in 1872-73 his feelings about England galloped off in directions too varied even for him. Like most working journalists he had now and then twisted the lion's tail since the Civil War. Yet, though he was interested in British history and literature and swayed by the Yankee intellectuals who were eager to close the widened breach, his preface for a British edition of *The Innocents Abroad* played on the "mother-country" theme with a fervor beyond the call of politeness or profit. One enduring side of Twain paid homage to tradition, the more bejewelled and escutcheoned the better. When he trod British soil in 1872 for his first visit, he lingered awestruck in famous abbeys or castles to exclaim eventually, "God knows I wish we had some of England's reverence for the old & great."[21] His awe flowed over into admiring the Victorian present and confiding to his wife that he "would rather live in England than America—which is treason." British audiences made the affection mutual when he started to lecture.

But he was weighing more than the nobby guards at Buckingham Palace or the crowds at his lectures. A few years afterward he claimed that he had not written a breezy book on England because he had been able to think only about "deep problems of government, taxes, free trade, finance" during his visit.[22] If this was tomfoolery it even took in the Hartford *Courant*, the newspaper least likely to misunderstand Twain. If he had typically overstated, his next comments made sober sense: England was perhaps the "most real republic" in the world, with shortcomings no worse than ours and a civil service less infested by party leeches. Over-reacting against the miasma of Grantism, he admired the British blend of elitism and democracy much more than he expected to when he asked Nast to become his illustrator.

This does not mean he had been undiscriminating as he affably raked in his lecture fees and looked after his copyrights. Anyway, he could not ignore party lines if he wanted to: the Tory-Conservative element was hostile to Yankees and quick to say so. After allowing for casual socializing it becomes clear that, like most American visitors, he gravitated toward Liberal circles, especially in his contacts with newspaper men. He was taken to Parliament by a political editor who wanted him to write for a Liberal weekly; and Frank D. Finlay, owner of the Belfast *Northern Whig* (which stuck to the Gladstone banner in hostile territory), soon rated as "one of the closest friends I have."[23] The effect of such friendships probably underlay both the six hostile pages about Prince Albert in his notebook and his cautious sympathy toward the Tichborne claimant, supposedly a prime example of the freaks that fascinated him.[24] Though he had several reasons for compiling a special scrapbook about this fight over a titled inheritance, it had become a favorite subject for Radical orators, who charged that Tory prejudice and Catholic influence were swaying the courts and denied that the claimant's sloppy manners proved he could not be blue-blooded. Twain's general scrapbook for 1872 also saved other anti-Conservative clippings about a rally to oppose the state church, a non-Anglican who refused on principle to pay tithes, and the wastefully archaic game laws that the nobility kept in force.

Unknowingly, he had stored up ammunition for *A Connecticut Yankee*, but he did a little sniping even before he finally left England in 1873. The O'Shah letters chuckled over the knighting of nonentities who had well-placed friends; a speech before a London social club joked cuttingly about the new ruling that kept plebeians out of Hyde Park. No matter how humbly he looked up to the self-made prince of industry, he held on to a Yankee Doodle hostility toward social class that was based on birth, as he showed again in his parting shot. Nettled because the nobility failed to grace his lecture audiences, he had apologized—in a letter to a stiffly

Tory paper—for not arranging the "attendance of some great members of the Government to give distinction to my entertainment," and then swung into a mock alibi about having hired dressy wax figures that got ruined in transit. This was reprinted in Finlay's *Northern Whig* with the comment that "Mark Twain has been audaciously poking fun at the snobbish tendencies of the great British public."[25]

For the present this letter was his most forceful statement on England though he had time and energy to spare for the book he had counted on as his next bestseller. Disgusted by Grantism he liked what he saw there but vacillated between reverence for stability under Queen Victoria and enthusiasm for middle-class reform under Gladstone. Perhaps he was also baffled by problems more complex in many ways than those at home and posed along unfamiliar lines; while attracted to the Liberals mostly, he switched erratically to Conservative or Radical ideas. To complicate matters further, if he happened to think in terms of the Old World against the New he suddenly changed his tone, as when his preface for the British edition of *The Gilded Age* ended with a hopeful forecast on American politics. The fumbling in the O'Shah letters indicates clearly that his confusions would have sapped the fiber of any book he completed.

No major indecisions silenced or lowered his voice as he turned again to the latest affairs at home, picking up where *The Gilded Age* had left off. When a Hartford crowd met a hometown businessman after he was forced out of the cabinet by the sharks around President Grant, Twain chimed in with an appropriate bit of comedy.[26] The letter he sent to a supper for the local Knights of Saint Patrick was much less genial: imploring their patron saint to drive out reptiles like a secretary of war who saved $12,000 annually from a salary of $8,000, it witheringly scolded the President and the swarming grafters of both parties. Restlessly searching for the source of the widespread "ulcers" he settled more heavily than before on universal suffrage, elaborating his diagnosis with a paper for the Monday Evening Club and summarizing it with epigrams such as one sent to a Tammany satrap, "We know there is Unrestricted Suffrage, we *think* there is a Hell: but the question is, which do we *prefer?*"[27] His family and friends must have heard Twain's own answer many times. A house guest from Boston, who kept a diary, recorded about her host:

He has lost all faith in our government. This wicked ungodly suffrage, he said, where the vote of a man who knew nothing was as good as the vote of a man of education and industry; this endeavor to equalize what God had made unequal was a wrong and a shame. He only hoped to live long enough to see such a wrong and such a government overthrown.

After a visit filled with lively talk she concluded that this "growing man of forty" was in "dead earnest" about life.

As Howells always claimed, it seems that to know Twain well was to take him seriously. Yet his reputation in 1875 was far short of this discovery, and he had the *Atlantic Monthly* for October publish "The Curious Republic of Gondour" without his name, not to hide from rebuttals but to get a respectful hearing. This outburst charged that the "bottom layer of society"—the "ignorant and non-taxpaying classes"—had seized control through the ballot-box, raising the problem of how to reinstate the power of "money, virtue, and intelligence." Bowing to the demagogic realities Twain merely proposed a system of extra votes but allowed these votes so generously for more property or higher education that the "hod-carriers" and their cohorts from the "ginmills" and jails would become a minority on election day at least. It is cheering to note at least that women voted in his utopian Gondour and held office, that free education ran up through the colleges, that the educated served as a "wholesome check" on the rich and as "vigilant and efficient protectors of the great lower rank," and that a top quota of votes was a higher status symbol than money. Though he never said so again, some scholars gratefully emphasize the fact that Twain also suggested more votes for education than property and implied he would mostly go in for college degrees under such a system.

The best perspective, however, is to see how closely "The Curious Republic of Gondour" was connected with other warnings that natural-rights democracy had run aground. During the stock-taking for the centennial of glorious 1776, many disciples of Manchester Liberalism openly doubted that the mob could police itself or else refrain from a feckless tyranny of its own; since monarchy belonged to the outmoded past, they called for a new patrician leadership based on brains and wealth. In the context of this debate, which raged almost as hotly here as in England, Twain's scheme of plural votes was not eccentric—though simpler proposals for giving a vote only to property-owners got heavier support. The skeptics about pure democracy also found in Gondour related features that they had been talking up like permanent judgeships and a civil service system staffed by a career elite who ran the government impartially and stopped the extorting of bribes. Such reforms, it was fondly hoped, would protect business from pickpockets like Tweed and control pirates like Vanderbilt who hired politicians to sanction their raids and would clear the road for the grand march of technology.

By now Twain had an ungilded, twenty-four-carat right to class himself among the propertied and almost as much right to consider himself well informed, with more than enough leisure to think, talk, read—the house guest from Boston said "study"—and write about what interested him. To help support this leisure he could still drop back into empty vaudeville; though Howells' review found a "growing seriousness of meaning in the apparently unmoralized drolling," the items Twain chose for *Sketches, New and Old* (1875) were more often nonsense than meaningful satire.

Designed to ride a rising market for stories about boys, *The Adventures of Tom Sawyer* (1876) was another offering with a shrewd eye on his expenses though it showed more concern for ideas by quietly refracting his characters through his deepening moral skepticism. Also adult in effect, but conventionally so, was its close variation on the popular success story with the climactic boon of a fortune rightly earned. All except his best novels would assuringly end with a big cash award to somebody deserving: the emphasis on the treasure in *Tom Sawyer* as against Jim's freedom in *Huckleberry Finn* typifies the gap between the two books.

The explicit touches of social doctrine in *Tom Sawyer* were not always so reassuring. While Injun Joe fitted the local color, his cold cruelty was meant to spread the alarm about misguided softness toward criminals. In February, 1876 one of Twain's strangely assorted friends sent him a general petition already endorsed by Longfellow, Whittier, and men of matching stature. He jotted on the envelope, "From that inextinguishable dead beat who has infested legislatures for 20 years trying to put an end to capital punishment. No answer."[28] For Injun Joe's case a petition was signed freely, and many "tearful and eloquent" meetings produced a committee of "sappy" women to "wail around the governor, and implore him to be a merciful ass and trample his duty under foot." Such acidities kept *Tom Sawyer* from turning saccharine as they steadily played over the townspeople drifting behind its plot. When shiftless Muff Potter was framed the town discovered he was a murderous-looking rascal and talked about a lynching; when he was cleared the "fickle, unreasoning world took Muff Potter to its bosom and fondled him as lavishly as it had abused him before."

Intermittently, suspicions about mass man had assailed Twain almost from the start, long before he climbed up in the world—though his first fictional use of Hannibal obviously did not record memories from the bottom layer in that village. As for his broodings about the democratic process, they would have come no matter where he was living in 1875. Reasonable cause was available to anybody who read the magazines and newspapers, and Twain was making a dogged effort to think for himself. In religion he had already moved beyond the relaxed dogma of Nook Farm, and his later feeling that he had long hidden the boldest edge of his mind referred partly to these furtive probings. But he mainly used political examples to carry the point of his dark conclusion in 1905 that "free speech is the privilege of the dead."[29] If this included his ideas on government during his first years in the Hartford house, it is because he was aware of standing often to the right of his friends as a curious Republican—hot to pry into current events, but badly tempted to doubt that democracy was worth saving.

At least what he said in public made good sense to some people. The Chicago *Times* for January 27, 1876, reported:

Mark Twain was proposed as an independent candidate for the mayor of Hartford, Conn. . . . Mr. Twain, himself a considerable property-owner, would, it is intimated, accept the nomination. . . . The Hartford people believe that he would give them a decent police force, and would not be the tool of any caucus or set of politicians.

But snatches of his "Punch, brothers, punch," jingle were run in between these sentences. The country liked Twain as a funnyman and, considering his frightful monthly bills, he could not afford as yet to wish otherwise.

I mean to heave some holiness into the Hartford primaries . . . if there was a solitary office in the land which majestic ignorance & incapacity, coupled with purity of heart, could fill, I would run for it.

FOUR

Solid Citizen

Despite the Freudian premise that hot concern with public affairs only masks a personal imbalance, it is possible to criticize senators and presidents on rational grounds. In fact Twain's hold on political reality slipped most when his own snug situation inclined him to share the complacency of his prosperous neighbors. When they announced in 1877 that putting Rutherford B. Hayes in the White House had restored our public virtue, he agreed too easily. For the next five years he trusted the Republican party with as much faith as the solemn financiers who were making Hartford an insurance center. It must have been a relief to see politics their way, and they must have remarked at their dinner parties that he was maturing as a full-fledged asset to the community.

Actually he was much less of a political asset than they expected, both in the long run and in his broader ideas at

the moment. He would have swung few votes to any party
if he had finished his essay scolding the Americans who demanded the title of "lady" or "gentleman" even though they
were not qualified by "birth, social eminence or culture."[1]
Stubbornly holding on to the keystone of his mythical Gondour, he was still capable also of hoping to turn back the
clock by arguing that "unrestricted" equality at the polls "is
founded in wrong & is weak & bad & tyrannical." Along this
useless vein his notebooks set down sardonic proposals that
the banks should give an equal vote to every stockholder,
large or small, and that the "Lord & his judiciary" should
be elective to satisfy unswerving democrats who reached
heaven.[2] Just as unrealistically—without the relieving tone of
humor—he greeted as "mighty sound and sensible" a passage
in the *Atlantic Monthly* of November, 1878 that called for
suppressing most newspapers and teaching deferential manners in the public schools. In moments of utter despair he even
toyed with his first predictions that the New World was
drifting toward chaos. Though his darkest musings were kept
private, they cast visible shadows like "The Great Revolution in Pitcairn," a savage fantasy about how the hard-
working but happy descendants of the British mutineers on
the *Bounty* sank into partisan bitterness, dreams of conquest,
and an expanding government that invented new taxes and
how they won back their simple prosperity by shipping out
the demagogic agitator, Butterworth Stavely—an American.
It is surprising to realize that just ten years separate Stavely
and Hank Morgan, the Prometheus from Connecticut.

Twain went to the trouble of publishing his fantasy on
Pitcairn, and it did imply that disaster could be avoided.
Instead of muttering passively he shouted advice any time
he saw a chance to reset our political course. During the
free-for-all before the nominating conventions of 1876 he
added his voice to booming a patrician reformer for the
presidency. When this maneuver at least blocked James G.
Blaine from the Republican ticket, Twain was happy to

settle for Hayes and quickly built up steam over what he soon considered a "momentous" battle. The boiler was stoked now and then by Howells, who rushed out a campaign biography of Hayes while urging his literary circle to stand up and be counted. A few days after Howells assured Twain that the public would take him seriously for once, he staged an interview for the New York *Herald* of August 28 in which, claiming cold impartiality, he endorsed Hayes' stand on civil service, a single term for presidents, and "honest payment of the national debt."

This last phrase, fortified with dark references to "inflation," showed that Twain had become as firm a hard-money man, as any Hartford banker. Encouraged by such solidness, prominent Republicans pressed him for total commitment, and before long he was insisting typically that a narrow margin for Hayes would not be good enough, that nothing less than a "sweeping" victory would restore faith in the judgment and motives of the average citizen. It would turn out that Twain had picked an especially bad time to set this test; but, never one to hope quietly, he started breeding ideas on how to "stampede" voters away from the Democratic candidate and proved he had caught the spirit of a hard-hitting campaign by suggesting a book of postage-stamp size titled "What Mr. Tilden Has Done for His Country" that would be pasted to a much bigger one on "What Mr. Tilden Has Done for Himself." Busy as he was with writing to line his own pockets, he might well have carried out this idea personally if he had not been afraid the serious impact would be ruined by his working signature.

Yet, without any recorded groans, he was eventually pushed into giving a full-blown oration that was respectfully quoted all over the country and reprinted verbatim under a tall headline on the front page of the *New York Times*, which also praised it editorially as proof that men of "culture and training" were doing their part.[3] With a squad of such men sitting behind him on the platform but with Hartford's working class out in front, he had felt it best to ignore the hard-money argument and spent most of his time promising that Hayes would fight for a civil service system of filling federal jobs on the basis of "worth and capacity" rather than the "amount of party dirty work" somebody had done. After briefly endorsing the whole Republican ticket from the same high ground, Twain—as president of the meeting—handed over the dirty work of bruising the enemy to a Nook Farm neighbor. Clearly on his good behavior, he had avoided the slightest touch of clowning.

Coming out for Hayes so solemnly and publicly left him even less resigned than usual to the idea of losing. On November 8, when Democrats claimed the victory, he wired Howells:

> I love to steal a while away
> From every cumbering care
> And while returns come in today
> Lift up my voice and swear.

When Republican politicos found the loose thread that would snarl the election returns into tangled deals, he switched to orthodox hymns of joy and wired a "Praise God from Whom all blessings flow."[4] As the snarl threatened to develop into another civil war, he quieted down, preferring a peaceful solution above everything else. Not until thirty years later, when he was worried about Theodore Roosevelt's increasing power, did he denounce "one of the Republican party's most cold-blooded swindles of the American people, the stealing of the presidential chair from Mr. Tilden, who had been elected, and the conferring of it upon Mr. Hayes, who had been defeated."

He did not feel this way in the spring of 1877 after Hayes' path was finally cleared. Instead he exulted to Howells, "Come—it is high time we were fixing up the cabinet, my boy." As a matter of fact the New England literati, believing they had given Hayes crucial help, felt that their circle should get some of the better posts overseas, and Twain did his share of the lobbying. Even though there were slipups and mistakes he found enough signs of an honest change to emote about Hayes on the next Fourth of July: "He looms up grand & fine, like the old-time national benefactors of history. Well, it's a long time since we've had anybody to feel proud of & have confidence in."[5] At last, over forty years old, he genuinely admired a living president. When Howells, who had entree at the White House, carried the cheering news to Hayes, he sent back a general welcome, and Twain soon tried to pay his respects in person but was blocked by an uninformed secretary—whom he properly vilified. The day of political ghost writers not having arrived, nothing was lost by his failing to get chummy with Hayes, especially if Twain wanted to repeat his advice that Colonel Richard Dodge should head up the Indian Department partly because of his "humanity"—which opposed the white grafters on the reservations yet favored having the army teach the red man to expect swift punishment for any nonsense.

Still, Twain's advice was a sign that his glacial contempt for the Indian was thawing around the edges under pressure from his neighbors, who were ahead of national opinion on this score. Hartford, and especially Nook Farm, tempered its money-getting with ethical purpose and perhaps a touch of *noblesse oblige*; more and more, he had sterling reason to class himself in the echelon that earned its comforts but nevertheless ought to help out the unlucky. It was pleasantly complex to add up his wife's income and his own. Less pleasantly, the outgo for one particular year ran to $100,000 —though this included varied, sometimes careless investments. To keep his expanding budget in balance he began backing inventions of all sorts and speculating in stocks. Teetering between his old awe and a rising sense of being an insider, he also mixed socially with the local titans of finance and industry like the fellow member of the Monday

Evening Club whom he described as a "great manufacturer, an enterprising man, a capitalist."

His respect for Hartford businessmen made it easy to believe that the Republican party had been purged by electing Hayes when this was the consensus in the parlor of Marshall Jewell, a magnate in leathers but also an officeholder on state and national levels. Jewell did not play billiards every Friday night at Twain's house, but Henry C. Robinson usually came except when he was too busy running for governor again. The birthplace of Republicanism in Connecticut, Nook Farm itself stayed uniformly hostile to the Democrats as the party that had once defended slavery and now catered to the Irish hordes who were filling up the local factories. Twain's day-to-day political circle was completed by George the butler—fervent Republican, would-be boss of the Negro voters around town, and stealthy poll-taker as he helped guests shed their coats in the ornate hall (that comfortably holds a front office today for the group that has restored Twain's house and recaptured a sense of how grandly he lived in Nook Farm).

Behind the facade of well-to-do Hartford's discussion clubs, charity work, Republican loyalty, and esthetic interests stood the same steelwork of Manchester Liberalism that most intellectuals and businessmen in this country as well as England depended on for their firmest social axioms. Twain's friends were sincere when they used the catchwords of democracy but they were more strongly committed to a laissez-faire economics. Government was needed for protecting life and property and financing the few enterprises like road building that private resources could not handle; otherwise, it should keep out of the way, letting production guided by free investment do the rest. This philosophy could be and was widely held without cynicism. Self-respecting capitalists detested the reckless robber barons as just slightly less of a threat to supply and demand miracles than the Granger or Greenbacker.

In 1878 Twain thrilled a schoolboy audience by predicting they would see more to marvel at in the next fifty years than Methuselah did in his whole lifetime. For this Coney Island of progress the stockholder put up the capital out of his savings from hard work, the industrialist ran the rides, and the inventor supplied the magic ideas; Twain told his brother:

An inventor is a poet—a true poet—and nothing in any degree less than a high order of poet. . . . to invent even this modest little drilling machine shows the presence of the patrician blood of intellect—that 'round & top of sovereignty' which separates its possessor from the common multitude & marks him as one not beholden to the caprices of politics but endowed with greatness in his own right.[6]

Public schools did their part by training a sensible electorate and turning out craftsmen and mechanics, from whose workbenches still greater inventors would graduate—so argued a long speech Twain clipped for his scrapbook in 1878-79. To get his fair share of prosperity a man merely had to prove his ability. Though Twain did not donate it to the public until later, he was already giving friends and relatives his sure-fire formula for landing a good job: take it without pay and show you are indispensable.

The mid-1870's, however, were awkward years for this advice because a depression had thrown many thousands out of work even if they deserved their pay. Fully confident that the trouble was temporary, Twain pitched in to help the worst victims of the puzzling, unscheduled slowdown; he gave benefit lectures and took part in fund-raising plays, spelling bees, and a Martha Washington pageant. Still, like his friends, he was anxious to make sure the money did not go to "professional paupers" instead of "worthy and honest poor families and individuals who had fallen into poverty through stress of circumstances but endured their miseries in silence and concealment."[7] For the passages of his Captain Stormfield fantasy that he drafted during these years he created a sausage shop owner who, suspicious of anybody who begged, would shrewdly "watch hungry-looking men and women and children, and track them home, and find out all about them from the neighbors, and then feed them and find them work."

Sound middle-class opinion, however moved by the lingering depression, was afraid of corrupting the gospel of hard work. Though Twain would soon take a more relaxed position, his parable of Edward Mills and George Benton even carried this grimness into 1880. Mills did everything right and his foster parents therefore poured their time and money into reforming their other adoptive son, a worthless rascal who was next supported by benevolent groups while Mills made his way through steady effort; when Benton eventually murdered Mills during a robbery, he was almost pardoned by the governor and his last days were sweetened by visits from sympathetic women but his victim's family was left to starve. This warning that charitable groups often wasted their money or did more harm than good drew approving fan letters, one of which grumbled that "my only fear is that the officers and members of the 'Prisoners Friend Society' will not read it."[8]

The worriment about charity was complicated by the hobo, who had suddenly loomed into notice. This new class of drifters without a job or a home upset their solvent partners in the American dream; the frightened reaction in Connecticut and elsewhere was to pass anti-vagrancy laws and treat floaters as criminals. Twain shared the nervousness they aroused, and for his scrapbook he collected newspaper stories giving the box score of their petty crimes in 1877. By no means stone-hearted, that same year he got excited because our coast guard was too calm about a drifting shipload of Negroes. But the hobo raised problems that easily entrapped Twain's famous conscience. In "The Recent Carnival of Crime in Connecticut" he complained of feeling guilty whether he lied that his icebox was empty or "told a tramp the square truth, to wit, that, it being regarded as bad citizenship to encourage vagrancy, I would give him nothing"; if he did hand out a meal his conscience cried, "O false citizen, to have fed a tramp!"—even when he insisted that the food be earned first by an odd job around the house. His heart was warring with the head of a Manchester Liberal. Publicly at least, he resolved the conflict by brushing aside "your paupers, your charities, your reforms" and offering to supply medical colleges with the corpses of "assorted tramps."

This clowning mock violence cannot be completely laughed off. After he chased away a seedy character who claimed to be soliciting for a charity, he wondered if he had been fair but also thought sternly that he should have taken time to pin down a possible fraud—"that being the plain duty of a citizen in such cases."[9] His vigilance became almost frantic when the status quo itself seemed to be threatened. The Molly Maguires in the coal pits worried him as a "powerful, numerous, and desperate . . . devilish secret organization"; the railroad workers' riots set him to condemning our weak-kneed "sham" government; as middle-class confidence wavered under these violent side effects of the depression, he even believed in 1877 that sixty thousand "communists" were "drilling" in midwestern cities.[10] Nervously echoing grumbles that the hired protectors of law and order had failed to come through and professing to doubt that the ugly truth could be exaggerated, he furiously lashed out at the posturings, dishonesty, and hollow efficiency of detectives in "The Stolen White Elephant."

For a man who studies the news as carefully as Twain did, fresh worries never stop springing up. Despite the pinch on his wife's fortune in coal mines, he could compute in 1878 that his family had "more than income enough from investments to live in Hartford on a generous scale"; he wailed, however, "now that we are fixed at last, of course the communists & the asinine government will go to work & smash it all."[11] This foreboding most likely referred to the agrarian-labor agitation for a graduated income tax, a proposal E. L. Godkin was denouncing in the *Nation* as a Marxian scheme to equalize income. Twain's notebooks projected a relevant sketch. He planned to have communists buy an island after "robbing the rich men," divide it equally, and give everybody $10,000 in cash; then he would show the "smart ones" out-trading the "loafers" and eventually hiring them on wages— a process taking about ten years, even after new redivisions, and proving the "fallacy of community of 'start' where there isn't community (equality) of brains." While he was meditating this riposte Charles Dudley Warner, who lived next door, sent the *Atlantic Monthly* a more urbane version of the same idea, driven home with a complaint that too many people felt above working as domestic help. Nook Farm was discussing Marxian socialism even if nobody there had better than a horsehair-parlor conception of it.

Though Twain continued to rate Hayes a genuine improvement over Grant, the upthrust of this hopefulness had eroded badly under such discussions and other nagging problems. The fiercest sarcasm in "Some Rambling Notes of an Idle Excursion" concerned graft in the port of New York City; by contrast with home, Bermuda struck Twain as idyllically contented under the banner of "English prosperity & good order." Straining for excuses to justify a longer trip, he insisted that the spreading talk about relaxing the gold standard was "unbearable" and pretended to feel so "cowed" by American rudeness that he had to "go & breathe the free air of Europe & lay in a stock of self-respect & independence."[12] Actually he was willing to pack his trunks almost any time—after he considered himself settled down as a family man he spent nearly a third of his life abroad. In 1878 he went partly to learn more about art and music so he could better hold his own around Nook Farm; he also wanted to pile up experiences for a new travel book. But his political grievances helped dull the pains of getting ready.

Unerringly finding what he had meant to find, he soon

rhapsodized from Frankfort-on-the-Main, "What a paradise this is! What clean clothes, what good faces, what tranquil contentment, what prosperity, what genuine freedom, what superb government!" Just as he had once admired the Caesarism of Napoleon III for its material results, he now approved of the prosperous alliance Bismarck had welded among the German middle class, the army, and the aristocracy. The larger truth here is that Twain was moving with the Anglo-American current of sympathy for the Germans as the stable yet energetic force on the continent. But even Italy benefited from his recent disquiet over the New World; despite more of his anti-Catholic fumings he stayed far from his acid-throwing of a dozen years earlier. Anybody who matches *A Tramp Abroad* against the *Quaker City* letters must conclude that Italian manners and self-respect had improved with breath-taking speed.

Seemingly the French had changed just as fast in the other direction. Though Twain and his family were tired when they reached Paris only to meet depressing weather, nothing would have helped much; France's collapse before the German army in 1870 and the radical gestures of the Paris Commune had soured world opinion. During the 1870's the French were belabored here for their gyrations between monarchy and leftism, their love of martial pomp and their contrasting failure in combat, their Catholicism or else their agnostic heresies, and their immoral appetites that sapped the national fiber. This was a rich list of faults, but Twain indicated he now saw all of them except the religious free thought. For the rest of his life he sniggered especially over French sinfulness, and his notebook quipped in 1879 that "France has neither winter nor summer nor morals."

When two statesmen held a hollow, fumbling encounter at dawn, he could not wait until his next book was ready and rushed "The Recent Great French Duel" into the pages of the *Atlantic*. While it would have been more American to favor Léon Gambetta, a champion of the republican forces,

Twain made him the butt instead of his monarchist oppo-
nent; taking sides in French politics did not seem worth the
trouble—though the pro-royalist Paris *Figaro* quickly trans-
lated and published Twain's burlesque. If he thought he was
also swelling the rise of sentiment against dueling as a stupid
anachronism, his catcalls at Gambetta's craven bluster were
really no help. As for reforming the French in general, a
wildly contemptuous essay (sensibly left out of *A Tramp
Abroad*) concluded that the only hope was to send "lay
American missionaries," disguised as ordinary *citoyens* by
wearing the ribbon of the Legion of Honor.[13] However,
when Twain sent Hank Morgan abroad, it was to England:
France seemed too far gone.

As yet he had little to say openly against the British, though
he came back growling about their "pretentious" newspapers that snubbed our gestures of cordiality and predicting
that we would not put up much longer with being "looked
down upon by a nation no bigger and no better than our
own." Ignoring England, in rounded effect *A Tramp Abroad*
was not even as hard on Europe as Twain's first travel book.
He again deplored a sweep of Romish influences but this
time added much joking at myopic Americans who insisted,
for example, that the slowest glaciers in Switzerland were in
the Catholic cantons. His reading in French history made
him look a little more kindly on the "hideous but beneficent"
revolution of 1789 but left him critical of Louis XVI for
spinelessly cheating the future of a "well-stocked Communist
graveyard" by which to remember the storming of the
Tuileries. Twain was not yet ready to bless the old bonfires
lit by a "red-capped mob of miscreants" or to borrow Patrick
Henry's three-cornered hat and Americanize the Europe of
his own day.

Still, considering the mood in which he had boarded ship,
A Tramp Abroad was surprisingly gentle toward the New
World too. He enjoyed telling about the punishment of an
American who desecrated a famous Alpine cliff with adver-

tising, but his warm portrait of "Cholley" Adams, the chatty horse doctor, proved that his love for characters in his native grain was unweakened. Politically, closer acquaintance with Europe and the reading it led to cheered him up again about the situation at home: "Looking back over history, one is comforted. Bad as our gov't is, it is a mighty improvement on old times."[14] While conceding that Europe had many advantages, he had decided they did not "compensate for a good many still more valuable ones which exist nowhere but in our country," raising the average standard of living distinctly above the Old World levels; to wealthy Americans he recommended short, not long, visits abroad that would "intensify our affection for our country and our people." Rather than a sop for his home market this was a confession he liked Europe a lot less than he had expected.

Howells was right in saying that *A Tramp Abroad* would confirm an American's patriotism without feeding his "vanity." However, it was surprisingly less political than the usual travel book of the nineteenth century; its stress on lighter matters, such as the craze for mountain climbing, fell far short of Howells' claim that it shows clearly how the "grimness of a reformer" often welled up from the "bottom" of Twain's heart. From long visits and letters Howells knew the deep seriousness of that heart and wanted to see it respected, yet he should have held up his one-man campaign at least until the next book, already in the works.

The Prince and the Pauper (1882) seems doomed to a marginal life outside the cluster of Twain's enduring books and yet apart from the ones that will inevitably be forgotten; no responsible critic has praised or condemned all of it. Only his third novel, it is much less mixed in performance, however, than in purpose. Though Twain's recurring fascination with the horrors of losing personal or social identity and his release in using the uncomplicated child as spokesman pumped energy into its veins, it has many desiccating patches of stock sentiment and plotting as a beggar and a king accidentally switch places. These weaknesses have been blamed on his Nook Farm friends, who urged him to avoid rowdy humor and generally elevate his tone. But *The Prince and the Pauper* also owes some of its strength to their belief that worth-while literature often bears on public questions. Whatever its private sources, it drew vitally on an argument interesting to loyal residents of Connecticut.

As part of the continuing duel of scolding across the Atlantic, a writer for *Blackwood's Edinburgh Magazine* of April, 1870 had cited the political and religious despotism set up by the New World Puritans and had made their Blue Laws his detailed example in contending that majorities are more tyrannical than a hereditary ruling class. Spokesmen for New England were quick to answer that *Blackwood's*, because of its own religious and political bias, sneered habitually at the American tradition. When interest kept growing, Samuel Peters' trouble-making book was reprinted in 1876, the same year *The True-Blue Laws of Connecticut and New Haven* was published by J. Hammond Trumbull—private donor of the cryptic epigraphs for *The Gilded Age*. Twain at once read this scholarly answer to Peters' myth-ridden indictment of our colonial ancestors; in fact he bought and marked up two copies, as he sometimes did with books he used both in Hartford and Elmira. Trumbull alerted him to the debate if he had not followed it before and also chalked out the best rebuttal—an exposé of the severity underlying British criminal law. Within a few months Twain considered himself to be working on *The Prince and the Pauper*.

He first thought of setting it in modern England. A few years earlier he had been moved by seeing a British judge give fourteen years at hard labor to a "humbly clad young woman" whose husband had forced her into a petty crime. But, sensing sticky problems with the plot and British dignity, he soon dropped the notion of building his story around the living Prince of Wales; well read in history, he easily found an opening in the sixteenth century to highlight British practices that existed near the same time as the notorious Blue Laws and were much harsher. Fittingly, taking a closer look had a softening effect on Twain as well as on his royal hero, and he tersely jotted in his notebook for 1879, "I disfavor capital punishment." Though he still grumbled elsewhere about the opposite fault of being too merciful, he could now in better conscience act shocked because, even up into his own century, British law had carried a death sentence for two hundred and twenty-three crimes.

To pound in his point Twain even went on beyond the end of his plot to a "General Note" declaring that the maligned laws of Connecticut "were about the first SWEEPING DEPARTURE FROM JUDICIAL ATROCITY which the 'civilized' world had seen." For the reader who needed any further prompting, Howells' review emphasized that Twain had exposed the "stupid cruelty" of "those horrible good old times" in England. However, the debunking and its immediate purpose were clear to anybody who looked beneath the comedy and melodrama buoying up the grim passages. According to Rutherford Hayes—who was a more curious mixture of Liberal and conservative ideas than Twain himself—his older children understood *The Prince and the Pauper* as the "only defense, or explanation rather, of the Puritan codes of our New England ancestor," and a British critic growled that it meant to convict his country of a still lingering "barbarism" and "so, by contrast, whitewash this embarrassing Blue business."[15]

The British critic also growled at a "general Protestant tone." Twain might have answered that he had pulled most of his punch on religious matters, as *A Connecticut Yankee* would show by comparison. It is true that only luck stopped an insane Holy Hermit from murdering the young king, but ragged Tom Canty was helped and educated by a "good old priest." Rather than lighting up the past crimes of Rome when he showed some Baptists being burned for heresy, Twain was commenting on the rigors of intolerance. In 1881 he felt impelled to undercut a genial talk about our Puritan fathers by recalling their harshness toward the Quakers and their passion for "liberty to worship as they required us to worship." Spurred on by Robert G. Ingersoll's agnostic essays, he was becoming hostile to formal religion, Protestant as well as Catholic.

The strongest British complaint was that *The Prince and the Pauper* created a "misty atmosphere of Scott's chivalry in which floats all the flunkeyism, aristocratic oppression, and so forth, of all or any later period, as revealed to Columbia's stern eye." In other words, Twain had taken the stance of a New World republican more firmly than ever before, and hindsight shows that he had started to warm up for *A Connecticut Yankee. The Prince and the Pauper* was still many degrees cooler, however, than Hank Morgan's insults or the hot asides in *Huckleberry Finn.* Though it often patronized its characters from the heights of a superior present, almost as many other touches were wistful over the chivalric past; though its haughty prince was often laughable, he matured into an admirable king. In denouncing it as a "libel on the English Court" the British *Academy* went much too far.[16] Its only vigorous passages of satire pounced on the bevy of high-ranking assistants at the King's dressing and dinner tables, a pet Yankee peeve that Twain had voiced against the Hawaiian court in 1866. In 1882 these passages must have sounded like a provocative echo of the Radicals' groans about the expensive court circle supported in the budget for Buckingham Palace and must have speeded up if not caused the drop in the British market for Twain's books that started around this time.[17]

However, the basic idea of royalty is usually treated with respect throughout the entire novel, whose closing emphasis falls on the fact that the reign of Edward VI was a "singularly merciful one." His coldness before his own troubles begin seems mostly meant for proving that humanity grows out of experience teaching you to imagine yourself in the sufferer's place—a point central to W. E. H. Lecky's *History of European Morals*, which Twain reread several times. After his early blunders the sturdy little prince rises to a mercy and heroism that justify the loyalty of stalwart Miles Hendon, who humbly accepts his share of the royal largess scattered to help a happy ending; this well-born pair is many firm mental and moral cuts above the "delighted and noisy swarm of human vermin" making up the common people. Furthermore, within its solid pity for the poor *The Prince and the Pauper* draws a sharp line between the docile paupers and "tramps and ruffians," the fake beggars or thieving vagrants whose march across the countryside borrows from Twain's fretting about the drifters spawned by the American depression of 1873. Tom Canty and his father neatly typify this ambivalence toward the submerged masses, who are, in any event, loyal to the crown with Twain's blessing. Perhaps such undemocratic reverence was overridden for genteel readers when Tom—because he otherwise had to deny knowing his mother—cooperated in proving the identity of the true king, but his cheerful abdication also smacks of the theme that uneasy lies the head burdened with the crown's duties. The juvenile audience that continues to enjoy Twain's tale surely sees it in terms of high-minded, careworn kings and their faithful subjects.

Not that the juvenile mind ever was Twain's regular target. Less than a month after getting back from Europe in 1879, he had his bearings on the newest problems crowding the national scene and was dabbling in politics—privately and publicly. Though nothing memorable resulted for a while, a stack of unfinished manuscripts from between 1879 and 1883 shows his eager tries at steering the country toward the best channels. It took exploring and luck to find the best channels for himself as an artist, but all his important work during the rest of the 1880's was heavy with topical significance.

Among the earliest news Twain heard after getting home

was the report that John Hay, having added substance to his literary talent and starchy ways by marrying the daughter of a Cleveland millionaire, was going to run for Congress. This delighted the white-collar circles who had been calling for better educated, more principled candidates. As Twain put it, "When such men come forward, it has a good influence, for it emboldens other men of like stamp to do likewise."[18] Eager to "heave some holiness" of his own into the campaign, even before settling back into Nook Farm he took time to give Joseph Hawley a humorous but also glowing testimonial at a mass meeting.

Such an immediate leap into the melee helped start a rumor that Twain himself would offer to become a congressman. Despite his contemptuous denial it kept popping up in newspapers across the country; a mutual friend wrote from Cleveland that she and John Hay hoped it was true and thought Twain's soul would be "stirred and tested" if he held an elective post. If he had ended up in Congress many things would have been stirred and tested; however, he stuck to the role of a loudly thoughtful spectator. About this time an impartial outsider made an extremely apt analysis:

In politics he at first impresses you as an indifferentist, with perhaps a leaning toward pessimism; but . . . you soon discover that your first impression was very remote from the truth. The fact is, like many another thoughtful man, Mark Twain sees plainly the gravity of the present and future in the United States, and accordingly has very little patience with the spread-eagleism and cheap declamations of contending politicians. Probably his political creed is not very different from that of the Independents, a new and still unorganized party, which is daily growing among the citizens of the great Republic.[19]

Forgivably wrong about the long-range strength of his pessimism, this even correctly predicted his coming shift to the mugwumps.

For an independent, Twain's next political move was a

serious misstep. Trying to boom Grant for a third term as president, his managers drummed up a Civil War reunion in Chicago, and Twain agreed to make a toast at the climactic banquet—where he enjoyed the flag-waving with a fervor that would not have been possible before his last trip abroad. However, he had regained his balance by convention time, when the Republicans nominated James Garfield instead of giving in to the party hacks operating through Grant. Satisfied that there was a ticket he could support, he squandered his energy on sardonic doggerel about unpredictable Ben Butler, who had turned both Greenbacker and Democrat.[20] When Grant was persuaded to stump New England in spite of his setback at the convention, Twain joined the rush to make a winning display of harmony and honor his Civil War exploits again without the danger of putting him back into the White House.

Since Twain was on the committee to arrange for and kick off the rally at Hartford, a network of Grant's friends, working to ignite national opinion, got him to include a plug for a law that would allow the General a fat pension.[21] Of course his welcoming speech also took note of Grant's current march to save the country once more—this time from "dishonor & shame, & from industrial disaster." Just giving Grant a staged welcome, for that matter, waved the bloody shirt that even Liberal Republicans, disappointed with how the South had behaved after federal troops pulled out, were willing to brandish again. Though the Democrats tried to parry this tactic by matching ex-General Garfield with Winfield Hancock, another Union hero, their opposition pressed its advantage. Twain was quick to sneer about the scarcity of "Hancock veterans—in the South."[22]

In the final stage of the campaign, Republican tacticians, afraid the bloody shirt was losing its magic, decided to emphasize that the Democrats courted "industrial disaster"— as Twain put it in welcoming Grant—with their efforts to cut back the protective tariffs. Twain followed this somewhat cynical maneuver in a long speech on October 26. After posing again as a stranger to political rallies, he made a burlesque defense of the Wood tariff bill, which had been essentially killed two years ago. Lowering the tariffs, he argued, would do away with the nuisance of factory smoke, make poorhouses a common sight, and give a sound reason for being unemployed; to the middle class he promised that laws depriving them of the "improving, elevating, humanizing society of the tramp" would be voted out by tramps themselves as the new majority and that any prosperous households still left would find "our old, ragged tourists moving in eternal procession from door to door disdaining bread and demanding pie at the butt-end of the club"; as for sectional effects the Wood tariff bill would let the South build up foreign trade and eventually "buy and sell" the North, while its international effects would benefit the British, who did all they could to "injure us and cripple us and insult us" during the Civil War. With perhaps the deepest plunge into demagoguery Twain ever took, he appealed even to the local Irish by warning that lowered tariffs would reinstate England as their "hard master" after they had migrated here to escape "seven hundred years" of such oppression.

Because of his genius at handling an audience this speech may have sounded better than it reads today, but the burlesque approach is awkward and the tone overwrought. After the election he was just as shrill in a mock funeral oration for the Democratic party—"a hoary political tramp, an itinerant poor actor, familiar with many disguises, a butcher of many parts." His crowing at a Garfield dinner in Boston was much more effective: "The Republicans won a substantial victory in my state despite the fact that I made a few speeches. The most important part of the victory was the election of Republican Sheriffs in seven counties out of eight. That is as it should be. Have officers and criminals on opposite sides!"[23] Far from really believing any more that his support was a liability, he felt he had earned a stronger right to back his favorites in the scramble for jobs under the new administration; he especially pushed a petition to have Howells made minister to the Netherlands. Though Washington circles surely admired him more as a humorist than as a politician, he got headlines with his campaign speeches and therefore rated some influence. When Howells later called for help because greedy hands were after his father's consulship, Twain was able to save it by working through Grant.

The best example of Twain's ramifying influence reached out to the Far East. In late 1880 he asked Grant to dissuade the Chinese government from closing its Educational Mission, a school it had set up at Hartford to steep some of its bright young men in Western culture; he took high ground but was well aware that Yung Wing, the Chinese minister at Washington, was fighting to save this school because he would like to see his country eased into the orbit of American capital. By the spring of 1881 Twain also became a go-between in a more direct drive to undercut European control of investment in Chinese railroad building and similar projects.[24] Thinking big, this busy ring worked next at dominating the appointments to our foreign service in Japan. They lost on keeping the Hartford school open, won on the diplomatic posts, and dreamed about profits that would have satisfied even Colonel Sellers. Eventually Twain took Yung Wing to meet Grant and propose an American railroad syndicate for operations in China.

But his career as an influential Republican had started to crumble with the shooting of President Garfield, whose slow death stretched feeling to an excruciating pitch. Agonizing over the news in his "house of mourning . . . like all the others in the land," Twain violently joined the tidal wave of revulsion against the spoilsmen. In his notebook he savagely damned the Stalwarts or machine politicians whom the psychotic assassin had claimed to serve, indicted their system of squeezing campaign funds from state and federal job holders as "Fijian slavery," and urged himself to "write a novel with a *real* M.C." who would waste hundreds of millions if he was promised a thousand-dollar bribe.[25] Gloating with revived zeal over every beating that "bossism" took at the polls, in late 1882 Twain chortled at length over a rout that the Republican machine suffered in New York after running "paltry" men. Always ready to see issues in terms of personalities, he got even more emotional because Whitelaw Reid was prominent in the squabbles that darkened Garfield's few weeks as president. As the New York *Tribune* had moved further and further away from the Republican faction who fought the grafters in their own party, Twain had projected a biography that would compare Reid to one of Boss Tweed's notorious errand boys. But when Reid proved to be giving orders as well as taking them, he was not dumfounded; during the bitter tug of war around Garfield he drafted a venomous attack on Reid's ambitions and his "coarse" taste in "volunteering to help the President of the United States conduct his government."[26] This may have been written after some trouble maker assured Twain that the *Tribune* was regularly slandering him, a story he could believe without checking. Before he learned it was untrue he filled pages of his notebooks with ideas for counterblasts; some were brutally personal but many dealt with the time-serving policies of the *Tribune* or magnified the gossip about Reid's backstage moves and his obligations to Jay Gould.[27] Twain must have been relieved when his honor did not require publishing any of this or a charge that the editor of the *Tribune* had indirectly caused Garfield's death.

Though Twain stayed out of newspaper columns in the months after Garfield died, his friends let it be known that he was worked up. Prompted also by an essay in which faithful Howells praised his "burning resentment of all manner of cruelty and wrong," the editor of a big monthly magazine asked for "three papers on the permanent sources of corruption in our government . . . a serious exposition of the ways that are dark of the professional politician."[28] Because Twain's answer that he was too busy went on to an outburst against railroad passes for congressmen as petty but flagrant bribery, the editor pressed him until he flatly decided he would put all his time into finishing his next book. That he did not refuse from lack of interest is shown by passages cut from *Life on the Mississippi* in the final editing. On the pretext of comparing antebellum and present society they complained about the continued graft, the repeated failures to set up an honest civil service system, and the unending control of Congress by "thieves" and "pauper intellects." These criticisms were cemented by an appeal for an individual sense of responsibility, for faith to a "citizen's duty" of supervising the public welfare.

Increasingly, Twain had been fulfilling this duty. If he relapsed now and then to the brink of pessimism, he always plowed back into battle; since 1876 he had fought vigorously and had even become hopeful that the level of civic morality could be raised. After the shock of Garfield's murder, the national reaction against bossism gave him "new confidence in the soundness of our republican system." His old-fashioned political terms, however, betrayed his naïveté about forces that would prove far too powerful to be guided by past formulas. And though slowly learning humanity toward the suffering caused by business cycles, he still believed that laissez-faire economics, energized by technology, would soon bury it under a flood of consumer goods. Almost a rich man already, he confidently expected to increase his own family's share of solid comfort. Yet he was not satisfied to relax in his expensive house while the world's problems screeched past: within the limits set by nineteenth-century Liberalism, he was trying hard to be a responsible citizen.

There is hardly a celebrated Southern name in any of the departments of human industry except those of war, murder, the duel, repudiation, & massacre.

FIVE

The Scalawag

IN THE MIDDLE of distractions like frothing about Whitelaw Reid or Captain Duncan, the *Quaker City* skipper who was now a political vulture preying on the ships that docked at New York, Twain went back to and finished *Adventures of Huckleberry Finn*. His mounting involvement in public affairs marks how far he usually or at least often was from the nostalgia that some have sensed as dominant in his greatest novel. While steamboating down the Mississippi in 1882 he must have added his share to all parts of a gabfest that "began with talk about horses, drifted into talk about astronomy, then into talk about the lynching of the gamblers in Vicksburg half a century ago, then into talk about dreams and superstitions; and ended, after midnight, in a dispute over free trade and protection"; but probably nobody on board argued harder about free trade than Twain. His crony Howells recalled, "Upon most current events he had strong opinions, and he uttered them strongly."

In postbellum America any serious concern with current events had to include the status of the South, though Twain needed no prodding on this subject. Most of the time he considered himself a southerner by birth and felt blessed with a special ability to prescribe for Negroes. As late as 1877 when his in-laws were debating whether to give their handyman a silver watch for stopping a runaway horse, he pontificated, "I know the colored race, & I know that . . . this fine toy will throw the other more valuable testimonials far away into the shade."[1] This sounds as if he had not learned enough from accepting Frederick Douglass as a friend when they met at Elmira, as if his cordiality toward this former slave and crusading lecturer had been primarily a tactic in an all-out campaign to win over Livy Langdon's parents. Humbly politic right down the line, even about his cigar-smoking, perhaps he saw a special need to prove that he disowned the mistakes of his Virginia and Kentucky ancestors. When he became an owner of the Buffalo *Express* in 1869, he started swinging a Republican cudgel like the most opportunistic scalawag.

Dutifully swelling the outcry that the South was still backward or even barbarous, much of Twain's earliest writing for the *Express* ranged from squibs like "Education is said to be the great hobby in Tennessee at the present time. Will it outlast the velocipede?" to editorials like "Only a Nigger," which played up the crudity of "mob-law."[2] Already building up toward his famous diatribe against Sir Walter Scott, he blamed lynching on "chivalric" posturings and elsewhere sneered at a Southern vogue for tournaments among mock knights as "absurdity gone crazy." If handled roughly, the ex-Rebels were good copy in the North. The opening chapters of *The Gilded Age* carefully placed its hopelessly ignorant settlement of poor whites in Tennessee, and the main story line used a Confederate colonel who was bold at seduction but finally a coward otherwise. At first Twain was, in part, merely profiteering in the sectional war of words; but as he settled deeper into Nook Farm his criticisms became wholly sincere. A few days before the election of 1876 he privately yet heartfully castigated the average southerner for "opaque perception" and a "dense and pitiful chuckleheadedness" that allowed "social ostracism" of anybody who voted Republican. Reacting to every rise or fall in the road toward reunion, after the compromise of 1877 he briefly trusted the idea of lulling tensions; but when the campaign of 1880 brought out the bloody shirt again, his major speech for Garfield would have satisfied a survivor of Andersonville prison. Stockpiling insults for other barrages, his notebook recorded a gibe that the South was good only at "war, murder, the duel, repudiation, & massacre."[3]

A close look at the election returns showed that southerners were voting Democratic as overwhelmingly as ever and, more largely, seemed to show that there was no basic hope of cleansing the Republican party so long as the bogy of a Solid South—as it quickly came to be called—could scare the North into tolerating the leadership of Roscoe Conkling and his sort.[4] As this flurry of analysis grew stronger Twain got around to retracing the channels of his pilot days. The trip had appealed to him for the last ten years, even before he started writing for the *Atlantic Monthly* about old times on the Mississippi, and when he did go steamboating again he naturally drifted into remembrance of things past. However, the fact that he finally put this trip above other demands and projects was partly due to the live debate that sent a thickening parade to gauge the liberated South's doings. His firsthand report had obvious topical value in the marketplace. Along with better examples, it refutes the notion that none of his books between *The Gilded Age* and *A Connecticut Yankee* has "anything like a contemporary social implication." Such a notion about *Life on the Mississippi* assumes that only its first and now classic chapters were important to Twain and the readers of his day.

After the first third of the book, which reworked the cub

pilot episodes written earlier, Twain surveyed the river-valley South of 1882. Though he carefully whipped up plenty of the froth that made him a giant in the subscription trade, he left a trail of serious opinion, mostly with constructive praise for any signs of rising industry, but also with flickering sarcasm for any vestiges of the cotton kingdom. Later chapters drew an implicit regional contrast that he pointed up now and then, as by writing, "From St. Louis northward there are all the enlivening signs of the presence of active, energetic, intelligent, prosperous, practical nineteenth-century populations. The people don't dream; they work." This reproving approval of the "go-ahead atmosphere which tastes good in the nostrils" covered the rest of the river valley all the way to Minneapolis, and he summed it up with: "Solicitude for the future of a race like this is not in order." For all its sighs about the lost romance of a steamboating past, *Life on the Mississippi* marks the first full blare of Twain's modernism.

Without feeling beyond his depth he even gave the lagging South some very specific advice, based on oracles like Edward Atkinson, a New England manufacturer and self-breveted economist whose word "upon any vast national commercial matter" struck Twain "as near ranking as authority as can the opinion of any individual in the Union." *Life on the Mississippi* solemnly cited Atkinson's proposals for building levees or using cotton stems as feed and fertilizer, echoed the scolding of his banker friends about the South's failure to find a better economic pattern than the crop-lien system, and praised a cottongrowing syndicate—financed in Boston—that planned to do away with sharecroppers by hiring Negroes outright or else giving them a chance to buy small farms. Twain also offered a firm theory on why the old Confederacy was so slow to enjoy the "wholesome and practical nineteenth-century smell of cotton factories and locomotives": it was infected with a "maudlin Middle-Age romanticism," caught mainly from Sir Walter Scott's still

popular novels. Breaking the tone of genial tact his hunger
for big sales dictated, he raged that the ideals set by these
novels were keeping the South "in love with dreams and
phantoms . . . decayed and swinish forms of religion . . . decayed and degraded systems of government" and thundered
on to his notorious charge that Scott's influence was "in great
measure" responsible for the Civil War—though he instantly
conceded this was a "wild proposition" and spent no time
arguing it. Hotly intent on the present he instead wailed—in
something of an anticlimax—that a South without this
"medieval" legacy would be "fully a generation further advanced than it is."

He made a spotty try at detailing his indictment. Though
he mentioned Scott's fondness for "caste," he did not press
this point and also saved most of his anger toward Catholicism
until he wrote *A Connecticut Yankee*. He had planned to
ridicule the mock tournament again but publicly decided that
its "puerility" was small and scarce game. He likewise decided that the Mardi Gras carnival, while spreading locally,
would never beguile "practical" people, because Northern
newspapers would deflate its "girly-girly romance" with
"merciless fun." But he berated Southern editors for their
failure to do so and, more generally, for their "flowery and
idiotic" diction that aspired to Scott's "swell, medieval bulli-
ness and tinsel"; he also inveighed against the "sham castles"
that southerners were still building for houses, colleges, and
state capitols. It is intriguing to wonder how much this passion for plebeian simplicity drove Twain to found his next
two books squarely on a vernacular spokesman for the first
time.

Of course he did not make a convincing case against Scott,
and his theory on the Civil War has often been derided as a
typical eruption from his shallow crater of thought. More
and more, however, it appears that no theory on what caused
the war is going to attract a majority. The broader charge
that Scott fed reactionary forces is almost as hard to prove

or disprove, but it had enough basis to merit revivals up to the present. For that matter, Twain had a fair amount of encouragement in the 1880's; even cautious and peaceable Howells was accusing Scott of teaching love for hereditary class and aristocratic pomp.[5] Reading other primary sources in the argument about the Solid South will dredge up countless references to lingering "feudal" or—especially if introduced by the defense—"chivalric" patterns.

Twain did not load all the blame on the sets of Scott novels that graced Southern parlors: he had just as pungent opinions about the overpowering strength of the Democratic party below the Mason-Dixon line. Brusquely declaring that the Southern white was "as far from emancipation as ever," *Life on the Mississippi* argued that it was contrary to "nature" when all of exotically diverse New Orleans voted on the same side. Nature seems to mean cosmopolitan reason here, for Twain went on, "Given a 'solid' country anywhere, and the ready conclusion is that it is a community of savages." This "barbaric" unanimity, he argued further, was tied to various kinds of coercion and—ultimately—an uncivilized toleration of violence. During his visit to New Orleans in 1882 he sampled attitudes toward the duel. When a shady character with several victories to his credit was shot in the "backside," Twain gleefully recorded this unheroic turn.[6] Though he decided that the duel was fading even in a South hanging on to worn-out dreams of chivalry, he saw political reason to work the Darnell-Watson feud into his book as well as to compliment the "independent race" along the upper river because they "think for themselves."

The hottest criticism of the Solid South was eventually cut from the manuscript for *Life on the Mississippi*, because its publisher had got worried about offending possible customers. There were some Southern grumbles anyway.[7] But the larger hubbub kept gaining force, and Twain had something more on his mind. He had said little about the Negro in *Life on the Mississippi*—even during its advice on cotton economics—and had said nothing that revealed he was increasingly gripped by a passion for the freedman's welfare.

There had, however, been signposts along the way like "A True Story," which improved the quality of the *Atlantic* for November, 1874. Though readers of today find it stiff with Victorian sentiment, in context it refreshingly treated the Negro as a sometimes troubled adult rather than a fun-loving darky and recalled poignantly how the cotton kingdom had ignored the fact that slaves could feel deep love for their families—Howells later praised it as "one of those noble pieces of humanity with which the South has atoned" for its "despite." When Northern newspapers and magazines began to feature material on the ex-slave, Twain was a willing buyer. Also a very early admirer of spirituals he preferred the most dolorous plaints about bondage and sang them himself with luxurious emotion. By 1881, impressed by mounting complaints that the Bourbon Brigadiers had nullified the advances for which the Union army had bled, Twain had firmly come to feel that the freedman needed help. He urged keeping Frederick Douglass as marshal to the District of Columbia and claimed him as a "personal friend" whose "brave, long crusade for the liberties and elevation of his race" was to be admired. With almost no grumbling Twain became a soft touch for Douglass' race, even supporting one Negro through four years of college. Howells' impression that his crony was consciously making the "reparation due from every white to every black man" is confirmed by a letter in which Twain argued that nine-tenths of the guilt fell "upon your heads and mine and the rest of the white race" whenever a Negro went wrong.[8] The fever stage of this expiatory ardor bracketed the time when he was completing *Huckleberry Finn*—the same time that his wife suggested a motto for curbing his temper: "Consider every man colored until he is proved white."

The practical pull of such an attitude is indicated by his friendship with George Washington Cable. A month after their first meeting in 1881, Twain was full of praise for Cable's *Madame Delphine* and soon spoke just as warmly about *The Grandissimes*, from which Howells and he read aloud to each other. Letters between New Orleans and Hartford built up to house visits and, at the end of 1884, to a joint tour of the lecture circuit. If Twain could not see immediately that Cable meant his fiction to comment on current race relations in spite of its antebellum settings, the clamor it set off surely opened his eyes. By the time of their lecture tour Cable, who had come out to fight openly for the Negro's legal and political rights, was almost notorious as a reformer. However, especially before friction rose from the grind of one-night stands, the "Twins of Genius"—as posters called them—were so compatible that Cable's ideas may account for some of *Huckleberry Finn*.[9] The probability that there was a direct influence shows clearly how Twain stood, though his humane concern was feeding on sources broader than private friendship.

In even the literary world Cable had lusty cohorts like Albion W. Tourgée, whose novels were much more openly partisan and used contemporary settings, while the unreconstructed camp bred apologists who skilfully founded the plantation myth in the short story and novel. Northern editors would not buy unmasked defiance, but some of them printed Joel Chandler Harris's stories implying that the Southern Negro was contented, understood by his white folks, and able to defend himself. Thomas Nelson Page capped this soothing approach with his version of the slave who was unready to face the cold rigors of freedom and unreconciled to losing the glamor and love that once radiated from the pillared mansion. Perhaps wanting a sauce for its popular but heavy series of Civil War memoirs, the *Century Magazine* accepted fiction from both sides. It printed Page's "Marse Chan" in April, 1884 and in December started running excerpts from *Huckleberry Finn* with the Grangerford-Shepherdson feud as a natural first choice.

Unfinished manuscripts reveal that Twain had been struggling to get an appropriate story under way. While chiding at a "little too much of the old Abolitionist legend of the Deep South," a foremost authority believes that *Huckleberry Finn* came when it did through "no mere accident."[10] Good enough to last a long time, it owes much of its luminosity to a flaming social and literary debate of Twain's own time. There are exceptions—some of them illusory—but all in all Huck spoke for Twain in remarking, "I don't take no stock in dead people."

Despite the critics who have charted intricate tunnels beneath the surface of *Huckleberry Finn*, the reader who comes to it without a thesis is interested keenly in the fate of its runaway slave. Twain publicly exclaimed in 1888 that "we used to own our brother human beings, and used to buy them and sell them, lash them, thrash them, break their piteous hearts—and we ought to be ashamed of ourselves."[11] *Huckleberry Finn* projected this emotion with strategies worthy of his close neighbor in Hartford, Harriet Beecher Stowe. By the middle of the book it is easy to accept Jim as a brother human being and share his heartbreak from the callousness with which slave families were separated and to feel that the whites were hardened, even brutalized by owning their fellow man—a common argument in the 1880's but epitomized perfectly in an otherwise decent Aunt Sally's notorious relief that nobody was hurt since "only a nigger" was killed in the explosion on the steamboat. It is just as easy to feel vicariously shamed because helping Jim forces Huck to fight inner battles, especially against his awareness that he is inviting the deepest social disgrace and his conviction that he is damning himself to hell-fire. For more than the last hundred years any short story or novel about antebellum society has at least implied a historical judgment, and *Huckleberry Finn* continues to deny in effect that the cotton kingdom was a defensible system. Howells remembered Twain as "entirely satisfied with the result of the Civil War and . . . eager to have its facts and meanings brought out at once in history."[12]

With matching eagerness readers of the 1880's saw the immediate use of implying that the Confederacy had deserved to lose and saw that to question the myth of the happy slave is to cast suspicion, by a weak but common linkage, on any later move the Deep South makes concerning the Negro. Those who believed Page's "Marse Chan" could stop worrying about the freedman; those who believed *The Grandissimes* would oppose abandoning him to the Redemptionists' custody. More forcefully than Cable's fiction and more expertly than Tourgée's, *Huckleberry Finn* gave a timely answer to Page and other romancers about the idyllic plantation. However, it did much more than oppose the glamorizing of the Old South. Gracefully moving in and out of the antebellum context to suit the purpose right at hand, it managed also to judge the South's conduct after being paroled to its own conscience by the compromise of 1877. Analyses of the novel that ignore the context Twain himself was living and writing in can never explain all of Huck's wanderings or some memorable passages during which Jim's flight to freedom is sidetracked.

Even before moving the action away from St. Petersburg, Twain drew Huck's father with a uniqueness beyond its needs. Pap Finn was more than a casually invented villain to his creator, whom a friend recalled as "assured . . . of the social truths behind Pap's diatribe on negro suffrage"; he stood for a class excoriated by name in *A Connecticut Yankee* and later in Twain's comment that slavery had a "hardly less baleful influence upon the poor white." Already puzzled by how willingly the mudsills of the Confederacy had died for it, Republicans began fretting about "popular ignorance" as the Democratic party made a fast comeback; and after 1880 there was even talk of excluding illiterates from the polls in order to cancel the "solid ignorant vote of the South"—this meant whites, of course, since few freedmen went Democratic. More realistically, the Republican faction that was best versed in Liberalism proposed federal aid to education as a way of helping not only the Negro but also the poor white to improve himself. But to their dismay many politicians in the South blocked such legislation, sharply cut the state funds for schools, and still kept winning elections.

Contradicting the sentimental novelists who were rising to the poor white's defense, Pap showed noisomely how his class resisted progress. Superstitious and shiftless, on his first appearance he raged againt the "hifalut'n foolishness" of his son's learning to read and write in defiance of family tradition. The only other time Huck quoted him at length, Pap was angry about what happened when he was on his way to vote—"if I warn't too drunk to get there." He had been upset by seeing a mulatto who "was a p'fessor in a college in Ohio, and could talk all kinds of languages, and knowed everything"; on hearing that the welldressed mulatto could vote at home, boozy Pap had "drawed out" and sworn never to touch a ballot again. His outrage because this "prowling, thieving, infernal white-shirted free nigger" could not be seized and sold led back into his favorite tirade. Though Huck reported that "whenever his liquor begun to work, he most always went for the govment," this time Pap outdid himself in disowning a meddlesome "govment" that even kept him from grabbing the fortune Huck had earned in *Tom Sawyer*. To readers in 1885, Pap vividly typified how the poor whites served the South's reactionaries by opposing education, insisting on white supremacy, and lining up against "governmental interference of any kind."[13]

Though Pap never got another chance to rasp his magisterial opinions, by getting killed in a brawl he swelled the violence that forms a dark undertone throughout *Huckleberry Finn*. In putting together a plot Twain almost always used plenty of mayhem, and even idyllic *Tom Sawyer* had its share; but he deliberately stepped up the flow of violent episodes in its sequel. The handiest proof lies in *Life on the Mississippi*, finished less than a year before *Huckleberry Finn*. When he covered the country just below Memphis, his account of a killing over a small matter was prefaced with,

"Piece of history illustrative of the violent style of some of the people down along here." This point was expanded in the long footnote that—he told his publisher—ticked off "some Southern assassinations"; running well over a page, it reprinted the damning details on many current cases of homicide or assault.[14] *Huckleberry Finn* continued this emphasis on the Southern proneness to climax a quarrel with shooting or stabbing or to lend a hand at lynch law.

To make this emphasis simply a clue to Twain's neuroses is to ignore again his sensitivity to current events. As early as August 24, 1869, he had fantasied in the Buffalo *Express* about a convention of Georgia editors, "Their revolvers and bowie-knives have been transported thither at reduced rates by the express companies. The convention ought to consult economy a little further, and through 'sealed proposals' to the undertakers, let their funerals to the lowest bidder." This special angle was soon given detailed play in "Journalism in Tennessee," a raucous burlesque that ends with the battered and maimed outsider saying, "I came South for my health, I will go back on the same errand, and suddenly." Twain was already convinced when, around 1880, Republicans began to complain more loudly than ever that intimidation was helping to keep the South a Democratic preserve and when the New York *Evening Post*, his favorite newspaper, began playing up reports of Southern feuds and other kinds of homicide. E. L. Godkin plugged away so vigorously that he gave the *Post* a "decided mortuary flavor," but Carl Schurz, his co-editor who was a Civil War veteran as well as a sworn enemy of machine politicians, emerged as the leader of outrage over the Homicidal Side of Southern Life (as "Marse Henry" Watterson wryly put it).[15] On the day after Twain told his publisher he was adding the long footnote to his travel book, the Savannah *News* objected to the garish spotlight being wielded by the *Post* and also the *Nation*—though Schurz denied he was exaggerating and stuck to his crusade through the election of 1884.

Instead of firing off more letters to some newspaper Twain had been trying to have his say through his books. His abortive Simon Wheeler novel used a Kentucky feud that senselessly raged on long after everybody forgot how the trouble had started; *Life on the Mississippi* carefully spotted the Darnell-Watson affair in westernmost Kentucky because "in no part of the South has the vendetta flourished more briskly, or held out longer." The Grangerford-Shepherdson feud in *Huckleberry Finn*, also between quality folk who could not recall "what the row was about," took place at the same spot. These three episodes rested on a memory from Twain's pilot days, yet it had been evoked and shaped by recent issues. The timeliness of the massacre in *Huckleberry Finn* was confirmed by an admirer who wrote that it was "in so far as the facts go but a leaf from the daily record of our day" and enclosed an item from the Cincinnati *Enquirer* describing an incident "directly in point" against the "*lunkheads* who disbelieve in the reality of the southern *vendetta*."[16] While Twain later threw away most of his letters for 1885, he preserved this one after jotting "Southern feud. answer" on the envelope, instead of "damphool"—his usual tag when he was irritated by stray mail.

The feud, especially between families of any status, was nevertheless waning by the 1880's. So was the duel. Twain's notes show he thought of weaving at least a relevant anecdote into *Huckleberry Finn*, but he apparently decided that even Southern duelists were a vanishing breed.[17] These notes also show he hoped to work in a lynching. For that matter Pap's townsmen talked of stringing him up for Huck's "murder." When Huck met the Duke and the King they were both running from mobs that meant business and the three of them barely escaped manhandling at the end of the Peter Wilks episode; later, tarred and feathered, the sharpers rode on a rail—to Huck's disgust. As part of the climax in the plot another yelling mob was even threatening to hang innocent Jim until it was stopped by the question of who would pay his owner. Though the height of the antilynching furor lay ahead, the Ku Klux Klan's nightridings—actual and rumored —were already touching off startled criticism that Twain magnified and exploited.

His concern about Southern violence found its most vigorous outlet in the Sherburn-Boggs episode, which directly echoed one of the passages cut from *Life on the Mississippi*. Noting that the South was commonly thought of as "one vast and gory murder-field" where "every man goes armed, and has at one time or another taken a neighbor's life," Twain had charged that its better element, while mostly law-abiding, was encouraging defiance of civilized codes because it failed to insist on convictions "even in the clearest cases of homicide" and therefore tacitly let some "hot head" defy the "hamlet." Such a hothead was Colonel Sherburn, who publicly killed an unarmed, drunken heckler in *Huckleberry Finn*. When a mob surged out to Sherburn's house in daylight, he met it with a contemptuous lecture:

Your newspapers call you a brave people so much that you think you *are* braver than any other people—whereas you're just *as* brave, and no braver. Why don't your juries hang murderers? Because they're afraid the man's friends will shoot them in the back, in the dark—and it's just what they *would* do.

He went on to sneer that after a spineless jury acquitted a murderer, some firebrand raised a lynching party from bystanders too cowardly to resist the misguided cry to manhood. Before routing the mob with a cocked gun, Sherburn gratuitously taunted, "If any real lynching's going to be done, it will be done in the dark, Southern fashion." Though Sherburn's passing gibe that in the South "one man, all by himself, has stopped a stage full of men, in the day-time, and robbed the lot" sounds like period-piece detail, in another passage cut from his travel book Twain had given as an example of the average southerner's instinct to cringe when he should be doing a citizen's duty: "The other day, in Kentucky, a single highwayman, revolver in hand, stopped a stage-coach and robbed the passengers, some of whom were armed—and he got away unharmed."

While the reader of today still finds the Sherburn-Boggs scenes especially vivid, their power came partly from the debate that Schurz had kept boiling and he must have admired how well they fitted into it. Involving "a heap the best dressed man in town," the killing nevertheless turned out a cold assassination in which Colonel Sherburn—whose patrician airs suggest a planter ruined by the war—obeyed a cruel, hypersensitive code. As for the community, it enjoyed the break in its sleepy routine; nobody called for the sheriff, who never stepped forward. When a mob gathered impulsively and swirled out to the murderer's house, it melted before his defiance. And there the matter ended to the harm of the South. This harm Twain, who stayed a fervent Republican until the final electioneering of 1884, had recently spelled out: because the average southerner did not "band himself with his timid fellows to support the law," his section was disgraced by "unpunished murder, against the popular approval, and the decay and destruction of independent thought and action in politics."[18] Without rigidly equating violence and the Solid South, Twain subscribed to the idea that they were more than casually connected.

Less obviously and vividly, he also traced other interlacings of backwardness and reaction in the Redeemed South. Though experts admire the rich folklore embedded in *Huckleberry Finn*, Twain did not use it merely for realistic detail, much less warm humor; his notebook for 1882 tautly complained that "human nature" makes "superstitions and priests necessary,"[19] and *A Connecticut Yankee* bludgeoned any notion of omens or witchcraft. Perhaps the crude medical lore in *Tom Sawyer* aimed at only a casual smile, but the cross of nails in Pap Finn's left bootheel fitted into the pattern of benighted ignorance. Stimulated in 1879-80 by Robert G. Ingersoll—the great agnostic and iconoclast—Twain had intensified his scorn for outdated ideas and mores. His spurting rationalism likewise made him quicker to ridicule the shouting fundamentalists who grew most rankly in the South, as freethinkers well knew. After generalizing earlier that "there was plenty other farmer-preachers . . . down South" like Silas Phelps who "never charged nothing for his preaching, and it was worth it," Huck went out of his way to note that Silas—"drunk" with bewildering news—unleashed a "prayer-meeting sermon . . . that give him a rattling ruputation because the oldest man in the world couldn't a understood it." Certainly intending his own public to be more outraged than robustly amused by the camp-meeting Huck saw, Twain ordered his illustrator to ignore it because pictures would tell the "disgusting" truth "too plainly."[20]

The social history in *Huckleberry Finn* was sometimes nostalgic and sometimes reeking with Twain's latent contempt for men everywhere; but much of it filled in the darker half of the contrast that *Life on the Mississippi* had sketched between the lower and upper river valley. Dead serious also about the business advice he had given, he perhaps meant to say more on the Southern economy, which upset the modern investor because of its inefficiency: Huck found the Phelpses living on "one of those little one-horse cotton plantations," and during the farcical rescue he now and then noted its lackluster, sleepy ways. However, the main exposé of backwardness had already come through Twain's hard stares at Arkansas.

Celebrated unkindly by the antebellum Whig humorists, Arkansas also became a favorite target for Republicans because it acted like the other ex-Rebel states while lacking their traditional glamor. In 1878 Twain labeled as the Arkansas of Switzerland a "lazy" and "worthless" canton that he thought no better than an "inhabited privy."[21] Soon afterward, he judged that the tag of Black Jack, Arkansas, was best for the setting of "The Second Advent"—a freethinker's updated account of the virgin birth in a town where "there are no newspapers, no railways, no factories, no library" and "ignorance, sloth and drowsiness prevail."[22] Pokeville, and its degraded campmeeting, apparently belonged to Arkansas in *Huckleberry Finn*; at Bricksville came the trenchant vignette of a rural slum, the shooting of Boggs, and the Royal Nonesuch that the Duke billed with LADIES AND CHILDREN NOT ADMITTED, chortling "if that line don't fetch them, I don't know Arkansaw!" It turned out that he was all too right about the vicious, gaping stupidity of the only Southern state actually named in the whole novel.

The setting for the last fourth of *Huckleberry Finn* was likewise played up to fit Twain's topical point. Though he had no compulsive ties with Arkansas either, the still popular idea that he was "imprisoned" in his personal past has prolonged the mistake of assuming that the action of *Huckleberry Finn* was unrolled against a Middle South essentially like antebellum Missouri. But at the start of Chapter 31 Huck recorded: "We was down south in the warm weather, now, and a mighty long ways from home. We begun to come to trees with Spanish moss on them. . . . It was the first I ever see it growing." Aunt Polly more precisely located the Phelps place as eleven hundred miles from St. Petersburg. When it is recalled that Twain had just brushed upon distances along the river, the last part of *Huckleberry Finn* must be taken as set no farther north than Natchez or possibly even Baton Rouge—the area tagged with the sneering footnote about violence added to *Life on the Mississippi*.

The fictional date of *Huckleberry Finn* is around 1845. If Twain had planned to enshrine his boyhood he could have kept the story in Missouri without giving up the slavery angle, but he had insisted on writing about the Deep South. Recently there has been carping at the sense of letting Jim drift farther and farther past Cairo, Illinois, and therefore deeper into slave territory. Though Twain planted sound excuses for this, the basic truth is he misrouted Jim's flight to freedom so he could work in many key episodes that are incidental to the escape plot. After the war Missouri was increasingly thought of as midwestern; Jim and Huck could not stay there or in Illinois if the novel was to have its say about the Solid South. Fifteen years later Brander Matthews, a sane and cosmopolitan critic, still read it partly as a report on regional patterns "important for us to perceive and understand": "The influence of slavery, the prevalence of feuds, the conditions and circumstances that make lynching possible —all these things are set before us clearly."[23]

Since he wanted a money-making sequel to *Tom Sawyer*, Twain carried over its antebellum framework; however, he used this framework with attitudes he had formed lately and for purposes tied to the 1880's. There should be no surprise that he also made it fit questions new to the postwar period: the sniping at the protective tariff in *Tom Sawyer Abroad* shows he could give up-to-date missions to the surrogates for his boyhood, and *A Connecticut Yankee* proves he commanded the subtlety of talking about the past and present at the same time—a pattern much more familiar to Twain than some of those wished on his books lately. As the Negro's civil rights crumbled before massive pressure in the 1880's, which moved Cable to protest militantly that the separate but equal doctrine was pernicious, *Huckleberry Finn* wasted no time on the fieldhand writhing beneath an overseer's lash or the other standard antebellum motifs more evident in *Pudd'nhead Wilson* (1894). Instead it stressed innate dignity and created a shrewd, loyal, generous Jim who deserved more respect than perhaps any Negro preceding him in American fiction and cast doubt on the gathering tendency to negotiate peace with the Bourbon Democrats by taking up their version of race. And, intentionally or not, when Twain made Huck and his brown comrade share bed and grub with growing mutual trust, he resisted the rising tide of Jim Crowism.

Unfortunately, the climactic emphasis did not stay on Jim's claims to fairer treatment: Twain was in a mood to attack the chivalric legend savagely, though his attitude toward it was usually ambivalent. *Huckleberry Finn* is at its firmest in the fake rescue burlesquing "Scott and Dumas and the phantasies of the Southern gentry"[24]—the lingering chivalric ideal that Twain felt was encouraging the notion of caste and the penchant for a code tolerant of violence. If he deserves the reader's confidence at all, the length of this burlesque must be taken as a measure of its urgency, already clear in the borrowed names of the King and the Duke. But callow Tom could not really carry off the part of a cottonized Miniver Cheevy; and Huck, already switching between rural ignorance and the humanity latent in a "Silent South" that Cable hoped to arouse, could not stand impressively for the practical, "go-ahead" frame of mind. Their inadequacy grew with every wilder turn of satire that also misused the self-respecting and respectworthy Jim who, before the rescue episode, had earned status as a man rather than just a "good nigger."

Because Twain's mind was as marvelously rich as it was fitful no glosses on *Huckleberry Finn* can exhaust its charm or its meaning. Some of its pages lingered over the escape from civilization; others burned with his conviction that meanness exists wherever there are people or, less frequently, with his feeling that some decency survives the grind of selfishness. *Huckleberry Finn* also had political bite aside from the Southern question, as when the King and Duke provoked comments that work toward the nub of *A Connecticut Yankee*. The more Twain's mind is studied, the more clearly a chain of solid purpose looms behind Huck's words. Distaste for fundamentalism guided the fooling about Solomon's thousand wives, and impatience with "superstitious" Christian burial colored the irreverent handling of Peter Wilks' corpse.[25] Twain was moving toward the mugwumpery he embraced in 1884 from motives wider than just voting for the public servant instead of the party hack.

Perhaps no analysis of *Huckleberry Finn* can fix its proportions of abstract ideas, elemental warmth, nostalgia, clowning, and political commentary. But its convincing effect was tied strongly to concrete social attitudes, which helped save it from the softness Twain so easily fell into at times. A respect for the latent dignity of even riffraff that makes Huck a natural gentleman is balanced by Whiggish suspicions about the masses. The human average is kept low as pikers and suckers parade through the novel, and Pap Finn is a reeking symbol of the poor-white's foulest depths. Another acidly indelible touch comes from Twain's irritation at naïve reformers, whose joy when Pap claims to swear off liquor makes Huck wonder why "rapscallions and deadbeats is the kind . . . good people takes most interest in." *Huckleberry Finn* is a blossomy tree of humaneness, but it was toughened by cold gusts from Manchester Liberalism.

So far as the Negro is concerned Twain's grounding in his time and place had less admirable results, both in the quality of his realism and the impact of his humaneness. A number of anecdotes in *Life on the Mississippi* carelessly pandered to the sense of innate white superiority still felt in almost every quarter. At the same time that he praised Cable's fiction, he praised Joel Chandler Harris for revealing the "negro estimate of values by his willingness to risk his soul & his nightly peace for ever for the sake of a silver sev'mpence."[26] Because Twain's sympathy for the freedman had a condescending base, *Huckleberry Finn* could mistreat Jim so crudely at the end that its total effect is seriously weakened. Twain had come far from Hannibal's attitude toward the Negro but not far enough, even if almost anybody today would rather travel with Jim on a raft than Uncle Tom on a steamboat.

Like other great novels *Huckleberry Finn* has been reinterpreted whenever fashions in ideas have changed. Yet nobody has given a convincing reason why, in spite of many flaws even before the weak ending, it so clearly outshines *Tom Sawyer* as well as their several sequels. Though Twain certainly had psychic tensions and though he liked to speculate (in an eighteenth-century way) about generic man, his interest in public affairs was also powerful. *Huckleberry Finn* took at least part of its drive from topical urgencies that suggested a goal for the stalled manuscript. In 1885 it unmistakably read as a commentary on the Southern question; to believe this was accidental is to be naïve. It is more realistic to suspect that a fear of losing touchy buyers led to his disclaimer, "Persons attempting to find a motive in this narrative will be prosecuted; persons attempting to find a moral in it will be banished."[27] Huck's raft floated down the currents of a churning debate, and, despite the bromide that art and politics must flow in two unrelated channels, its fame depends heavily on the skill with which Twain navigated both on the same trip. At that moment, old friends in Hannibal must have thought he looked more like a scalawag than a homesick native boy turned novelist.

Despite the surprising calm that followed the election of Grover Cleveland, tremors from the Southern question went on, as anybody can see by glancing at the newspapers and magazines of the later 1880's. Quite unaware he had gotten off a masterpiece, Twain flirted with a new idea—an ironic fantasy about the Negroes coming to dominate Dixie through sheer numbers and, in their turn, enforcing segregation on the whites.[28] This tactic of putting the chain on the other foot eventually made its way into *A Connecticut Yankee*. Ignoring historical fact, Hank Morgan found a slave system in sixth-century England; and as white men suffered the cruelties of being sold, he pointed up the parallel with "our own South." Thinner traces of the storm that had pushed *Huckleberry Finn* toward greatness turned up in several outbursts on how slavery ossified the feelings of the owners, in quips that Guinevere's warm glances at Launcelot "would have got him shot in Arkansas, to a dead certainty" or that a crude tabloid named *The Weekly Hosannah and Literary Volcano* showed "good enough Arkansas proof-reading, anyhow."

Before *Huckleberry Finn* was available to the public, Twain left more proof of how topically he could use his famous boys: he started a story that would take them out among the Plains Indians. The public conscience was building up toward the Dawes Act of 1887 that would begin the policy of turning the Indians into citizens instead of "pacifying" them by force, and many signs indicate that Twain was trying to see their point of view as well as the Negro's. His exulting over Cleveland's election included the prospect that the spoilsmen would be kept off the reservations; in 1886 he sent the President an angry note about the report that a New Mexico town was paying a bounty for Apache scalps.[29] *Huck Finn and Tom Sawyer Among the Indians* was left incomplete, however, and the existing fragment is mostly hard on the redman. Perhaps Twain broke off because he was unhappy with the harsh tone it fell into, though *A Connecticut Yankee* let Hank Morgan sneer at King Arthur's circle as "just a sort of polished-up court of Comanches." Twain was never to focus directly on the dark agony of the American Indian, a subject fit for his most trenchant insights.

While orders for *Huckleberry Finn* were being extracted door to door, Twain took up current politics in person. Since 1876 and even before he had leaned toward the Republicans who argued their party was losing its idealism and was being used by the professional boss; and his "Let's Look at the Record" letter in 1879 had caustically run over the shady side of James G. Blaine's career. When the machine faction put up the soiled "knight" from Maine for president, Twain decided right off to bolt the party, declaring before his daughters, "I am a mugwump and a mugwump is pure from the marrow out."[30] Unshaken by Cleveland's liaison with a "consenting widow," he found the morals of the campaign clearer than the course to take, for he joined the Democrats with deep reluctance; in fact at first he merely signed petitions asking "our fellow Republicans" not to become "camp followers" and felt that chastely keeping away from the polls would be enough. But he could not stay on the sidelines of a fight that excited much calmer men. By October he had heard and said so much that he ended up presiding over a huge mugwump meeting in Hartford, though still professing belief in the "greatness and righteousness of the principles of the Republican Party" and promising he would vote its ticket except for Blaine. It was only when his last-minute idea of a write-in candidate fell flat that he grimly resolved to vote for Cleveland and even the rest of the Democratic ticket all the way down to constable.[31]

Like Huck he had obviously fought an inner battle before he could humble himself this way. Years later, betraying how deeply he had been troubled, he was still wincing over the hostility that whitecollar Hartford showed toward its mugwumps in 1884.[32] Again like Huck, however, he "warn't never sorry afterwards" that he opposed Blaine with a freshness and sincerity missing in his oration on Garfield's behalf, as if he was now speaking his own mind rather than lines cued by feelers of the public pulse. Cleveland's election seemed to confirm Twain's rising hopes that "clean men, clean ordinary citizens, rank and file, the masses" would vote right if they had a real chance, and he publicly acclaimed it as overdue proof that at least some Americans could put the "State" above the party.

This conclusion was nevertheless hemmed in by the two-party system. Though he agonized at the station and then boarded the mugwump car, it was coupled to the Democratic train, and in December, 1884 a "person in authority" brought word that the President-elect "had expressed a strong desire to have me call, as he wanted to get acquainted with me."[33] With clear entree at the White House, Twain soon felt closer than ever before to national policy-making. He also picked up some new supporters of his own. *Puck*, a comic magazine backed by Democratic money, realized suddenly that he was our "*best* humorist . . . something more and better than a mere 'japer of japes' . . . a thoughtful, sincere and suggestive literary artist." When the public library in Concord, Massachusetts, banned *Huckleberry Finn*, the local Free Trade Club named him an honorary member. If the banning was not a devious result of the election, the free traders—who were anathema to orthodox Republicans—made it look that way.

Actually, Twain had been much more against Blaine than for Cleveland. Like many who deserted the Republican cause despite the last frantic waving of the bloody shirt, he was surprised to find that the country could run smoothly under a Democratic president, while the pardoned Rebels stayed a vocal minority and nothing more. With this reassurance he felt free to ride the fad for Civil War memoirs with "The Private History of a Campaign that Failed." Five years sooner he could not have treated his Confederate soldiering as an escapade by young lads whose hearts were in the right place; earlier versions of it, which started coming with the light thaw of 1877, had harsh and almost hypocritical satire beneath the broad comedy. But his "Private History" was a firm step toward his speech in 1887 advising Union veterans to believe that "there is no North, no South any more."[34] Later he corrected this overstatement without rushing back to the other extreme.

More than most men, Twain is hard to pin down neatly; he had the habit of dropping an opinion for several years and then suddenly taking it on again. Yet it is helpful to say that he changed from a scalawag to a mugwump and, no longer worried about why a New South did not slough off its cotton chrysalis, shifted the brunt of his advice in other directions. The election of 1884 had been a pivotal and deeply stimulating experience. Soon afterward, his essay on "The Character of Man" defrocked the platitude that society admires the courage of mavericks who defy it on live and important matters; and his essay on "Consistency," flaunting a label he welcomed the rest of his life, argued that mugwumps are always the spearhead of progress. Though with less of a change than it may seem, he began to stress the power of the free-thinking leader rather than the stupidity of the masses. Huck is kept busy fooling society in self-defence; managing to pick up a few brave recruits along the way, Hank Morgan in *A Connecticut Yankee* often dominates society for its own good.

The feeling of forceful independence left Twain more inclined than ever to tackle public questions. Explaining to his wife why he had agreed to go down to Washington and lobby on copyright laws, he insisted that "one must not refuse an office of that kind when asked—a man who prides himself on his citizenship *can't* refuse it."[35] He obviously was fancying himself a vital integer of the republic. He was not marching alone, however, even though he avoided the mistake of becoming a regular Democrat; the mugwumps were well-defined politically as the American branch of middle-class Liberalism. Since the 1860's he had been loudly critical of machine politics and financial buccaneering and of the alarming ways in which they meshed to misuse the state for plunder. No longer hobbled by loyalty to a major party, he was fully free to work with a group that attacked these evils as barriers to the drive of laissez-faire economics, and, more sincerely than many others, he used democratic catchwords to plead the case for giving technology a clear road. Turning mugwump was a big step toward Twain's writing *A Connecticut Yankee*.

That government is not best which best secures mere life and property—there is a more valuable thing—manhood.

SIX

Uncle Sam

OF ALL TWAIN's books *A Connecticut Yankee in King Arthur's Court* (1889) stands in the most peculiar position today. The general reader enjoys it and keeps it in print with almost no encouragement from the professional critic. Though Twain did sternly remind himself to put in plenty of "fun," there is rich evidence that he took it more seriously than anything he had published before and worked harder only on *The Personal Recollections of Joan of Arc*. More than once between start and finish he referred to it grimly as his swansong or his frank valedictory. After he had his manuscript in proof he still throbbed with surplus ideas he would have liked to mix into its smoking tide.

From the day it reached print, there has always been some rigid dislike of its ideas or brash tone; and after praising many passages the typical critic decides that it fails as a unified work of literature. In part Twain is clearly to blame for this last verdict. Though the transfer is not complete to the last

feature, Hank Morgan comes the closest of his major characters to being Twain himself. This means that Hank's attitudes
cut in many directions, sometimes confusedly or erratically.
However, *A Connecticut Yankee* had a basic coherence of
plan as well as a simple foundation: Twain was more hopeful
about the American system than he had ever been or would
be again. Actually, it looks as if he had been pathetically
eager for the lift he got from the election of 1884. As early
as September 23, 1885, he gushed to Grover Cleveland at the
White House:

Every one of us in this town who voted for you last fall would
vote for you again today. And would be glad to do it, too; glad
to testify that the good intentions which they saw in you have
been ratified by your acts; glad to testify that they believe in you,
rest in you, stand by you, & are day by day increasingly proud
of you & grateful that you are where you are.[1]

He kept writing about and to the President in this ecstatic
vein and once even gave some money to the Democratic
warchest for Hartford. He very firmly considered himself a
mugwump instead of a regular Democrat, but this only meant
a still warmer duty to fight for the right side. Most important
of all, it implied there was a side in human affairs worth fighting for.

The mugwumps' faith in Cleveland was solidified when he
ignored safe politics for the coming election and lambasted
the protective tariff in 1888. This must be the point when
Twain finally moved over to the free trade camp, where most
of the mugwumps already were because they held that to
interfere with what could be imported was to compromise
the spirit of laissez faire. His change of position took effort.
As he had done himself in 1880, Republicans still claimed that
anybody against high duties was a tool of British policy; and,
at the moment, Twain was especially inclined to avoid any
such suspicion. He must also have been embarrassed when
parallel columns in the Hartford *Courant* matched what he

had said earlier and what he now argued in behalf of tariff reform at a Hartford rally. Still *A Connecticut Yankee* defiantly led Hank Morgan through a long routine to convince voters that while a protective tariff brought fatter pay-checks it brought even higher prices and therefore lower real wages.

Though it enraged Republican manufacturers, free trade was not leftist doctrine, nor was the single-tax plan to expropriate the socially created margin of land value. At other crucial points, Henry George's system merged with safe economic theory; and some of his leading disciples merely wanted to free industry from the drag of conservative landowners. How strongly Twain favored the single tax is not clear. On July 27, 1889, the New York *Standard*—a single-tax weekly—ran a sketch titled "Archimedes" that it credited to a Twark Main living in Australia. "Archimedes" was patently done by an American hand, however, and had even more familiar touches. Probably genuine Twain, it made the usual Georgist case against high rents. But the text of *A Connecticut Yankee* does not bear out the claim of Twain's favorite nephew that it raised the "feudal land-question" to show the "present evils of land monopoly."[2] Only the drawings by Dan Beard—later a founder of the Boy Scouts—lend a measure of sense to such a reading, though Twain sent a copy of his book to George, and the *Standard* announced several times that he had joined the cause. He was not even as dissatisfied with the basic economic framework as Beard, whose novelette *Moonlight* (1892) had a coal operator make wide concessions to his miners without waiving the right to a handsome profit. In spite of some emphatic social criticism *A Connecticut Yankee* was rooted in middle-class Liberalism and the faith that the United States had become its Rome.

Liberalism was nevertheless changing with the time. During the long depression of the 1880's, the rigidities of supply and demand dogma had softened around the edges. This softening was speeded by an anxiety that the unemployed might listen to the leftist agitator if their miseries were ignored while the piratical entrepreneur kept plying his trade without the least sense of pity. Though Twain's "Letter from the Recording Angel" was aimed at the hypocrisy of the tight-fisted Christian, it also sneered at the businessman who squeezes out every ounce of profit wherever he can, no matter how much blood is mixed with it. Twain began making notes for another essay on Vanderbilt but soon switched his ferocity to Jay Gould, who was still busy manipulating railroads for all they were worth and was very much in the news for his troubles with exploited help. Beard drew him as the slavedriver in *A Connecticut Yankee*, making a good likeness that would have been obvious even if Twain had not grimly pointed it out to a reporter.[3] In his review Howells dutifully noted "there are passages in which we see that the noble of Arthur's day, who fattened on the blood and sweat of his bondmen, is one in essence with the capitalist" of 1889 who "grows rich on the labor of his underpaid wagemen."

For the first time in his life Twain had just spoken out directly and heavily on the side of these wagemen. As late as *Life on the Mississippi* his admiring memories of the steamboat pilots' union had overlooked the deckhands or chambermaids with much more to groan about than the elite at the spoked wheel.[4] And when he began investing in the typesetter he gloated that it did not get drunk or join a union. However, he dashed off "The New Dynasty" as a tribute to the rising Knights of Labor, who had called and won a strike against Gould's companies. Extreme enough to enrage conservatives even today, it accused the capitalist of political as well as economic oppression and exultingly welcomed the signs of a change.[5] Uncooled, this enthusiasm carried over into *A Connecticut Yankee* where Hank Morgan predicted a time when "the 'combine' will be the other way, and then how these fine people's posterity will fume and fret and grit their teeth over the insolent tyranny" of unions that settle a "long and bitter account of wrong and humiliation." Though Twain would soon drift back closer to the employers' side

again, "The New Dynasty" marks a basic shift in his attitudes.
Well-to-do Americans had at last faced up to the size and
suffering of the least fortunate class and started questioning
the cosy axiom that everybody gets as much of the world's
goods as he deserves. Where Twain once would have reported a rude conductor to the company he now cooled his
temper by remembering that the average pay on a railroad
was only twenty dollars a month.

His harder look into the American depths did not, however, keep him from still assuming that the Old World was
the model for poverty and cruelty on a mass level. In fact,
as his political faith in the New World rebounded with
pent-up energy, he steadily became more excited, along with
Howells and Warner, about the evil influence of imported
literature. Their case was stated cogently by H. H. Boyesen,
immigrant author and a lecturer at Columbia University.
Taking a line popular long before he arrived on the scene,
Boyesen accused British novels of corrupting too many naïve
Americans into a "bitter aristocrat at heart, sighing for the
picturesque splendor of feudalism, and looking with ill-dis-
guised contempt upon the unpleasant equality and dreary
monotony which society presents under a republican form of
government."[6] In *Life on the Mississippi* Twain had warned
that chivalric romance-novels caused just such a syndrome,
but he was only warming up to *A Connecticut Yankee*. When
it was done he told a reporter that the United States needed,
more than ever, a "national" literature "preserving" our way
of life.[7] Busily whipping up free publicity for his own novel,
he told another reporter that "America with its floating scum
of fools who are fond of aping aristocratic ideas and actions,
is pretty well Europeanized." In a late stage of composition
he had particularly itched to lash out at the "American
heiresses buying up rotten dukes" or, more specifically, to
burlesque the recent marriage between a Huntington of the
Southern Pacific family and "her Sauer-Kraut Prince Hatz-
feld"—the disguise would have been thin because the work-

ing notes read, "Mr. Skunkington railroad thief—daughter marries Prince Hatfeldt."[8] Even Twain, however, may have decided it was too awkward to lug a German prince into Arthurian England; Hank Morgan managed only the comment that "dudes and dudesses" in the United States had too much "reverence for rank and title."

Twain's humane feelings and hatred of fixed social rank both took on added force from the freethought movement, which preached the duty of challenging any agency that repressed or coerced the human spirit. His admirers will find many familiar arguments if they read Robert G. Ingersoll's essays. Though "Royal Bob" was a staunch Republican and corporation lawyer, his agnostic philosophy drove him to heckling on varied fronts; he was especially fierce in defending the scientific mind against the clergy, and Hank Morgan's exploiting a solar eclipse to seize control of the sixth century matches up closely with Ingersoll's taunts about how priests once mistook rare natural events for miracles. However, it fits just as well with passages from Andrew Dickson White or John W. Draper or the popularizers of their school. Plowing through Draper's *History of the Conflict between Religion and Science*, for that matter, turns up many other specific arguments that look like Twain originals when they are dressed in the catchy idiom of *A Connecticut Yankee*.

Draper and Ingersoll—and White, to a lesser degree—accused the Roman Catholic church of leading the hostility to the march of science and also continually trying to recapture the broad political power it once held. For the late 1880's this line of suspicion was epitomized by Ingersoll's essay on "Rome or Reason"—the crux of a running debate in the *North American Review*. Henry C. Lea, a Philadelphia publisher and mugwump, put the anti-Catholic case with heavier detail in such studies as *Superstition and Force* and a dark *History of the Inquisition of the Middle Ages*. As soon as it came out Twain pored over this last polemic, which taught him nothing basically new, perhaps, but let him feel that his hatred of the medieval rested on sound and rich historical data. Even before it came out and just before the gestation of *A Connecticut Yankee* he scribbled in his notebook, "For a play: America in 1985. The Pope here & an Inquisition. The age of darkness back again. Pope is temporal despot, *too*. A titled aristocracy & primogeniture. Europe is *republican* & full of science & invention—none allowed here."[9]

Like so many ideas seemingly hatched in cigar smoke over Twain's billiard table, his belief that the Pope could seize the upper hand in the United States reflected a common attitude. As the Roman Catholic church entered a period of militant growth after 1870, newspapers and magazines quivered with forebodings that parochial schools were undermining the public system. This eventually swelled up to a new thunderhead of prejudice, whose murkiest part became the American Protective Association. Orion Clemens added it to his long list of memberships, and in 1888 brother Sam jotted down this reminder: "Speech advocating 21 years residence for citizenship. . . . Exactly as a minor is. Look at the movement for parochial schools. 'Let me educate your children & I will determine your ultimate form of govt'—instead of the 'songs'—make a paraphrase."[10]

Except to complete reactionaries the most dramatic example of danger was the official Catholic hostility toward the Knights of Labor and then toward Father Edward McGlynn of Manhattan, spellbinder about the virtues of a single tax. When the Pope excommunicated McGlynn for his political ideas after Catholics who belonged to the Knights of Labor had been threatened with the same sentence, public reaction was hot and prolonged under the lash of angry headlines even in newspapers that hated unions or Henry George. Admirers of Lea's *Studies in Church History* (1883) could recall that its main essay showed how popes had often wielded the interdict from Rome in civil affairs elsewhere—just as it was wielded in *A Connecticut Yankee* to smash Hank's popular support after he had bowled over all the other enemies of progress. Alertly on top of the situation, Twain tried to land a book by McGlynn for his publishing firm.

On some pages, like those about free trade, *A Connecticut Yankee* lectured explicitly to modern America; other pages made points it could profit from if it liked. But the hot humanity, the economic criticism, the bursts of leveling democracy, and the religious satire were mainly for export: Twain was jumping into the family quarrels of John Bull and Brother Jonathan. His attitude strained fraternal limits, however; he acted more like an impatient uncle. Besides sketching a free-thinker's version of what the Old World past had really been like, the narrowest focus of *A Connecticut Yankee* projected a rich, bustling, inventive United States as the living example of what our British relatives had failed to accomplish. Twain had been surprisingly slow to feel this way. All in all he had resisted the waves of anti-British talk since the Civil War, and when he finally started sniping at John Bull's island nothing at first promised an all-out barrage. As he was well aware, his market in England was still lucrative—early in 1886 he told a Senate committee that his books earned a third as much there as at home. In spite of the typical energy with which he eventually lunged into the name-calling, he vacillated so long he missed out on its noisiest rounds.

Trans-Atlantic interplay during the 1880's has not yet been untangled except where it involves Matthew Arnold, and Twain's sudden animus toward England has generally been explained away as a private grudge. But the enveloping debate was more than a tiff in overfurnished parlors and was in fact basically impersonal, centering on the question of what England could learn from our experiences. In November, 1882, Howells answered Arnold's unfavorable "A Word about America" with the old Yankee position that a democratic society naturally tops whatever can grow on monarchist soil. Warner, who was still Twain's neighbor, found it necessary to publish two essays—one the same month and another the next year—deploring the "lingering feudal con-

ditions and prejudices" among the British and suggesting
they could take some cues from the United States. Asked
for his own answer by a magazine Twain never finished either
of two tries, one of which merely argued defensively that
though England was "greatest among nations" we were as
capable a people "if you scrape off our . . . crust of shabby
politicians."[11] He was by no means ahead of local opinion.
When Arnold came over in 1883, Hartford newspapers were
outstandingly hostile throughout his lecture tour.

Arnold was an inviting target in the larger melee. "He was
culture, and he was suspicion of democracy; he was amenity,
urbanity, the Church of England and aristocratic manners."[12]
Yet Twain kept his noisy temper at a low hum even though
Arnold insultingly held him up as the "jovial, genial man
of our middle-class civilization." The first time he openly
showed anger was when Arnold wrote a carping review of
Grant's *Memoirs*. As publisher of the expensive, two-vol-
ume set Twain was of course touchy about it; furthermore,
Grant's recent death had seemingly elevated him to national
sainthood, and many worshipers hurried to shush Arnold.
Still "General Grant's Grammar," which began with a sincere bow toward Arnold as a "great and honoured author,"
was relatively mild for Twain.[13] The manuscript of *A Connecticut Yankee*, it should be noted, was already well along
by this time.

The loudest and fiercest blasts at Arnold came in the spring
of 1888 after his essay on "Civilization in the United States"
made more news than it should have and inspired supporting
attacks in England. The rebuttal here was at the very least
matching in size. Proclaiming Arnold's "lapse as a cult among
us," Howells accused him and his clique of "snobbishness,"
and Twain's private notebooks began at last to register complaints about British fault-finders and Arnold in particular.
In 1889 he got off an effective speech, "On Foreign Critics,"
that asked caustically, "Must all the advice be emptied upon
us?" He worked on another speech challenging Arnold's idea

of culture and still another comparing British and American manners, which resurrected the gossip about Arnold not offering a lady his seat on a Boston horsecar.[14] But Twain's fury against foreign critics boiled mostly too late to affect *A Connecticut Yankee* and, surprisingly cooled, left its heaviest traces on his next book instead. *A Connecticut Yankee* was made of finer alloys than injured pride and would have been written, in about the same tone, if Arnold had never lived.

In its usual form the Arnold story prolongs a key mistake —the lax habit of talking about the British as if they pretty well agreed among themselves. Actually, their two major parties differed much more crucially than ours; and though Americans had always kept close track, during the 1880's they followed the seesaw between Conservatives and Liberals more intently than ever before or since. In his notebook for 1885 Twain could speculate about Lord Rosebery as "probable—no, possible—future prime minister of England." Arnold, here on another visit, was amazed at interest in the British election of 1886, which made the president of the University of Pennsylvania get up "at some unheard-of-hour in the morning" just to see the latest returns and made George William Curtis—a leader of the New York literati and a political oracle for the genteel—declare that England was undergoing its tensest crisis since Waterloo.

As Arnold noticed with pain, opinion here very solidly hoped the Conservatives would fail in their drive to push over the Liberal cabinet. Only typical was the New York *Herald's* tribute to Gladstone: "The scholarship of England, in great part, and the aristocracy and the landed gentry have fought against him with desperation. Nevertheless, he represents, as no other man in the United Kingdom does to-day, the cause of progress." The high spots in the career of the Liberal's champion, who had turned down a peerage to carry on his long fight against "vested wrong," were reviewed again and again. Wherever he had fallen short, there was the

The Slave Driver

Jay Gould, represented in *A Connecticut Yankee in King Arthur's Court* (above).

Merlin (below) was drawn to represent Alfred Lord Tennyson (above) in *A Connecticut Yankee*

"HE UNLIMBERED HIS TONGUE AND CURSED LIKE A BISHOP."

same warmth toward his party instead; in fact its left wing held the Englishmen dearest to Uncle Sam—the Nonconformists and republicans who agitated for erasing every vestige of a state church, cutting the power of the House of Lords, and replacing the king with a president someday. Praising what the Liberals had already done and pleading for the reforms still in doubt, *A Connecticut Yankee* overlooked no major part of their record or program.[15]

If there had been no doubt, Twain might never have finished his book. But the Conservatives posted a solid victory in 1886 even though the Liberals expected to gain ground because the latest Reform Bill had enfranchised masses of new voters. Other Americans felt as Hank Morgan did when he saw the "large and disenchanting fact . . . that the mass of the nation had swung their caps and shouted for the republic for about one day, and there an end! The Church, the nobles, and the gentry then turned one grand, all-disapproving frown upon them and shriveled them into sheep!" When Queen Victoria's Jubilee of 1887 was an elaborate success, reaction in the United States mostly ranged from disgust at the crowds who cheered the reverent parades to anger at the Conservatives who staged them.[16] Still, revealingly, the liking Twain had taken in 1872 to the journalist Frank Finlay was strong as ever. Two months before *A Connecticut Yankee* came out he was happy to put up Finlay as a houseguest and introduce him around as honorary secretary of the Reform Club, the Liberals' social center in London. There was no intended offense to them in Twain's fantasy about King Arthur or his private comment that it was mainly meant to "pry up the English nation to a little higher level of manhood."

Many touches in *A Connecticut Yankee* could strike Finlay as topically sound. All too familiar was Hank's sneer that the British army was overloaded with officers, whose rank depended on their degree of noble birth rather than merit; his immediate move to ease the tax burden on the poor by adjusting it more efficiently in other ways seconded a demand that extreme Liberals as well as the fewer Radicals were making loudly and regularly. With squalid detail the family in a rural hut testified to the poverty of their class and the heavy grip of landlords, while the young farmer who writhed in a torture chamber because he had killed a deer that was molesting his crops was a witness to the fact that the Ground Game Act of 1880 had not gone far enough in curbing the gentry's old hunting rights. Morgan Le Fay's private penal system also suggested the evil of letting the gentry administer the law in their neighborhood. In his notebook Twain wrote on July 1, 1888, "The Liberals welcome the passage of a Local Government Bill through committee as almost a revolution which transfers the control of county affairs from the privileged few to the people. . . . There—the handwriting on the wall! There's a day coming."[17] The Tories must have thought that day had about come instead with the London dockers' violent strike in 1889 and must have shuddered at Hank Morgan's defense of trade-union militancy.

Though *A Connecticut Yankee* managed to plug most of the Liberals' program, its emphasis was shaped around the main problems—as many Americans saw them at least. The year it was published a New York City newspaper declared, "So long as either of the twin relics of feudalism—a state church and a hereditary aristocracy—shall continue to exist, England must halt in the march toward democratic liberty, founded upon the truth of the equal rights of men."[18] This is a fuller clue than Howells' comment that while Twain is working the reader up to a "blasting contempt of monarchy and aristocracy in King Arthur's time, the dates are magically shifted under him, and he is confronted with exactly the same principles in Queen Victoria's time." Howells pussy-footed, just as Twain's own firm did in advertising his book as a "satire on English Nobility and Royalty." It was grounded on the conviction that priestcraft and kingcraft go hand in hand. It attacked them separately and at their intertwinings before concluding that a state church was actually the more dangerous enemy.

Still the first part of *A Connecticut Yankee* did imply that the aristocrat was the archenemy. Aside from some incongruous praise of Launcelot and Arthur it sternly repressed Twain's sneaking taste for chivalric froth. Respect for ancient trappings, which the Conservatives were trying to build into mass support through Primrose Leagues of "knights" and "dames," had to go. Even softspoken Howells charged that awe of nobility, an "ugly relic of feudalism," had sapped the self-respect of the English people and sunk them into "open and undeniable . . . spiritual abasement."[19] To deflate this awesome tradition Twain hinted at the courtesans in its lineage, and the Launcelot-Guinevere liaison echoed his private rumblings that adultery was a habit with high-bred loafers. More openly, he made an accusing point of the coarse chit-chat between Arthurian knights and their ladies and expanded this vein with tidbits lifted from the racier history of continental royalty. But he went beyond prudishness to grim examples of blue-blooded cruelty. Hank learned ruefully that the Earl Grip was not too proud to turn a quick profit by rescuing strangers from a mob only to sell them as slaves and that Morgan Le Fay never doubted her right to knife a careless servant. With Beard using Tennyson's face as a model for Merlin's,[20] Twain also made sure that Hank met knights who were brutishly different from the hero-saints in Tennyson's *Idylls of the King*.

Twain was obviously hunting with the fiercest critics of the House of Lords. The only hereditary chamber left in European parliaments, it was being widely deplored as an anchor of reaction, particularly after its drag on the latest Reform Bill. In a trial preface he explicitly needled the Lords for "once in a while in a century taking care of Number One to the neglect of the rest of the numerals."[21] More often their stubborn holding on to a lopsided and antiquated margin of power drove their critics far beyond such understatement, and Hank Morgan, who gleefully massacred most of Arthur's knights, called for the return of a "Reign of Terror and a guillotine." This was not really meant to set off another

bloodbath but only to challenge squarely the favorite example of people who opposed swift action or even loud
debate.

Because the French Revolution was held up so widely as
a dire warning, many shades of reformers kept trying to put
over a countering version. Switching sides very slowly during the 1880's, Twain finally insisted he was a latterday
Sansculotte, indeed a Marat. Without any reservations Hank
hailed 1789 as "ever-memorable and blessed" and, turning the
tables, called life under the Bourbon kings an "unspeakably
bitter and awful Terror which none of us has been taught to
see in its vastness or pity as it deserves."[22] Twain underlined
the use of still cheering for the French Revolution by grumbling to Howells that the "gracious work" of this "immortal
benefaction," usually clouded by being seen through "English and other monarchical eyes," was "not done yet." Aware
that his novel was being published during its centennial—
which some British leftists ached to celebrate with new victories—he declared in another of his trial prefaces, "Human
liberty—for white people—may fairly be said to be one
hundred years old this year."

Deep in a melee over the past's meaning, he was throwing
type instead of cobblestones. For his publishing firm he out-
lined a series of documents like the memoirs of the Duke of
Saint-Simon and the "English printer's little book." This
printer, who has escaped the notice of scholars, was George
C. Standring. He met Twain in the 1870's, and when he began
putting out a shaky magazine named the *Republican* and
later the *Radical*, he mailed over some issues as well as other
material on freethought and anti-royalist causes. His "little
book" was a packed *People's History of the English Aristocracy* that retailed every bit of gossip about immoral courtiers
and kings. Having seen chapters in the *Republican*, Twain
asked for a copy several times in 1886 and 1887 and wanted
to reprint it under the title of *An Englishman on England*.[23]
Then he thought of expanding it: "Carry down George

———'s Exposure of English society & publish it at 25 cents."
Two weeks before *A Connecticut Yankee* was available he
sent Standring's book to his assistant, telling him to rush it
into paper covers and have it for sale at the same time; he also
wanted a copy for every newspaper that got the *Yankee* to
review. Somehow the reprinting did not come off after he
had already drafted a title page himself, yet he stayed in touch
with this obscure crusader. On a letter dated December 8,
1905, Twain inscribed, "Standring is a practical printer & a
radical in politics & religion. I have known him 30 years—a
fine man."

But judging or writing history objectively was not among
Twain's many talents, and in puncturing the bubble of feudal
glamor he could stab too furiously for best results. *A Connecticut Yankee* was deadliest, unsurprisingly, when he aimed
to make the nobles look more ridiculous than vicious, more
like the Duke and the Dauphin during the scenes in *Huckleberry Finn* where they grab petty privileges on the raft. In
many memorable passages Hank's laughter blows away the
gentle mist around feudal lords and ladies. Some readers enjoy most the great tournament (which had incidental satire
of the duel); others specially enjoy the knights who sport
ads for toothpaste or volunteer as conductors on the new railroad and then pocket the fares. If much of this denuded the
chivalric legend in general, some of it was quite timely.

When Twain introduced the Baron of Barley Mash, en-
nobled for building a brewery, he adapted the Radicals'
choicest example of dubious new peerages.[24] He also added
lift to complaints that pensions and honorary posts, as well
as grants to the Queen's relatives, added up to a "gigantic
system of out-door relief" for bluebloods. King Arthur, said
Hank, "had something like a religious passion for a royal
grant; he seemed to look upon it as a sort of sacred swag, and
one could not irritate him in any way so quickly and so
surely as by an attack upon that venerable institution." The
mighty "Boss" staunchly turned down a sinecure or even a

court title. By thus letting the puniest baronet—said Howells —have social "precedence of him, just as would happen in England today," he made his beribboned inferiors look all the sillier and their admirers all the stupider. After several wry lessons Hank decided that the average Englishman rated a titled oaf over any commoner "though he were the mightiest production of all the ages in intellect, worth and character" and that it would "remain so, as long as England should exist in the earth." However, Twain had marshaled his unmatched talent for ridicule in the effort to encourage a change.

Such changes seemed unlikely so long as the throne still made a rallying point for the myth of hereditary class. In private letters and notebooks Twain was raging about monarchy as the "grotesquest of all swindles ever invented by man" or scrawling heavy-handed gags in the same vein. When the king of Brazil abdicated in 1889, he gloated, "These are immense days! Republics & rumors of republics, from everywhere in the earth." Hoping that the time was also ripe to disenthrall the mobs who had cheered during Queen Victoria's Golden Jubilee, he coldly informed his British publisher that he must "say a Yankee mechanic's say against monarchy and its several natural props," and Hank explicitly proposed: "First, a modified monarchy, till Arthur's days were done, then the destruction of the throne, nobility abolished, every member of it bound out to some useful trade." This bowed to the fact of Victoria's popularity but rejected the idea of even a figurehead as a stabilizing tradition. Though Twain fumed privately that the "English human herd are as dumb & patient as their cattle," Hank tried to inflame their confidence:

The master minds of all nations, in all ages, have sprung in affluent multitude from the mass of the nation, and from the mass of the nation only. . . . Which is to assert an always self-proven fact: that even the best governed and most free and most enlightened monarchy is still behind the best condition attainable by its people.

The Prince of Wales, later Edward VII, (left) and Kaiser Wilhelm II (right) were drawn as the top and bottom heads in the "chucklehead" drawing of *A Connecticut Yankee*

Picture Post Library

From *A Connecticut Yankee in King Arthur's Court*

"THIS WOULD UNDERMINE THE CHURCH."

Supposedly ungifted and untrained except in practical skills, Hank usually symbolized the potential talent of the masses; more average than Arthur he was, therefore, without deliberate paradox, more capable.

Once Twain had decided to help stamp out royalty in England he typically tried every approach he could think of and ominously took notes on the scandals about the current Prince of Wales, whom his illustrator posed for the drawing of a "chucklehead."[25] His own running picture of Arthur, however, was guided chiefly by the impersonal, star-spangled attitude that "you can't tell a king from a cooper except you differentiate their exteriority." Leveled by their disguise in ordinary clothes, Arthur and Hank do not even end up equals when they wander across the countryside; the American mechanic has to look after the King, who impresses nobody and finally brings a much lower price on the block. Despite the blow to Hank's own pride in being sold for a slave, he cannot hold back another one of his frequent Yankee Doodle smiles.

This irreverence was actually the most deliberate quality in Twain's handling of Arthur and the knights. It came easy to him, but at the moment he was giving it full play according to plan. In 1888, when accepting a master of arts degree from Yale, he proclaimed that the humorist follows a "worthy calling" by deflating "superstitions" and "privilege." Elsewhere he broadened this to a national habit: "No, there *is* no reverence with us. I remember once in a dream I went to Heaven, & noticed there that it was an ordinary thing for Americans to hail Michael the Archangel as he went by with a hearty & friendly 'Hello, Mike.' "[26] Still another tentative preface for *A Connecticut Yankee* proposed to make a key issue of reverence, which is "forever masquerading in new disguises, & doing devil's service in the name of righteousness."[27] Head on, he was defying the Conservatives who, fighting the breakdown of a graded society, preached that respect for tradition and authority is a cardinal virtue in itself.[28] As a shrewd tactic, Hank was made to surprise himself with his first reaction to the Camelot *Weekly Hosannah and Literary Volcano:* he had lived in a "clammy atmosphere of reverence, respect, deference" too long of late and was "unpleasantly affected" by pert squibs about higher ups. Though a passionately explicit salute to the undeferential American press was held over until *The American Claimant,* the feeling that had inspired it pulsed through the arteries of *A Connecticut Yankee* where, more gingerly, ridicule invaded even the monastery.

There were strong, diverse reasons for going slower here. Yet Twain's anticlericalism was triplebound by black Protestant folklore about Rome, his early reading in the school of Voltaire and Thomas Paine, and his recent gusto for the school of Draper and White. He was more than ready to discover that consecrated hands were holding back progress, as when he computed, "Deceased Wife's Sister's Bill: 24 Bishops in House of Lords & 27 majority against the bill. Without the Established Church the bill would have had a majority."[29] This line of arithmetic had lately become busy as many Liberals and Radicals started to agree that the Queen was not vitally powerful and the nobility must soon give in to having less power but that the Church of England held on unshaken—to the peril of the future. By 1888 Twain had essentially decided on his ending: "I make a *peaceful* revolution & introduce advanced civilization. The Church overthrows it with a 6 year interdict."[30] Ready to burst into full prosperity, Hank's industrial network was blocked by "that curious invention of machine politics, an Established Church."

Ignoring the dates of his facts from Twain's favorite historians, bitterly disappointed Hank accused the church of not only failing to oppose slavery but spreading a slave mentality. More specifically, he charged that "in two or three little centuries it had converted a nation of men to a nation of worms" by defending the divine right of kings while preaching meekness to the commoner, and he reported back from the future, ". . . down to my birth-century that poison was still in the blood of Christendom." Even active cruelty was added to the indictment; and Beard's drawings played up this count, especially when the abbot in the Valley of Holiness menacingly offered to "persuade" Merlin to close shop for a while. Still, the text implied elsewhere, Merlin and the Church stood united on superstition and mumbo-jumbo learning in a stagnant society whose logical end was the hermit. Though Twain gave—with Beard's help—a few glimpses of the fleshly monk that the Reformation had shuddered over, he gave much more space to his scenes of the posturing holy men in foul caves. Ironically, they were the heathens who needed Ingersoll's "gospel of water and soap" most, but neither Ingersoll nor Lecky should get special credit for shaping the attitude behind these scenes.[31] It was easy for any middle-class Protestant to feel that the hermit who did nothing useful and denied the virtues of family life was wilfully mad and that Twain improved on Tennyson in his guffawing treatment of Saint Simeon Stylites.

Agilely shuttling between the past and present, Twain also made specifically modern points wherever he could or dared. Sneering at how long the British would keep religious limits on who could hold public office or enter the universities, the Boss set up elementary schools free of the state church as Nonconformists were asking in the 1880's. Twain also thought about a satire on the selling of advowsons (the right to the revenue from a parish) and a direct protest against exempting the Church of England from taxes. He did squeeze in a secondhand quip against tithing—the passage about the Welsh mother who offered her tenth child to a priest after he took the tenth pig.[32] Though Hank knew he was facing Roman Catholic knights and abbots, he often growled simply about the Church or even the Established Church. At least once, before friends warned Twain to be less specific, the manuscript singled out the Protestant Established Church.[33] Still, in an England where the Roman hierarchy had lost control long ago, his criticism ran no danger of missing its closest target.

Trying to sound objective, he conceded that "not all priests were frauds and self-seekers" and even that most of the priests "down on the ground among the common people were sincere and right-hearted." This also seemed to say he did not oppose religion but only its influence as an "Established Anachronism." In another concession, whose sincerity is clearly weak, he let Hank encourage Sunday schools for Arthur's realm; inwardly closer to agnostic doubts than at any other time in his life, he was wooing the Nonconformists, who exerted the most effective pressure against the Church of England. But his real concern was not for Protestant freedom to worship. Beard caricatured a clergy who rode financially on the commoner's back, worked hand in silken glove with the gentry, and kept monarchy in power. And though Twain was reported to feel that "some of the illustrations tell their tale too plainly for the British people,"[34] he had not stopped Beard from making the vestments of his prelates more Anglican than Roman or printing "High Church" under a priest blown skyward by dynamite.

Worried about counterblasts that would hurt his sales, Twain wrote at least six different prefaces as he looked for the right blend of frankness and business tact. Some referred unequivocally to current British affairs; at the other extreme he was tempted to pretend he was merely praising how far society had risen above the dark past. A compromise approach hid behind little Tom Canty and made the new novel another reminder that the Blue Laws were more lenient than their British models.[35] This idea came perhaps from E. C. Stedman's comment, after reading the galleys, that "to some extent, this manuscript is an extension of the text called *The Prince and the Pauper*." Yet Stedman, who subsidized his skimpy poetic talent with coups on Wall Street, saw that the "little book was checkers: this is chess." The preface Twain settled on was a mixture of craft and innuendo suited to his more complicated game. Its first paragraph claimed only that the laws and customs in his sixth-century story "existed in the English and other civilizations of far later times"; glancing at Lady Castlemaine as well as the Pompadour its second and last paragraph puzzled over the divine rights of royal blood.

When proofs arrived from England this last paragraph was missing. Growling he had "modified and modified" his book until he "really couldn't cut it anymore," Twain stirred up some free advertising on both sides of the Atlantic by calling European publishers a breed of "cowards."[36] He also started planning to export an "Appendix" that would include material from Standring and British newspapers.[37] But Andrew Chatto, his publisher in England, soothed his rage by rushing over a copy of the British edition to prove that the main text was uncensored and by arranging for other editions on the continent. Just as soothing was Chatto's news a little later that sales were good.

Still the British sale was bucking a headwind. Fondly recalling Tennyson's *Idylls* and frowning at Yankee "irreverence," most reviewers either ignored its serious point or went no further than the *Athenaeum's* icy nod recognizing that "not a few of the historical privileges that still exist do not suit the ideas of the great Republic of the West."[38] The Conservative magazines were the most clearly offended but even the usually Liberal *Pall Mall Gazette* was cool. For his advertising Chatto could lift phrases only from a few newspapers and *Truth*, Henry Labouchere's Radical weekly, which briefly noted the satire on "King, Nobles, and the Church" and hinted that Twain's "admirable preaching" was "needed still so sorely in England and Ireland." The most space given *A Connecticut Yankee*—as book of the month—came in the *Review of Reviews* run by William T. Stead, who voted Liberal though no party was broad enough to hold his interests that ranged from world peace to reclaiming London prostitutes. Letting an angry cat out of the bag, Stead classed it with Henry George's *Progress and Poverty* and other books "whereby Americans are revolutionizing the old country."[39]

While claiming too much credit for the printed word, this recognized another major side of *A Connecticut Yankee*. The products of American technology, which was picking up steam daily, and the freedoms of an open society were attracting a wide range of British admirers, from manufacturers to workingmen who felt class resentment. Tories invariably disliked the idea of imitating upstart Yankees, but most Liberals did not mind; and their gadfly, the Radical party, welcomed it.[40] Americans were just as aware of their influence and much more agreed in thinking it a fine thing. *Little Lord Fauntleroy* (1886) rang up a rich profit here partly because it assured them that a boy reared by Uncle Sam could give his titled grandfather a lesson in manners. They so enjoyed reading about not only their exportable virtues but also the coming shift in world leadership that there was a crescendo of debate around 1890 on whether they "hated" England.

This debate cannot be traced back very far without crossing Andrew Carnegie's trail. Having decided his mounting profits should go, partly anyhow, into making Great Britain a republic, he got himself so well known as the Star-Spangled Scotchman that Twain's book reminded the *Scots Observer* to take a swipe at "renegade Europians—Europians of the stamp of Mr. Andrew Carnegie."[41] The steelmaster's *An American Four-in-Hand in Britain* (1883) lacked no major point urged later by the machineshop wizard from Hartford. Ramblingly, it discussed the "sham" of royalty, the barons who "robbed and ravished in the good old times" and the "women who were even worse than their lords," the "feudal" holdovers, the perquisites of the Established Church, the need for secular schools, and the snobbishness toward "vulgar trade" even though for "a great deal of beer a peerage is not beyond reach." Along with many other fillips of democratic slang, one passage made the affinity with Twain explicit: "But the old land must come after a time up to Republicanism! I make a personal matter of that, Lafayette, my boy, as Mulberry Sellers says. No monarchy need apply."

Carnegie next signed his name to *Triumphant Democracy* (1886), which totted up our expanding production for everything from pigs to pigiron. Singling out our political system as the vital factor behind this energy it mercilessly pounded in the moral, beginning with its title and even its covers— besides a broken scepter and overturned crown they flaunted a toppling, inverted pyramid labeled "Monarchy" and a solidly based one labeled "Republic." Just as boldly the text appealed to the "people, the plain, common folk, the Democracy of Britain." Carnegie told friends that he hoped to start a Radical surge and impatiently sent his ghost writer abroad to give away copies wherever it would help; though, in a bad year for books, *Triumphant Democracy* actually sold over sixty thousand in England and did still better here as very pleasant doctrine. Not everybody read it, however; Carnegie was asked to contribute for the Queen's Jubilee in 1887 and, in spite of his habitual cordiality, felt bound to answer, "I should stultify myself were I to celebrate the reign of any hereditary ruler."[42] When the Carnegies went to look on without celebrating, among their first callers were the Gladstones. A few days later the Liberal champion came back alone to extract $25,000—then a new high in political donations.

Carnegie could spare it; he was making money even from British politics. When he started financing Radical newspapers the common man could afford, they did so well that he ended up with a network of eighteen; though wrong about the future of the Radical party he was right about the future of journalism. Aimed at wider sales and modeled on American tabloids, the cheap newspaper shot up in England as well as Europe during the later 1880's. Of course spokesmen for the staid tradition of columns packed with heavy and sober wisdom loudly resented this change they had deplored long before their own island was overrun. Arnold's last essay warned that "if one were searching for the best means to efface and kill in a whole nation the discipline of respect, the feeling for what is elevated, one could not do better than take the American newspapers." Fifteen years earlier Twain had sounded the same warning more sweepingly, but in this new context he wrote "The American Press," which arraigned British editors for lulling the masses with solemn clichés. Just as anxious as Carnegie to set a better example, Hank insisted on starting up a newspaper as soon as possible. Though his *Weekly Hosannah and Literary Volcano* also burlesqued our own backwoods press so vividly that Arnold seemed not so wrong after all, Twain was primarily saying that even this smeary tabloid was an improvement for England.

Perhaps with a margin of flattery, because he was about to ask Carnegie to invest in his sagging enterprises, Twain wrote in 1890 that *Triumphant Democracy* was a "favorite" of his and went on, "I am reading it again, now & firing up for a lecture which I want to deliver on the other side one of these years."[43] But Carnegie had only stiffened the transatlantic storm; its sources were innumerable. For instance Twain most probably knew about the very popular *King Solomon's Mines* (1885)—which got further publicity from an argument over whether an eclipse that its heroes exploited the way Hank did was astronomically on time. In any event Hank contrasts neatly with Rider Haggard's Englishmen: they use science and modern gadgets against an African tribe to get at a diamond mine; he wants to spread the light of progress. This role as a Prometheus, it should be noted, likewise contrasts with and soon dwarfs the passages of objective fiction that hint at his brash "circus side."

A titan in practicality also, Hank brought along the technical skill that is, Twain implied, a special talent of his country. In his doings the telephone, Edison's lightbulb, and the Colt revolver get more play than the steam engine or spinning jenny. At the time most of his pet devices were impressively new; New York had just put in electrocution as more humane than hanging, and the barbed wire on which the knights died had just proved its worth out on the cattleraising plains. The ending—which desperately solved the problem of leaving the chain of history unbroken after all—did not mean technology is a menace, however.

Pumped by high pressure advertising, a flood of the latest American gadgets had been ready to irrigate a parched Britain; Hank's proposal to establish a "Republic on the American Plan" was baited with the lure of solid comfort. He did not stop with patentable, workaday devices. His skill with a lariat reminded Londoners how they had enjoyed their first look at Buffalo Bill's Wild West show; the knights he taught to clank awkwardly around a baseball diamond were proving that Americans had come up with a better game than gentlemanly cricket. When the All-Stars got back from spreading the news through a world tour in 1888, Twain was there to salute baseball as the "very symbol . . . of the drive and push and rush and struggle of the raging, tearing, booming nineteenth century!"[44] Hank's message was pointed up with a vibrant idiom that also fitted such an era. His sixth-century friends, who talked in murky circles, soon envied his forceful vernacular, and when Sandy imitated it she was gaily thumbing her nose at complaints that American influences were corrupting Victorian speech. If Hank found any feature of old England really worth saving, he never let on. Like Carnegie, he had given clear warning—heave the inefficient past overboard or miss the wave of the future on which Americans were steaming ahead.

The parallels with Carnegie included what was left unsaid to England and what was ignored at home. *Triumphant Democracy* had shown the partisans of laissez faire that they could appeal to natural rights as profitably as anybody. Unsuspecting that his name would soon stand out in labor troubles more starkly than Carnegie's, George Pullman acclaimed it as a model of soothing and faultless logic; but beneath the skyscraping rhetoric lay shallow footings. Carnegie assumed that the ballot-box held all the equality needed, that only a formally entrenched class got unfair advantages and so progress—as Twain put it—came "at the expense of royalties, priesthoods & aristocracies."[45] Carnegie also assumed that democracy should be judged by the pile of steel and steel appliances produced. By this standard it was criminal to doubt the rightness of a society whose industrial graphs had risen so far from the day when there were no railroads and factories or, as Hank found, not even matches or mirrors.

Though the Whig party in the United States sorely missed having a titled class to inveigh against, Daniel Webster had covered up its conservatism by hurrahing for the anti-royalists in Europe. Without his trained shrewdness Carnegie and Twain came close to the same effect. Instead of challenging abuses that were straining the seams of American laissez faire, Hank's best fighting speeches faced across the Atlantic, just like Twain's hardest sally at the doctrine of a negative state:

The English laws don't allow a man to shoot himself, but you see these people don't want to make a law to prevent a man's committing half-suicide & being other-half murdered by overwork— & his family left destitute. No legislation to strengthen the hands of the despised strugglers. Why doesn't the Church (which is part of the aristocracy) leave tithes and other robberies to "voluntary action"?[46]

Enraged, he was invoking the specter that would soon haunt laissez faire—the use of the state to protect victims of unguided supply and demand or to equalize the power balance. Yet he never spoke out for the campaigns to get an eight-hour day here, and his appeals to lowerclass militancy were shaped to the ears of the Old World "commoner" rather than the captives of New York City sweatshops.

This does not mean that Twain was insincere or connived at a diversion: he believed he was fighting evil's crack regiment. In the heat of desperate battle he could rush beyond the old Lockean contract and argue, "That government is not best which best secures mere life and property—there is a more valuable thing—manhood;" and he could propose to judge any system strictly by how it serves the "whole people."[47] Though many a conservative was finally ready to shout agreement with such ideas if they were kept abstract, Twain could even sweep on to ringing statements about writing not for the upper crust but for the "mighty mass of the uncultivated who are underneath," for the "Belly and the Members" of the social organism. Until his assistant convinced him that they would lose money, he thought seriously of putting *A Connecticut Yankee* and possibly *Huckleberry Finn* and *The Prince and the Pauper* into twenty-five cent editions as a major shift from his long policy of holding the price of his books distinctly high.

Yet Twain's sympathy for the underdog never went seriously beyond orthodox limits, which were relaxing under not only a spreading demand for fair play but also a sense that unions—as Twain's "The New Dynasty" said—might be "our permanent shield and defence" against the leftist "agitator for 'reforms' that will beget bread and notoriety for him at cleaner men's expense." If Twain was discussing politics with his best suit on, he could get painfully close to putting himself in the very cleanest group, and if their expense was concerned he could be all business. When the Paige machine looked like a sure bet to take over every big printing plant, he bridled at protests that it would throw human typesetters out of work and coldly insisted that technology has been "Labor's savior, benefactor; but Labor doesn't know it, & would ignorantly crucify it." The most disturbing fact is that he could just as easily waver toward man in general or even relapse into believing the "majority of all peoples are fools." Like Voltaire, in hating superstition he often despised the masses for holding on to it. In his novels most of the mob that the self-reliant thinker tries to enlighten are dull and unwilling pupils, easily scared into quitting school; friendly and plebeian Hank sometimes changes suddenly into a superman outwitting a species that is basically despicable.

Twain's attitudes toward the common man finally make sense only within the pattern of Liberalism, which—even when it was not dubious about the average voter's wisdom— kept a wall between political and economic democracy. As he was writing *A Connecticut Yankee* he carefully denied that he meant more than giving every man the same "legal right & privilege." More positively, he praised the United States as an arena "where inequalities are infinite—not limited, as in monarchies; where the inequalities are measured by degrees & shades of degrees of difference in capacity, not by accidental differences in birth; where 'superior' & 'inferior' are terms which state facts, not lies."[48] As to what happens if some men turn out too superior at amassing money, he was unclear. From the vantage point of a mild socialism Howells later concluded his friend "had not thought out any scheme for righting the economic wrongs we abound in."

If pressed, Twain would have answered that technology will take care of most wrongs. Though Hank used raw coercion now and then, Twain felt guilty about it, blaming religious knots that were too deep for applied science to smooth away.[49] Hank's legislative program was very simple, and he almost never mentioned it after bragging that the "very first official thing I did, in my administration—and it was on the very first day of it, too—was to start a patent office; for I knew that a country without a patent office and good patent laws was just a crab." In 1888 Twain visited Thomas Edison at his laboratory with the zestful respect for applied science that let Hank beat Merlin hands down. Clowning over the quirks of a burglar alarm or storming impatiently at a sick telephone did not keep Twain from believing that the inventor was the supreme wizard, the catalyst, the dynamo, the solar engine that turned loose rays into profits if it was not wrecked by priests and kings or unions or the stock-market wolves who cause disturbing panics in Wall Street and grab too big a share. Unhumble Carnegie went so far as to say that the industrialist also gets too much more than the practical genius who spins wealth out of his brains. Hank was a grease stained cousin of Carnegie's ideal rich man who, with a hardheaded sense learned in the factory, handles his money as a trust fund piled up by applied science.

The inventive genius seemed to need some ink stained disciples too, especially for clearing away the mental cobwebs and false idols. In time there were enough volunteer iconoclasts to sound like an organized movement, with Twain considering himself a head executioner at "this wholesome and merciless slaughter-day" for the outmoded.[50] Yet the fetish of a negative state rode safely above the slaughter, and rooting out the old obstacles to laissez faire carried over into opposing any plan for setting up a safety code. Confidently, Twain was willing to have the present and future ride on the same few principles with which he judged the past:

Let us say, then, in broad terms, that any system which has in it any one of these things—to wit, human slavery, despotic government, inequality, numerous and brutal punishments for crime, superstition almost universal, and dirt and poverty almost universal—is not a real civilization, and any system which has none of them is.[51]

As a guide for federal policy after 1890, this left the main circuit open to a new kind of baron who soon made the public clamor for trust-busting.

For that matter Twain had livewire ambitions on his own. Paying taxes during the 1880's on property assessed at over a hundred thousand dollars, he needed a big income, and he got into the stock market with both feet. Among his bad buys was a holding company organized to plant Yankee capital in Europe. Thinking big in an expansive age he even wrote to Leland Stanford and General Grant about chartering a railroad from Constantinople to the Persian Gulf. Doubtless he had visions of this line carrying progress along with the payload, just as he was stubborn in backing the typesetter because it would benefit mankind as well as his bank account. As a publisher, however, he was too busy shoring up his list prices to worry about improving the world: "Macy has Grant books for sale cheap. We must assault him, next." Because he—too hopefully—scented a big killing he promoted an official biography of Pope Leo XIII and looked for other manuscripts that were good gambles "in these piping times of pious pow-wow."[52]

As always Wall Street and business proved sadly unpredictable. It was a comfort to have one major front covered with a nerveless, homegrown Liberal like Grover Cleveland in the White House. Cleveland stood unbendingly for cash and carry government and against any kind of "paternalism," even federal seed-grain for Texas counties baked by drought. His narrow defeat in 1888 stunned Twain almost beyond profanity. However, for longer than any other period in his life, Twain felt public affairs were moving well enough and dabbled in them with pleasure. To say that *A Connecticut Yankee* falls into nostalgia for a pre-industrial Eden is to play up a minor thread instead of the bold, obvious pattern. When he gave a public reading from the first batch of manuscript, he ended up with liplicking about how much power and money a modern man could swing if he were dumped into the benighted past.[53]

Beneath Twain's unique verve and the bizarre plot *A Connecticut Yankee* was inseparably entwined with its times. In 1886 an ex-congressman and friend from Washoe days sent Twain a clipping of his latest Fourth of July oration, which declared we had improved on our British heritage so evidently as to set an example for the mother country; Twain passed

it on to his circle after jotting, "It is fine. . . . Preserve it."
A Connecticut Yankee said almost nothing new as it leaped
back thirteen centuries to look forward: the very gimmick
of bringing the past and present face to face was common
property. In another variation, Charles Heber Clark's *The
Fortunate Island* (1882) imagined a floating bit of England
that had drifted away in Arthur's time. Revering tradition
and wallowing in a devil-ridden ignorance complete with
hermits, its natives are mystified by a ship-wrecked American whose suitcase full of scientific devices puts the official
conjurer out of business. Given to plundering raids by habit,
the nobility are tamed by the castaway, who deflates a pan-
oplied bully with his revolver. Twain insisted he had not
borrowed from this thin fantasy. It is easy to believe him after
finding the same basic ideas in many other sources including
the later fiction of Bret Harte[54]—whom he despised too much
by then to borrow anything from.

Indeed *A Connecticut Yankee* fitted current ideas so well
that it was virtually a manifesto summing up the Gilded Age
just before times changed with a vengeance. It assumed progress as a booming fact; and, ironically adapting the classic
Whig historians by using England as the zero mark, gloated
over the rise of science and political freedom. Set against
the ludicrously feudal past, the United States needed no
defense beyond loud cheers emphasizing mostly its wealth
and technical skills. Because it had come so far and was
pounding ahead so fast, the American system was obviously
sound in spite of minor flaws. In the grand perspective its
flaws did not justify criticism from the inside by the leftist
or even the Populist, and it towered over the Old World as
the model for industrial republics of the future.

A popular manifesto must slide over the tangles caused
by man's imperfect nature or the tensions of unregulated
progress. The chance that the masses and industrialism may
clash was just dimly suggested; Twain still did not doubt that
social harmony will be sweetest if everybody is encouraged

to make as much money as possible in almost any way. The chance that the elements of human nature may clash was made much clearer—without his intending it to be. Hank exults in his appeal to reason; yet he expects his struggles and declares that the finest quality of Arthur's knights was their spirit of "emulation." Seemingly, man is both rational and fiercely competitive. But self interest, it turned out, can be short sighted and work for the wrong side along with heredity and conditioning. At such moments, when Twain's dark view of character blocked his optimistic theory of history, Hank raged he would like to "hang the whole human race and finish the farce." How could he be sure about the future if people were so intractable? And if they were not, society was supposed to roar on improving—into what? The smashing logic of *A Connecticut Yankee* worked best at hindsight. By 1890 most Americans, while committed to worshiping progress, were wary of predicting any serious change in social and economic patterns. Ironically, the changes in the next ten years would take the bounce out of Twain's confidence.

Of course *A Connecticut Yankee* also holds the stamp of Twain's personal emphases and interests. In some places his old fondness for burlesque is uppermost, in others his old ambition to recreate the past from an insider's viewpoint. Always driven to chart man's basic makeup, in 1883-84 he started a novel that—besides tracing feudalism in Hawaii—would show the lifelong grip of whatever religious system the child is taught. The crucial fact is that, once again, topical interests won out. This novel soon limped to a halt and the guiding ideas took third or fourth billing in *A Connecticut Yankee*, which was finished with enthusiasm to spare. Even as literary burlesque it had immediate point as an answer to Tennyson, who jarred Liberals everywhere by accepting a baronetcy in 1884 and next publishing an indictment of modern progress in "Locksley Hall Sixty Years After."

Twain began *A Connecticut Yankee* by 1886, kept it moving along fairly well, and made final revisions during the summer of 1889. If he had a shaky spread of motives at first, he aimed more and more at the current situation in England as he went on.[55] In the prospectus his firm gave its salesmen, the heaviest weight fell on the trans-Atlantic message:

The book answers the Godly slurs that have been cast at us for generations by the titled gentry of England. . . . Without knowing it the Yankee is constantly answering modern English criticism of America, and pointing out the weakness and injustice of government by a privileged class. . . . It will be to English Nobility and Royalty what Don Quixote was to Ancient Chivalry.

Unquestionably, Twain edited this prospectus if he did not write it. While the comparison with Cervantes needs excuse as the usual exuberance of publishers' claims, he lavished much effort on *A Connecticut Yankee* with much success. Its teeming imagination, its parade of vivid characters, and its often sensitive pacing deserve more praise than they have had. Its sweep is finally uneven, as every reader knows, but the troughs feel so low partly because the crests swell so high. Though Twain must have piloted a steamboat better than his books, the mistakes in *A Connecticut Yankee* can too easily be exaggerated. A critic should make sure he questions its art rather than its attitudes and at least understands them before he brushes the book off as confused if not chaotic.

Like a majority of Americans at the time, Twain fits reasonably well within the school known to the nineteenth century as Liberalism, though it will not pass as liberal today, especially after the realignments of the 1930's. At most, *A Connecticut Yankee* sometimes took positions staked out by British Radicals like Labouchere, who busily defended the gulf between himself and Marx or the utopian socialist or any kind of defector from private enterprise. Yet humanity and a sense of fair play led Twain so far that some labor groups in the United States decided his book was on their side.[56] When he snatched up the banners under which the middleclass was forcing the nobility to disgorge, he was eloquently sincere; his flaming calls to revolt against self-appointed masters are great statements of that right, and his genius at phrasemaking left memorable appeals for self-respecting manliness and political equality. Their immediate purpose has gone down the stream of time but they will be useful for years to come.

I have been reading today . . . that little work of Prof. Sumner's What the Social Classes Owe to Each Other. *So far I like it extremely. Oh dear me! such political truths are a little chilly nichts? Not so warm as* Looking Backward. *But doubtless much truer & healthier.*

Olivia Clemens in 1895

SEVEN

The Bankrupt

WHEN *A Connecticut Yankee* was ready for the printers, Twain found time to read Edward Bellamy's *Looking Backward*, which he impulsively praised as the "latest & best of all the Bibles." At the moment it was easy for him to cheer on a middle-class revolution that would follow a line marked out by education and industrial change. However, he did not commit himself to Bellamy's program and it soon dropped out of his mind: *The American Claimant* (1892) would show a surprising retreat in the militancy of his Liberalism.

Though *A Connecticut Yankee* had its strand of uncertainty or even savage disgust over human nature, the immediate causes of this retreat were mostly personal. For a while longer, when he could get his mind off his own problems, he was in fact still enchanted with the "imagination-stunning material development of this century, the only century worth living in since time itself was invented"; and he still believed that Bellamy's paradise of technocracy was just about here already except for some backfiring in the social machinery, which the self-made man could fix better than the intellectual. *The American Claimant* finally put on record Twain's mutterings about how poorly the "college-bred" type stacked up against graduates of the university of hard knocks: awed by our material progress, a migrating young nobleman granted that it was beyond the abilities of "Oxford-trained aristocrats." More broadly, Twain must have originally thought of his new novel as neatly reversing *A Connecticut Yankee*. Running under social handicaps, Hank Morgan leaped to the front of the steeplechase; Lord Berkeley, who had all the advantages at home, trailed in the American sprint for success where nobody got a head start.

The attitudes behind *A Connecticut Yankee* had obviously —and unsurprisingly—carried over, if in ebbing strength. However, a hubbub about czarist cruelties had led to a target even more infuriating than Queen Victoria's court. One account has it that after a lecturer described the penal mines in Siberia, Twain stood up from a Boston audience and said in a "voice choked with tears": "If such a government cannot be overthrown otherwise than by dynamite, then thank God for dynamite!"[1] These tears had already washed away the gratitude born in Civil War days that let him, during the *Quaker City* jaunt, help compose a formal tribute to the "grandest monarch of the age, America's stanch, old steadfast friend, Alexander II, Autocrat of Russia!" By the time Howells and he wrote their luckless play, it was probably his idea to include—among Sellers' inventions—a "Nihilist bomb" disguised as a sugar plum that could be served for dessert at royal tables.

Violently serious in principle, Twain was moving a little ahead of a tide that speeded up after George Kennan, a conservative who had nevertheless been shocked by the flesh and blood realities, came back to spread the details. Along with his stirring lectures, once given two hundred week-nights in a row, Kennan's magazine articles excited even the casual public, which took up Siberia and its "salt mines" as colloquial tags that Twain was quick to exploit. He wove them into *A Connecticut Yankee* and also drafted a preface pairing the "civilizations of hell and Russia" and charging that exile to Siberia "concentrated all the bitter inventions of all the black ages for the infliction of suffering upon human beings."[2] Failure to use this preface did not spring from second thoughts about the Romanoffs. Sometime in 1890 he assured the editor of *Free Russia*, the organ of the anti-czarist exiles, "Necessarily I am with you . . . it goes without saying. . . . It may be months before I get an article written for you, but be sure I shall not drop the matter out of my mind, or my heart, for even a single moment."

He meant to keep his promise. One attempt—tied in with a campaign for better copyright laws—had the Czar joking about Siberia as a summer resort and aching to get his hands on Kennan. A longer manuscript scolded the "liberation" parties for protesting so humbly to the "granite-hearted, bloody-jawed maniac" and advised them to "keep the throne vacant by dynamite until a day when candidates shall decline with thanks."[3] This was extreme doctrine for even an American bourgeois, and seemingly Twain never gave *Free Russia* a chance to publish it. But he kept trying out approaches such as "The Answer," which cloaked his violence with a little artfulness. In this hoax reply to "Impertinent Republican Scum," Alexander III, freely admitting the cruelties Kennan accused him of, laughed at the over-respectful petitions of his subjects; he also sneered at the restraint of his foreign critics and declared he would send his lackeys to learn the American knack for servile patience with tyrants. Twain was easy game when Sergius Stepniak, a seasoned leftist, arrived to organize the Society of American Friends of Russian Freedom.

Stepniak bustled down to Hartford with a note from Howells and spent a "most delightful" and profitable day at the Clemenses, reporting that "they *all* signed our appeal— the paterfamilias for print, the rest for my personal use and gratification [—] and promised their hearty cooperation."[4] This visit happened to catch Twain in the middle of putting together *The American Claimant*, but even without it he probably would have lugged in the anti-czarist crusade through Sellers, whose wife said Russia was his favorite topic. With the mad grandiosity that made him a dubious asset to any cause, Sellers planned on buying Siberia—to which Alexander III had exiled anybody who showed "manhood, pluck, true heroism, unselfishness, devotion to high and noble ideals, adoration of liberty, wide education and *brains*"—and setting up a republic that would entice away the Czar's "slaves" and leave a "vacant throne in an empty land." This was not just comic relief. Around 1891 Twain could hardly write anything without giving the Czar a vicious dig.

His animus toward the British lion, however, had waned even before he could finish *The American Claimant*, which started out to heckle foreign critics such as Lord Berkeley who, as soon as he reached the hotel, undertook the "first and last and all-the-time duty of the visiting Englishman— the jotting down in his diary of his 'impressions' to date" and—sleeping with it handy in case new impressions came during the night—grabbed it before anything else when a fire-alarm sounded. After so overwrought a beginning Twain forgot about this diary except to quote parts he agreed with —in only one of the many inconsistencies that, in spite of stiff competition, make *The American Claimant* the most jumbled piece he ever published. Unfortunately, there is no reason to doubt he dashed it off within less than two and a half months though his mind was often taken over by business affairs and the typesetter that spelled out bigger and bigger losses.

Pinched for cash no matter how he figured his long range assets, he was probably tempted even to play up cynically to his English market, which began a decline with *A Connecticut Yankee* that spread to sales of his older books. Some of the unprinted passages in Lord Berkeley's diary had tart gibes about the extremes to which anti-British prejudice carried here, as in a plumber who plotted to kill the interest in billiards after he saw the unbeatable English champ. (Nobody who knows what dominated the top floor of Twain's house will under-rate the emphasis of this flourish.) With the manuscript of *The American Claimant* there is also a short essay that warns against the closed mind, giving as an example: "By habit our people have come at last to imagine that a democracy is the only perfect form of government & that the monarchical form is thoroughly bad."[5] Never going this far explicitly the novel once sympathized with Lord Berkeley because he "was glaringly English, and that was necessarily against him in the political centre of a nation where both parties prayed for the Irish cause on the house-top and blasphemed it in the cellar." Twain had a perfect right to his example at least. Without achieving anything memorable he had been openly berating our Fenians for twenty-five years.

The story line of *The American Claimant* epitomizes the basic wavering in attitude. When Berkeley's father cynically growls, "Going to renounce his lordship and be a man! Yas!" readers of *A Connecticut Yankee* are sure the old earl will eat crow eventually. As far as halfway through, they are reassured by finding a long editorial on how easily the British people could either vote or laugh the nobility into dropping their titles; but the earl, erect and poised, turns out fully likable at the climax and does not even mind his son's marriage to an American girl of plain family. Already dashingly handsome, the son turns out to be an excellent boxer and a sterling hero—in effect a physical and moral as well as legal aristocrat. Furthermore, with the prompting of the most

sensible American he met, his Radical posture has slumped
into tolerance toward the lucky few who "naturally decline
to vacate the pleasant nest they were born into" and contempt
toward the "all-powerful and stupid mass of the nation for
allowing the nest to exist." This tongue-lashing of the docile
masses partly renewed Hank's crusade to arouse them against
vested rights and social rank. In the same vein Sally Sellers
fumed at Rowena-Ivanhoe College where "unAmerican
pretentiousness" was taught to the "Colonial—Dutch-
Peddler—and Salt-Cod—McAllister Nobility" among her
classmates. Yet when Lord Berkeley concluded that respect
for rank was widespread here, Twain's tone became more
jeering than hortatory, and he made the crowd at the boarding house seem hopelessly stupid, petty, and eager to look
down on anybody who could not pay his bills.

By the early 1890's some reformers could foresee the shape
of twentieth-century problems. The best Twain could do
in *The American Claimant* was to sigh at "what being out
of work and no prospect ahead can do to a man." Even so, a
belated discovery of social Darwinism undercut his recent
tendency to oppose the severities behind supply and demand.[6]
Though vacillating here too, he now implied that a fight for
dominance rages inevitably and the weak must go under
without too much meddling from unions. Revealing inciden-
tally that he knew as little about them as John Hay or Thomas
Bailey Aldrich, two of his good friends who had given
slanderous pictures of a labor organizer, *The American
Claimant* was at first respectful toward the "decently dressed
and modest" members of a "Mechanics Club" but then turned
downright cool. Meanwhile, the eager British immigrant
found he could not land a job without a union card and decided there was a blue-shirted "aristocracy of the ins as
opposed to the outs"; if he had heard of a "right to work"
law, he would have been all for it.

In Twain's fiction *The American Claimant* is behind only
The Gilded Age as his closest approach to a contemporary

setting. Its curiously minor and even tangential scope must have surprised the admirers of *A Connecticut Yankee*, who had reason to expect a look at central problems in the United States. As Twain handled it the boarding house could not begin to stand for the national arena, and Sellers now operated much further from the heart of affairs than he had done as a friend of Senator Dilworthy. The biting wind that met the English visitor soon died to a zephyr in love's garden. To the pettiness of effect was added a series of reversals as, except for the anathema on the Czar, the second half of the novel took back or neutralized almost every progressive touch. The only lasting results were a deservedly small sale for *The American Claimant* and frustration for anybody who takes it seriously. Indecision would run deep through *Pudd'nhead Wilson* too. During these years Twain was not balancing his books very well in either business or literature.

One British reviewer could heartily praise *The American Claimant* for its satire "against the young aristocrat playing at social equality, and against the democracy, which, when it comes to putting theories into practice, is so very anti-democratic."[7] Nevertheless, Twain still fancied himself a nemesis of royalty. Having arranged to write six travel letters from Europe during the summer of 1891, he did not want them syndicated abroad because they would be "robbed of their freedom."[8] Particularly after the first two, there was actually little in them that he need regret because of the social triumph he scored in Berlin during the winter, though he did have a fresh skeleton in his closet. Reflecting American disgust at the new Kaiser's arrogant greeting to "My Army," *A Connecticut Yankee* had declared sourly that "there is plenty good enough material for a republic in the most degraded people that ever existed . . . even in the Germans," and Dan Beard drew Wilhelm II as one of the "chuckleheads."[9] Unaware of these insults the self-satisfied Kaiser condescended to meet him at a dinner, which was not a success because—Twain said later—he dared to disagree with Wilhelm's praise of increasingly generous pensions for our Civil War veterans. But other high-toned affairs went much better, and his notebook blandly set down a few instances of noble hauteur that would have made Hank Morgan reach for his hand grenades.

It would be unfair to suspect Twain of selling out for an elegantly served glass of beer. Like most Americans who could afford the trip, he admired the way Germany combined its industrialism with Junker firmness and honest bureaucracy. With utility companies under fire at home for their reckless profiteering, he even praised the publicly-owned telegraph and telephone systems. Despite his satire on fussy officials in "About All Kinds of Ships," his letter on "The German Chicago" also praised the tidy patterns forced on Berlin by the businessmen who had made it their stronghold. He especially liked the laws against public begging and the socal security program that relieved the worst cases of poverty while sweeping the rest under the rug with an iron broom; and he showed no pain when he mentioned seeing some "proletariat" riots quashed.[10] Not charmed, yet impressed by a close look at the Kaiser, he said nothing more against the Prussian cast of mind that grew stronger and stronger before World War I.

Though the Boss was supposed to shake off Merlin's spell in due time, his spirit was getting groggier: reversing the effect of his last trip, Twain liked Europe much more than he had expected. In a more cautious balancing of credits his essay on "Some National Stupidities" admitted our debt to the Old World's ideas—meaning inventions—and only complained that it was slower to learn from us. He was giving ground, even if there were periods of homesickness when the New World looked better than ever; on the whole he and his family clearly enjoyed moving around Europe as his business affairs went from bad to worse at home. It is surprising he could produce a book during these months that was so deeply in our native grain as *Pudd'nhead Wilson*.

In the ten years since he last set a story in the South, Twain's attitude had veered, leaving along the way some revealing touches in *The American Claimant* with the Sellerses' housekeepers, old Dan'l and Jenny. Helplessly gravitating back after the war, these ex-slaves were now waited on by a young girl hired for the purpose while somebody else was brought in to do their job—a situation worthy of Thomas Nelson Page. So was the spirit of "The Snow-Shovelers," a dialogue between Negro handymen who are supposed to be clearing the sidewalks but loaf while agreeing fervently on the virtue of hard work and obviously floundering beyond their mental depth when they touch on political and economic theory.[11] Drifting even further with the swelling stream of fiction, cartoons, and space-filling jokes about the inescapably ridiculous Negro, *Pudd'nhead Wilson* chuckled that the "coloured deacon himself could not resist a ham" in an unguarded smokehouse. It helped very little to explain that Negroes "had an unfair show in the battle of life, and they held it no sin to take military advantage of the enemy—in a small way; in a small way, but not in a large one." Such a defense recalls Twain's own anecdote about the woman who excused her illegitimate baby as a tiny one.

As the flaws in his portrait of Jim proved, he was undependable in even his most humane mood; since then public opinion had become almost solid for the other side. Caught in a current so wide and strong that only a latter-day Garrison could resist it completely, *Pudd'nhead Wilson* at times even moved close to the less genial vein of the unreconstructed school. Unlike Jim, Tom Driscoll had a "native viciousness" and Roxy said of the Negro fraction in his make-up, " 'Tain't wuth savin'; 'tain't wuth totin' out on a shovel en throwin' in de gutter." At the other end of the Southern ladder, Judge Driscoll and Pembroke Howard got a much better press than Huck would have given them, especially for their stiff-necked loyalty to the code duello.

But Twain was working haphazardly, as he confessed in

the preface to "Those Extraordinary Twins," which he also
published in 1894. This earlier version of his story punctuated
the dueling episode with heavy sarcasm. The sad truth is
that he had so much trouble finishing *Pudd'nhead Wilson*
that some minor effects got out of hand: indeed he had
trouble controlling his main point. His early drafts are
neeeded for making sure he meant to analyze the grip of
"inherited training" and show that slavery as a social institution is the basic "corrupting force" in Tom's character.[12]
Seen this way Tom's stealing, which goes far beyond the hen
roost, is chargeable against his masters rather than the
colored fraction of his soul. Since he had been brought up as
a respectable white, however, his criminal instinct looks like
the result of heredity; also, Twain used Roxy's whiskey
bottle for a stage prop too often, seemingly confirming the
racists' argument that Negroes are as much dissolute as
laughable. All in all, he obviously failed to draw the line
between inborn weakness and socially created sin—a tricky
job for the most careful novelist or sage. While she is as interesting to know as Jim, Roxy is distinctly less pathetic and
likable.

Still, Roxy was pathetic enough for a reviewer to growl
that *Pudd'nhead Wilson* slandered the contemporary South
and a reader to charge that its author was "sinfully recon-
structed."[13] Compared with other fiction at the time, it
actually was hard on the sugary antebellum legend. Though
Roxy said migrant Yankees made the worst masters, Twain
left no doubt that the southerner mistreated his slaves and
that owning human beings bred an ugly sense of caste, which
let Tom ask Roxy's supposed son, "Who gave you permission to come and disturb me with the social attentions of
niggers?" With irony that cut a genteel audience very deep,
Tom was unknowingly refusing to see his own mother; however, he merely overdid the haughtiness and bland cruelty in-
herent in the system. A stunted, warped conscience coiled
within the ruling families of Dawson's Landing, no matter

how they glittered when they strolled down the sleepy main street. And if they looked at Roxy coldly in public, some of the gentlemen had a warmer attitude in private. Sold down the river, she found a master who wanted her for a house servant, but his wife—who was "not right down good-lookin' "—objected "straight off" and sent her to the fields. As it was, buxom Roxy could brag to Tom that "dey ain't another nigger in dis town dat's as high-bawn as you is."

This last touch broke through an informal but wide censorship. Typically, after *The Grandissimes* Cable was told to submit no more fiction about mulattoes because they pointed to the sticky fact of miscegenation. Some southerners, however, kept inviting a rough and tumble fight as they defended lynching by claiming that almost every Negro lusts for white women and rejected his plea for civil rights as really a drive for interracial marriage. Cable was stung into answering that "probably not one in a thousand owes his or her mixture of blood to anyone suspected of advocating 'social equality'."[14] In 1892 Fred Douglass's vehement denial that Negroes are born rapists whipped up still higher waves of argument, though Twain had been aware for some while that more than one slaveowner took his female property to bed. Roxy's history made its point loud and clear—without a dulling veil of sentimentality for these scenes, it holds a spotlight on her illicit union with an F.F.V. and even rubs the truth in several times, as when she scolds her son for disgracing his father's high bloodline.

While Roxy usually stole the show when she was on stage, she was too often pushed aside by a ragged parade of other matters such as Twain's endless attempt to untangle determinism and free will or his growing fascination with the horrors of losing personal identity. The title he chose is an eye catching sign that he was brooding again about the good sense of the majority, who looked down on the brightest mind in Dawson's Landing. Less obviously, he also took up lynching again, but this time with relevance to a New Orleans

mobbing of whites in March, 1891 that brought a formal protest from Italy and nationwide criticism, particularly in New
England.[15] Craftily, he seemed to agree before trying to
shake the popular image of Italians as knife-wielding assassins.
Yet neither the topical touches he could never resist nor his
sprawling interests finally kept him from evoking and exorcis-
ing the spirit of the Old South and holding this effect to the
end (when Tom was pardoned and sold down the river because keeping an able-bodied Negro in prison was wasteful).
Pudd'nhead Wilson has solid virtues, though any case for its
greatness must assume that first-rate literature can come off
the top of the mind and a distracted mind at that.

As late as the middle of 1890 Twain thought his typesetter
was the big bonanza that made him "one of the wealthiest
grandees in America—one of the Vanderbilt gang, in fact;"
but he admitted he had no ready cash. Soon he had no credit
either and wasted many nights fighting rows of hostile figures. It is surprising that *Pudd'nhead Wilson* was any good
at all. However, he could cover more fronts at a time than
almost anybody else and, besides, kept writing because he
needed money. Desperately, he even tried to tap current
politics, suggesting to his assistant that parts of *A Connecticut Yankee* might be promoted as good campaign material
for the Democrats. More than ever, he also wanted to help
elections turn out right; even before the depression of 1893
gave the fatal tug on his overextended line of finance, he
knew very well that the public world could affect him seriously. There was vengefulness in his pleasure at the Republican upsurge that year after a Democratic Congress—he felt—
had wasted time in face of an "intolerable commercial con-
gestion."

Appeased for the moment he lectured to his wife, "*Now*
you understand why our system of government is the *only*
rational one that was ever invented. When we are not satisfied we can *change* things."[16] Like most people he felt mighty
democratic when the voters saw things his way, but his politi-

cal eye was basically as stern as ever. During the years he was heating up to Hank Morgan's attack on the Old World, he kept recording notes in the following vein, "Text for a mugwump speech: Goldwin Smith in London Times: 'The American . . . politician is in most cases a political slave.' Change that to *all* cases, & change 'politician' to 'voter,' & the statement is exactly true." A related quip he never used was, "Papa's been in the Legislature—there now! That ain't anything. I've got an uncle in hell."[17] He would have raged to his large limit if Cleveland had not made good on a comeback in 1892; for Cleveland still carried the hopes of the mugwump Liberals, unbothered by his recent hobnobbing with big bankers and industrialists who did not fit into the Republican camp.

Though Twain carefully avoided a party label and felt free to damn any Congress, he always got cordial treatment from Cleveland's palace guard. Over the years he had built up a reputation for speaking out, acidly and impulsively, on current issues; it was a relief to have his support and sometimes rather helpful. For example, *Tom Sawyer Abroad* (1894) suddenly swung into an anti-tariff routine. Tom and Huck were all set to take back a load of Sahara sand for the souvenir trade when they thought of the import duty, so named because governments consider it "their duty to bust you if they can." Tom predicted glumly that the impost on desert sand would be unbearably high because businessmen at home could not compete. More than any other passage except perhaps Jim's claim to an indemnity from Egypt, this fits Twain's comment in August, 1892—at the opening of the presidential campaign—that he was undertaking the book merely to lead up to one episode in an "effective (and at the same time apparently unintentional) way."[18] In his notebook for 1895 he wrote starkly, "The man that invented protection belongs in hell."

Twain also delighted the Cleveland faction because his faith in the gold standard was unshaken by the pressure from the mining lobby and spokesmen for the small debtor. When he concocted a trick sentence to test the Paige typesetter, he came up with, "Through consecration of the nation to inflation the degradation of the nation is occasioned."[19] When the mining states were holding up repeal of the Sherman Silver Purchase Act during the late summer of 1893, he started "The Facts Concerning the Late Disturbance in the Senate," a throwback to maneuvers he had used in 1867-68. Posing as ghost writer of the speeches that had "lately been chocking the wheels" of the drive for repeal, he dropped into mock praise of Nevada's William Stewart for orating on senatorial courtesy rather than the languishing bill that the public thought more important.[20] He did not finish this sketch, but not because he had wavered as yet on the silver question. Published in the same year, "The £1,000,000 Bank-Note" may be taken as a homily against diluting the money pool: credit was eagerly available if a man showed he rated it, and the penniless hero soon had a fat account in the Bank of England.

Because Twain was anxious to rebuild his own bank account, this story had as much hollow glitter as solid purpose. In the context of his business troubles it was also a wistful projection of his belief that all he needed was generous credit until his big deals paid off. He still ached to emerge as an American-style grandee with the gold seal of approval, and his notebook stoutly rejected foreign jeers that our millionaires were merely a crasser kind of nobility: "Their own work & talent gave them money—& it's the work & the talent that are respect-worthy, not the money. The money merely *represents* the work & the talent, as paper represents gold."[21] Taking a more sardonic posture "The Esquimau Maiden's Romance"—about the arctic "Vanderbilt" of twenty-two fish-hooks—denied that we were the high-priests for the worship of wealth. Though this story also raked the populace for servilely gaping at rich men, Twain later made its main point explicit in an essay that decided, "It was a dull person that invented the idea that the American's devotion to the dollar is more strenuous than another's."[22] No more strenuous in the fight for marks of status, the American tycoon looked much more sensible than the tribesman who gloried in an excess of fish-hooks, brass rings, or sloptubs.

Hobbled by his financial worries, Twain was tamely following the cycle of mugwump energy, which hummed in the 1880's but idled after that when Populists and leftists demanded changes too sweeping for middle-class caution. Having read Edward Bellamy and Henry George, he knew there were some trustworthy men behind this new upsurge, and Howells' account of a quasi-socialist visitor from Altruria was running in the same issue of the *Cosmopolitan* for December, 1893 that carried the enticingly titled "Travelling with a Reformer." But Twain sketched a crusader against "petty public abuses," a "Major" who went around cowing telegraph operators or surly brakemen into better conduct with his shrewd bluffing—though he knocked down three "boisterous roughs" on a horsecar without any diplomatic nonsense. If it is dismaying to find Twain excited again about insolent clerks and waiters, it may be a comfort to note that the Major flatly opposed firing them; aware of how serious losing a job could be, he was satisfied to remold them into useful employees. To allow Twain all the credit possible, it should also be noted that the Major insisted on getting as good a meal as the top brass of a railroad.[23] More courteous service of dining-car chicken, however, stood low on the want list of the unemployed.

Twain knew this yet was at a loss for substantial ideas that did not reach too far. Moved by the obvious suffering he reminded himself, "Go to Chauncey Depew—& propose my plan to raise $50,000 cash for the unemployed poor of New York. Another idea: have stage-boxes & sell them at auction."[24] Talking with Depew, the eloquent lawyer for Vanderbilt interests, left Twain way behind his friends who understood the size of the problem, the many thousands and perhaps millions of families pinched by poverty. While he was getting enthusiastic about the Salvation Army's rescue program, Howells was doggedly and publicly doubting that charity could take care of all deserving comers; in 1894 Warner's latest novel included a sweat-shop drudge who nearly starved on full-time work but Twain was still more worried about softening the fiber needed for progress. With awkward timing his *Pudd'nhead Wilson's Calendar* proclaimed, "Hunger is the handmaid of genius."

If Twain had a plan for curing depressions he never unveiled it. He was held back not by shyness but the common faith that laissez-faire business, the triumphant master of modern life, ran by unwritten yet—as he said—"exact and constant" laws that should not be "interfered with for the accommodation of any individual or political or religious faction."[25] When his extremely gentle wife read William Graham Sumner's *What the Social Classes Owe to Each Other*, she accepted its answer of very little as a good deal more reasonable than Bellamy's.[26] For convictions like this, Cleveland, who officially ignored the wide-spread hunger during his second term, was a fit president. Twain sometimes gets a cheap medal for predicting television among the wonders to come, but he did much worse when a nephew—a talented scholar and journalist who died far too young—sent him his *Suggestions on Government* (1894), which firmly pointed onward to the Progressive movement. Claiming to have read it carefully, Twain misused its ground-clearing criticisms to conclude "there is no good government at all & none possible."[27]

Politically, his hawk-like eyes were much better at seeing where society had been than where it would go or at judging countries that still lagged behind the ideal of an industrial republic. When Paul Bourget, a French Catholic and reactionary, dared to criticize the United States, he shelved his gloom and again rolled out the artillery that had lit up the pages of *A Connecticut Yankee*. When his cordial friend

Sir Henry Campbell-Bannerman, the Liberal party's new leader, introduced him to Henry Labouchere, he got along with that old-style Radical much more cheerfully than with his nephew. Not a born listener either, Labouchere held up his end of the talking while Twain helped him "walk off his mineral water" at a German spa. Before long Twain noted, "Make a book to be called 'English Justice.'" Eventually he took a handful of clippings from Labouchere's weekly *Truth* and drafted an essay at least.[28] Especially intrigued by *Truth's* "Legal Pillory," a column featuring the worst side of British courts, he found in it proof that the most grimly punished crimes were those against property and that the "man who lays his hand upon a Farthing save in the way of kindness is in deeper peril than he would be if he had committed three rapes." Pushing on to an even more provocative analysis, Twain also charged that British judges, descended from families of wealth and social standing, "must often be betrayed into unrighteous leniency where their own class and its interests are concerned, and into as unrighteous severity where the other class is concerned."[29] He did not, however, try to draw a contrast with our courts' handling of the very recent Pullman strike.

It was easier to stick to foreign cases; with them he could be firmly Liberal, even Radical, and prescribe bitter pills. In the spring or summer of 1894 he told himself, "Write Ambassador Wayne McVeagh—how to stop bomb-throwing."[30] Either then or a few weeks later, after an anarchist stabbed the president of France, he composed "A Scrap of Curious History," which warned that harsh measures egg on "wild-brained martyrdom" and finally—"in natural order"—the rioting and wars touched off by reformers "since the beginning of the world." This could have been applied here to pardons for those Haymarket anarchists who were still alive, but Twain was calling for cool action from European regimes harried by leftist factions which the United States had only in fleabite strength. He also wanted the French, who were worried about the lineup of world power, to stop working for an alliance with Russia. When their government played host to the Czar's retinue in 1896, he fumed about the "exhibition of bootlicking adulation" and asked, though he had settled on the answer years ago, "Is there anything that can insult a Frenchman?"[31]

Despite changing his mind on the revolution of 1789 Twain had become even surer about his answer and especially liked to play variations on the general Anglo-American notion that the French were immoral to the core. Still, with slightly dwindling energy, he followed the politics around him as usual, and from Paris his wife mentioned a change in cabinets to a Hartford friend as an event that "interests us all—you over there and we here—so much."[32] When the Third Republic finally began to look stable, he softened a little, particularly after the middle-class parties overwhelmed both the royalists and the left in the elections of 1893; under a sound premier a few details of French polity even seemed better than ours. However, when a right-wing Parisian suggested his country could give us lessons in manners, Twain revoked his concessions with a crude vehemence that keeps his answer to Paul Bourget from becoming a classic like the essays on Shelley and James Fenimore Cooper, done around the same time. The startling fact is that it came as he was also putting the final touches on *Personal Recollections of Joan of Arc* (1896), yet he had lived with this paradox since beginning work on the book in 1880. He admired Joan only in spite of her nationality—as he managed to show here and there, starting with the last paragraph of the "Translator's Preface." Though a diatribe against the French was not his chief purpose, it suited him if his reader ended up thinking they were slippery in political morals too.

It is well known that Twain pondered long about what he wanted to do in *Joan of Arc*. When he called it a companion piece to *The Prince and the Pauper* he partly meant he was still trying to catch the day-to-day feel of the past, but it had stronger linkages, both obvious and unexpected, with *A Connecticut Yankee*. Under his helmet of iconoclasm toward "shams" he had bristled at the sneer that he was incapable of reverence even where deserved. As if in penance *Joan of Arc* was often reverent beyond reason, and compliments to its heroine flew much harder than the wobbly cannonballs or papier-mâché broadswords of her battles. Among other superlatives that could set examples for the most solemn courtier Hank Morgan ever met, the preface crowned Joan as the "only entirely unselfish person . . . in profane history;" this theme kept recurring and hit a painful high in the "Conclusion." Though Joan's unique "purity from all alloy of self-seeking" could make the rest of the human race look all the uglier, Twain worshipped her while letting some of his favorite game slink by with hardly more than a frown. Sentimental readers had every right to think he had found pure sugar at the bottom of life's cup.

Whatever Twain's drive to show he could feel reverence, his undertone was still hostile toward kingcraft; but he had to let up on Joan's religion. If she was to be a heroine her visits from angels and even her prophecies had to be treated with respect. This may have come easier because of his stray moods of longing for the spiritual certainty of Catholicism. If accused of recanting *A Connecticut Yankee*, however, he would have said it attacked not the doctrines of Rome but its social policy and influence. The school of historians that he admired held up Joan's trial as a clear example of how the Inquisition had often masked political ends with the charge of heresy. Twain obviously agreed, and the darkest-dyed villain in his account was easily Bishop Cauchon. In October, 1894 he raged that the "English-French priests" had "burnt her" but their church now had the gall to propose a "tinsel saintship" for Joan.[33]

For a good cause Twain did not mind working both sides of the street, even in the same book. Sometimes it ripped at Cauchon for appealing to backward notions that woman was created only to play a weak second fiddle at home and for using Joan's military skill as evidence of her abnormal character; other passages poured scorn on the Bishop and his assistants for bullying a sweet innocent girl. The sentimental approach moved in much deeper grooves. All his life Twain revered the sanctity of femaleness like the most genteel son, husband, or father; reinforced by his delivery, many episodes in *Joan of Arc* were sadly comforting to the shawled, flouncy circle around his writing desk. Yet he had always kept them uneasy by breaking out of staid patterns, as in his strong leaning toward free thought. And freethinkers had started making a prime goal of woman's rights. Unable to agree heartily about the Negro they switched extra energy in this direction, further challenging because they saw a "medieval" attitude that churchmen did most to prolong.

Now that the feminist crusade has won out on many fronts without toppling the country into chaos, its uphill fight against ridicule is often forgotten. Twain helped to scoff before his Nook Farm days, though by the time he finished *Life on the Mississippi* he openly favored letting women into the state universities and Hank Morgan planned to give votes to "men and women alike—at any rate to all men, wise or unwise, and to all mothers who at middle age should be found to know nearly as much as their sons at twenty-one." In private Twain went beyond this position but held back for tactical reasons, irritated rather than dismayed by the white Uncle Tom ladies on the other side.[34] He kept up a flow of increasingly emphatic, shrewd comment before and after *Joan of Arc*. When his political scientist nephew grouped it among Twain's books that were "tales of the day," it is hard to imagine what he could have had in mind except the feminist movement.

By 1891 Twain cared enough to work on an essay that looked into how male chauvinism is handed on and, with a typical surprise, charged that most mothers unknowingly teach their sons to "despise" women as passive-minded and impractical.[35] Turning to an approach he knew better, his incomplete essay on "Have We Appropriated France's Civilization?" argued that the sacred cause of progress demanded equality for the American woman; perhaps with self-criticism he went on to predict, "She is reverenced, now; she will be respected, then—which is worth six of it." On this last tack, after seeing for himself how the tide of battle was running in New Zealand and Australia, he even suggested that feminists were proving to be the male's superior in drive because they fought so well against long odds.[36] Appropriately, he was later made an honorary member of the Joan of Arc Suffrage League, which felt it could genuinely recommend his book. His Joan testified to woman's intelligence and her ability to take a role in top level matters. Without desexing herself his Joan also testified dramatically that persistence and even courage exist outside the male frame. As a kind of homemade epigraph Twain used a separate page to feature the fact that she was the "only person, of either sex, who has ever held supreme command of the military forces of a nation *at the age of seventeen.*"

This was a direct challenge to the "Rob Roy"school, which could not have been better named to raise a glint in his eye. Supposedly indebted to Sir Walter Scott, it mainly argued that women deserve no hand in government because they cannot carry their share of the military burden. At its worst it accused them of resorting to tears in a close spot or even personal allure—unfair tactics conceding that man is the tougher half of the species. At its kindest it held that women lack the iron nerve needed to enforce law and order or are too soft-muscled and queasy about bloodshed to threaten war if foreign policy demands it. To deny they all belonged in the parlor and nursery, some feminists in the United States took to strenuous games and horseback riding while a few British ladies started military drills; but the majority settled for verbal answers like citing the Maid of Lorraine's career. By 1891 Twain was alert to the argument that, as he put it, a woman could not soldier "because she had no endurance and was a coward in the presence of danger." As late as 1894, intriguingly, he thought he might end Joan's saga with the smashing victory at Orleans.[37] His finished and lovingly polished product certainly played up her cool hardiness and her genius not only as a spine-tingling leader in the field but also as a strategist who, after she settled a council of war incisively, moved the once skeptical La Hire to thunder, "By God, she knows her trade, and none can teach it her!"

Its topical side does not make *Joan of Arc* an impressive biography. Uninspired at its best, it wavers toward tired confusion as rationalistic and cloyingly genteel attitudes mix in almost every chapter. Though George Bernard Shaw was unfair in laughing off Twain's peerless heroine as a "most ladylike Victorian," his own approach to Joan as a forerunner of ideas that would disrupt the medieval synthesis and as a genius fatally lacking in tact went much deeper, historically and humanwise. Twain's straining eulogy wasted his talent as obviously as if doughty La Hire were to take on the job of seeing that school-girls get across the street safely. Except for the style many a hack could have written *Joan of Arc*, which in fact competes poorly with a row of other biographies. Bowed down in homage Twain merged with the crowd; for the time being this was a relief if not a deliberate escape.

The early 1890's had brought the threat and then the ordeal of bankruptcy. Even loyal and calm Olivia Clemens wailed to her husband, "I have a perfect *horror* and heart-sickness over it. I cannot get away from the feeling that business failure means disgrace. I suppose it always will mean that to me." He would not have been cheered up by seeing that, for all his bad luck, he was only an acute case as the stoutest arteries of middle-class Liberalism, drained by a baffling depression, wavered close to the point of collapse. His confidence was badly shaken, and he pulled back on all fronts: *Joan of Arc* could not have come before this retreat nor *A Connecticut*

Yankee after it. Though he wrote much more than in the preceding five years, his output for 1890-95 includes nothing that will last except a few essays in literary criticism and perhaps *Pudd'nhead Wilson*. After 1895 some of his bounce came back but not all—he was over sixty years old. When he fought the rise of American imperialism he would slash and parry almost like a younger Twain while he would obviously be getting older and further behind his times on domestic questions. Emotionally, his bankruptcy left him in debt to Henry H. Rogers, who extracted the interest irregularly but deftly. Rogers was not, however, a Svengali. Twain moved down channels he had learned long ago, and it is best to be happy that Rogers helped him finish the trip in comfort.

" HANDS OFF! MY PERSON IS SACRED."

From *A Connecticut Yankee in King Arthur's Court*

I have filled the position—with some credit, I trust, of self-appointed ambassador-at-large of the United States of America —without salary.

EIGHT

Dollarless Diplomacy

WORRIED ABOUT the debts that also kept him aware he had gone bankrupt in a blaze of publicity, Twain began his world lecture tour of 1895 under an emotional cloud. Then before he could rest up from the grind of travel and get in a better mood for writing, the death of his oldest daughter shattered his family circle. Understandably, *Following the Equator* (1897) is not a happy or great book. But it deserves to be read if only because it shows that his values had firmed up in an unexpected way, typified by a maxim he set down during his tour: "The universal brotherhood of man is our most precious possession—what there is of it." He would sometimes reword this maxim with a much less cheerful cynicism and, less often, would even feel more strongly than ever that the brotherhood of the "damned human race" meant universal stupidity. However, the shadows over his final years were cut by many signs of a freshly vibrant humanity, making it sure there was at least for the moment no venom behind his saying in 1901 that the "hearts of men are about alike all over the world, no matter what their skin-complexions may be."[1]

His advance toward a new level of feeling for brotherhood is clear though it was a dogged, winding march. Anybody who wants to dramatize Twain's life after 1895 as a retreat into total darkness and despair can certainly use patches of his reaction to Asia. He was sourly depressed by the crowds plunging reverently into the dirty Ganges; also, thanks to the social Darwinists, he was tempted on his gloomy days to shrug off the suffering of India's millions as the inevitable struggle for existence. Nor were his hopeful moods always an improvement. Sometimes they only touched off angry bursts of impatience with primitive squalor or revived the greedy dreams that his trip to Hawaii had first stirred up thirty years ago. Overstating like a reformed sinner he confessed later that he set out on his lecture tour in 1895 as a "red-hot imperialist" who "wanted the American eagle to go screaming into the Pacific."[2] But, with a flexibility that would do great credit to any man as old as he was, he modified much of his mental baggage to fit the realities he met. Before long he was able to say in his best deadpan tone, "I have traveled more than anyone else, and I have noticed that even the angels speak English with an accent."

Greeted by European officials in every Asian and African port, he became keenly aware that the scramble for colonies was spreading like wildfire. As usual his first impulse when he got uneasy about the situation was to burlesque it with a "Sketch of the future, in which the Imperial trust, having seized & divided up all the earth, begin to gobble the constellations—fall out, & fight a devastating war over the Southern Cross."[3] *Following the Equator*, however, settled for a flippant analogy with stealing from neighbors' clotheslines and a complaint that "claim-jumping is become a European governmental frenzy." Though both of these figures—which understated the scale of operations—were hazy about the real victim, Twain had learned to put himself in the breech-clouted native's place on some counts at least. He was now firmly against any traffic in able-bodied coolies or Kanakas and sang the virtues of the Australian bushman though he never saw one; seeming to mellow as he went along, he sampled the strange smells and customs of Asia or Africa with much more tolerance than *The Innocents Abroad* had shown toward Italy though the cultural gap was much wider on this trip. The wry experiments in perspective that cluttered his workshop after 1900 would often use details from his sight-seeing jaunts between lectures in Bombay or Pretoria and would increasingly pierce through the illusions of ethnocentrism. As an omen his final travel book suggested: ". . . let us hope that when we come to answer the call and deliver [Asia] from its errors, we shall secrete from it some of our high-civilization ways, and at the same time borrow some of its pagan ways to enrich our high system with."

As yet such comments were only signposts rather than the groundwork of a new position. Slackly mixing principles with profits, he still believed at other times in 1896-97 that western enterprise deserved a wide-open track. Half seriously, he wrote to his wife when he heard the American consul at Johannesburg was quitting, "I suppose I could have the place for the asking. I might make a fortune, I might not. But a Consul there must have mighty good chances."[4] It was tempting to feel practical and argue that the Anglo-Saxon might as well get his fistful since the hunt for imperial loot was sparing no undefended country on earth. Even so, as an old Liberal instead of a global Jay Gould, Twain was eager to think that pulling these countries into the western sphere of influence would at least end the "dreary and dragging ages of bloodshed and disorder and oppression."

When he got down to concrete cases he was often uneasy, but he had been briefed along his lecture route by salesmen for Anglo-American unity and then petted in London as a

Portraits of HENRY V, the DUKE OF ORLEANS and the DUKE OF BOURBON, Copied by the Author from the Originals in the South Kensington Museum : : : : : : :

From *Queen Victoria's Jubilee* (1897). Notice Twain's "Private to the Engraver: Reduce these as much as you please."

favorite cousin who had in fact just been orating about a "great English-speaking family." In the current context this was far more than a bland cliché, as any private in the growing army of diplomats knew. Though Twain was willing to let the British take charge of the white man's burden, *Following the Equator* made a gesture toward sharing it and predicted that the "English-speaking race will dominate the earth a hundred years from now, if its sections do not get to fighting each other." Accordingly, more attuned to Rudyard Kipling than he had ever been to Matthew Arnold, he was ready to help make up for the way Americans had lately twisted the lion's tail in the quarrel over Venezuela's boundary. His account of the next Jubilee honoring Queen Victoria in 1897 bowed with heavy respect for her country; and he assured Howells, who noticed the same change of tone in many Boston and New York literati, "Beneath the governing crust England is sound-hearted—& sincere, too, & nearly straight."[5]

However, as these reservations show, the new chorus of friendship had not charmed him completely. When he arrived to cover the Jubilee he jotted, "Game laws remain. Poaching the highest crime then—& now."[6] Decorated by silly fashion plates that he labeled with the names of bluebloods, his syndicated account undoubtedly went over with Liberals much better than Conservatives, who could not be expected to like its closing point that the parades should have honored business and industry rather than their lordly "beneficiaries." He still took the British selectively on their home grounds, no matter how good they looked in India. And, after some indecision and double talk, he flared out at Cecil Rhodes' swashbuckling in South Africa. This was a warning that he would not excuse just any imperialist raid that hoisted the banner of progress or Anglo-Saxon destiny.

Whenever possible he watched too closely to be taken in. About the first sign that he was rebounding after Susy's death came in this outburst from London: "These are sardonic times. Look at Greece, & that whole shabby muddle. But I am not sorry to be alive & privileged to look on. If I were not a hermit I would go to the House every day & see those people scuffle over it & blether about the brotherhood of the human race."[7] Soon, unable to stay a hermit or even a sideliner, he began a series of "Letters to Satan" that went far enough to show their bite would have been partly political; the one finished letter closed with Satan's ambassador reporting that Rhodes "would serve you just for the love of it." Still, though honesty forced Twain to cut through Rhodes' smokescreen, best policy at the moment kept him from more than hinting at what it hid. He had lately decided that England was the "only comrade" the United States could count on.

It is just as well that Twain did not live to hear Americans suddenly hymn the virtues of *la belle* France in 1917. He kept moving toward hotter animosity, if possible, which even led him into an essay stuffily condemning glamorous Monaco as a gambling den run with Catholic blessings.[8] He had no policy to restrain him from racing far ahead of world opinion in concluding that Captain Dreyfus had been framed. A stream of public and private comments proves that the case eventually obsessed him as the Tweed ring had done in 1870 or the Czar in 1890; when all its grisly dishonesties were uncovered he rasped, "Oh, the French! The unspeakables! . . . I don't think they have improved a jot since they were turned out of hell."[9] After the victim himself was finally sent back from Devil's Island, Twain even offered to send Madame Dreyfus his latest surefire idea on perking up the sick.

In spite of his notorious literary blunders he was always better as a writer than as a medical adviser, and the Dreyfus affair posed fat targets for his irony. Unfortunately, his British publishers had been against his doing a book about it; as it went into its most sensational phase he ruefully insisted that the "first chapter—the only one finished—fits into today's news."[10] Since Joan of Arc's trial was fresh in his mind he saw Dreyfus partly as a victim of the French legal system, which he needled in a story with the harmless title of "From the 'London Times' of 1904." Built around a telectroscope, it is another good example of how his seeming froth often had solid purpose; published in the fall of 1898, it was really about the dilemma of officials who now suspected that Dreyfus was innocent but felt it impossible to pardon him without reopening some nasty dossiers. Though Twain did not make much of the fact that the whole affair pulsed with anti-Semitism, he knew it and disapproved heartily. When he proclaimed in "Concerning the Jews" (1898) that he had no prejudice against any race "bar one," this exception sneered at the French with ironic neatness.

Perhaps influenced most by eloquent Robert G. Ingersoll, who ripped at anti-Semitism as a vestige of the Dark Ages, he had started to take a sounder position about 1880. When Howells reported unhappily that some Jewish readers objected to a passage in *The Rise of Silas Lapham* (1885), he could say that a "distinguished" Jew had—without looking very far back—just rated Twain's books clean as a whistle. His notebooks and unpublished manuscripts prove he was soon wanting to go beyond this fresh virtue of omission, though his first tries timidly worked the angle that he had once seen a Jew risk his neck for a stranger.[11] When he finally took a public stand, his taunt that Jews are resented because of their sharper business sense and brains was not much help either; in fact the opposition found it could quote him after some unfair editing. But he had truly shown his heart was on the fair side, as his close-knit family knew; his daughter Clara later married a Russian Jew with his blessing.

If Twain's "Concerning the Jews" fell awkwardly short of seeing through anti-Semitism anywhere or its special uses in Austria-Hungary, the fault lay in his more and more outdated patterns of thought rather than in negligence. Drifting to Vienna in the fall of 1897, he was fascinated by his first look at the Balkans and especially the tangled affairs of state there. He very soon wrote, "If I had time to run around and talk, I would do it; for there is much politics agoing, and it would be interesting if a body could get the hang of it."[12] Naturally he took time after all to run around and talk, including a speech studded with references to the latest politics at hand, and during a stalemate in the parliament he cheerfully rushed to the gallery and gathered material for his *Harper's* article on "Stirring Times in Austria." This item stuck chiefly to reporting but he also drafted "Government by Article 14," which blamed the voting system for giving the Hungarian landowners too much power.

However, he was understandably slow to air many provocative opinions as his apartment in Vienna became crowded with eminent and titled callers. In turn he was invited to call on various princesses, and a baroness felt chummy enough to try bagging him for a peace society. She picked a good prospect who had always liked the classical economists' dream that world trade would make war look senseless. When the United States and England signed an arbitration treaty in 1897, he exclaimed that it was a truly epochal document, even holding out hope that the standing army would become an unpleasant memory. Along this vein that must have surprised his old friends at West Point, "The Austrian Edison Keeping School Again" (1898) fumed about the waste of talent where everybody, even a young inventor, was conscripted for training. Inevitably asked to comment during the debate over setting up a world tribunal for crises in diplomacy, Twain clowned a bit but also suggested a scale for cutting armaments. He gave the pacifist baroness further advice and let her convoy him to some meetings, grumbling that he favored her cause yet doubted that the ruling kings of Europe would dare to disarm.[13]

Actually he was ineligible to advise her because he was cheering on the United States against the Old World armies in Cuba. Though still opposed to the "average war" he insisted ours was righteous and growled half-seriously about wishing he could enlist. Pretending to offer a "word of encouragement for our blushing exiles" he instead scolded any fellow tourists who felt the home front had fallen into an imperialist mood. His own way of stating the same fact, when he published his essay on "Diplomatic Pay and Clothes" in the spring of 1899, was that the "Great Republic lengthened her skirts last year, balled up her hair, and entered the world's society." To make the debut more effective our diplomats, he proposed, should shake off the Ben Franklin tradition of simplicity and dress much more showily, perhaps as honorary generals or admirals. As the agents of a "trading nation," they also needed big expense accounts to coax orders for the goods and gadgets that Hank Morgan had counted on as his best selling point.

In fact Hank was now a blunderbuss whom it was best not to mention as Twain argued that the Spanish-American war had more than paid for itself merely by bringing us "close together" with the British, who had taken our side in the diplomatic jockeying. If an interviewer trapped him he was most likely to gush about the beauties of this alliance, and he announced he had worked eight days on a pun to be proud of: "Since England and America have been joined together in Kipling, may they not be severed in Twain."[14] Ignoring the record he even claimed that such unity "has always been a dream of mine." In part this was his timely way of saying thanks for being wined and dined almost beyond comfort after going back to London from the Balkans, though the onset of the South African war strained his public smile because his personal letters sided profanely with the Boers. As the handiest way out he tried to follow a policy of diplomatic realism: "Even wrong—& she is wrong—England must be upheld."

For the rest of his stay in London he kept the cheerful half of this policy facing up. Soon after getting home in late 1900 he was therefore asked to introduce a talk by Winston Churchill, fresh from his exploits in South Africa. If it is true that Churchill took over when they had a smoke together, Twain more than evened the score by stealing the show in public. Opening with the idea that he was a "self-appointed missionary" for unity and declaring that Churchill—with a British father and an American mother—was a "perfect" mixture, he carefully struck a courteous and friendly tone. But he went on to question the morality of provoking the Boers into a war they could not win; conceding we were just as wrong in our treatment of the Filipinos, he closed with the barb that England and America, already "kin" in blood and government and "lofty" purpose, were now "kin in sin."[15] This well-plated irony startled Churchill into a partial apology and gave full notice that Twain had decided the crusade against Spanish tyranny in Cuba was changing to raw conquest in the Pacific. During the days ahead he would startle and harry our State Department with much less regard for tact.

Its current secretary would have laughed off such a prediction. Twain had often singled out John Hay, a close friend since the early 1870's, as just the kind of man who ought to run things in Washington and had written from England on February 27, 1900, "I watch your onward & upward career with the interest & pride of one with a personal stake in it."[16] But when the Treaty of Paris made us owners of the Philippines, Twain came home full of doubts that he showered on shipside reporters. In time to catch the climax of a major election, he dutifully oriented himself among the whirlwinds of oratory and took a firm stand: hostile to Bryan's domestic platform, he could not support McKinley either after hearing the anti-expansionists. On election day he must have smoked many a cigar in restless anger. However, he could not lie low for long and was soon asking Grover Cleveland's opinion whether it was possible to have the Supreme Court pass on the legality of the treaty.

Historians agree today that McKinley's re-election put his side irreversibly on top, but Twain was just getting warmed up. Even after Joe Twichell, talking as a friend rather than a minister of the gospel, reminded him that keeping quiet would protect the sale of his books, he built up a drumfire against taking over the Philippines and crushing the nationalists there who had helped fight the Spanish. A mass of manuscript proves he doggedly tried out many approaches after combing newspapers and magazines for material. It also proves he held back very little or none of his venom on this score; most of the unused items were merely trial runs, few of them as daring as "A Defence of General Funston," which cut through a hail of smug editorials praising the victories over poorly equipped Filipinos. He published enough to make his position glaringly clear and give the tiring anti-imperialists a second wind. Since he had been loudly welcomed home as the avatar of American qualities, almost nobody had the brass to call him a traitor, and he helped vitally to keep the unpopular side respectable a while longer. There was much rueful comment about how our leading humorist had turned moralist, but this only pleased Twain's dearest self-image. An honorary vice-president, he stuck to the Anti-Imperialist League as long as it could afford stationery.

Leftist critics of imperialism like to quote Twain and would of course like to claim him as a fellow traveler. However, the Anti-Imperialist League was sparked by men from the right side of the tracks like E. L. Godkin, William Graham Sumner, Charles Eliot Norton of Harvard, and Andrew Carnegie —who paid for reprinting Twain's "To the Person Sitting in Darkness." In routine politics its hardcore members were veteran mugwumps, Cleveland (rather than Bryan) Democrats, or elderly Republicans who wished Rutherford Hayes could be president again. And in economics they were Liberals who still believed in the peaceful magic of inventions and industry and heartily favored sending American products over the farthest oceans. They were only opposing the use of force, because it led to more power for the scheming politician in Washington and the wasteful militarist. Rather than groping toward Lenin's analysis of finance capitalism as a glutton that inevitably touches off wars over the world market, their case against colonial empire went back finally to Locke's axiom that government must get its sanction from a contract with its subjects and their hottest pamphlets appealed to the spirit of '76. Far as ever from turning left, Twain followed their lead before going off on his own lines of analysis.

The captains of the Anti-Imperialist League kept their eyes on the Philippine issue; it was clearcut and, besides, they soon felt they were losing too much strength to spare any for China's troubles. Indeed Twain, taking Hay's manifestoes at face value, still believed for a while that the United States was "steadfast for humanity & justice in China when the other Powers would rob her & dismember her."[17] But one of his pet peeves, outranking even the claims of friendship, came into play. He had missed very few chances to complain that the United States was helping the "fat Spanish Friars" stay in the Philippines; later he would underline the irony that the greedy invaders of the Congo said they were out to spread the Roman Catholic gospel. Though he disliked papist missionaries most of all, the truth is that he had grown hostile to those of any church in any corner of the world. During his lecture tour he had often winced at the casual or unsuspecting brutality with which most Christians brushed aside the gods of the Orient; a letter he offered to the London *Times* in 1900 poignantly urged westerners to imagine themselves in the place of parents whose children were enticed away from their native religion.[18] So when American missionaries made ugly headlines from the Far East, it was easy for him to sign off—publicly—from our China policy too.

There has been elaborate comment on the "Great Dark" stories as the index to Twain's state of mind after 1896. Yet he finished off little and published even less of this material,

CAN THE MISSIONARY REACH THIS OLD SAVAGE?
— *The Minneapolis Journal.*

Inspired by Twain's controversy with American missionaries in 1901.

Having the Time of his Life.

From *Harper's Weekly*, February 23, 1901. The "schoolbooks" at the left are *Innocents Abroad, Huckleberry Finn, Following the Equator, Joan of Arc,* and *North American Review,* which had just carried "To the Person Sitting in Darkness."

which is matched by several other stacks of manuscript. One stack holds anti-imperialist essays and dialogues, many of them as complete as "The Stupendous Procession"—written at the end of 1901 to parade the contrast between Christian morals and the ways of colonial profit.[19] Tableaus for our actions in the Philippines were made as unsparing as those for France, England, Germany, and Russia in a disgusting spectacle that dragged along to the music of the "Spheres (of Influence)" under a bandmaster who had read his newspaper carefully and picked out the damning clues, however well hidden under official rhetoric. Whether Twain sent "The Stupendous Procession" to any of his regular outlets is not known. He may have assumed—correctly—that they would not want it because it was even more enraging than "To the Person Sitting in Darkness" (not a story of private gloom either but another broad attack, which Howells thought showed more nerve than was healthy).

Or if Twain did not try to publish it because he was spacing the risks he took, there is no doubt he kept taking them. His irony stung so hard that it could not be ignored or placidly admired. Ever in demand at banquets, he left a trail of tart ambiguities and sly preaching like his pun on the western attitude toward the Chinese Boxers, "Taels I win, Heads you lose." With the timing he had perfected long ago he exploited his old popularity and the new prestige he was well aware of, saying in 1902: ". . . for many years I have represented the people of the United States without special request, and without salary, as Special Ambassador to the World."[20] The appointment had been wise. Though he did not always speak for the majority, he had become a humane troubleshooter ready for service anywhere, and by October, 1904 the word that he was "whetting up" for King Leopold of Belgium surprised nobody.

Quite promptly his literary razor shaped up "King Leopold's Soliloquy," which the editors at Harper's were glad to refuse so it could be donated to the Congo Reform Association. Too excited about the brutality with which the Belgians were squeezing profits out of their African colony, it had hacked rather than sliced. But it caused a stir upsetting to Leopold's agents, who rushed out a forty-seven page pamphlet in direct reply. Adding another vice-presidency to his list, Twain took an active hand in guiding the Congo Reform Association so long as it had any weight. He also wrote to friends in the State Department, enclosing documents and leaflets, and made at least two trips to its offices, where he was treated with the courtesy due an important diplomat; eventually he drew an answer from Secretary Elihu Root himself, who argued that the United States had no right to enter a formal protest in behalf of the exploited natives. After a little grumbling Twain accepted this verdict because Hay, before his recent death, had held the same line.[21] Full of admiration to the end, in the fall of 1905 he had sent Hay an anonymous letter honoring his "long roll of illustrious services."

Because Twain knew so many of the world's movers and shakers, he thought too often in terms of who carried out policy rather than what forces shaped it. His blinding fondness for Hay was matched in reverse by a distracting contempt for Theodore Roosevelt, especially as the old Rough Rider bragging about his hour of glory at San Juan Hill. On matters more important to Twain than his taste in heroes, he was nevertheless grimly pleased if Roosevelt took the other side. Not a pacifist himself, Hank Morgan had started building a modern navy but now, suspicious of armaments, Twain was happy to protest that the money Roosevelt lavished on new battleships should be used for internal waterways. Such waterways did not include the Panama Canal made possible by "methods which might have wrung a shudder out of the seasoned McKinley." In the fall of 1904 Twain warned with an ungentle smile that Roosevelt, egged on by his high-handed coup in Panama, was likely to hold the White House by force if the voters did not give him another term.[22] When the President pounded on the Monroe Doctrine to justify his moves in Central and South America, Twain was not impressed. As coldly as a village atheist he answered that it was no more valid than any other manifesto "not gotten up by the advice and consent of the foreigner" and would hold good "as long as we are strong enough to take care of it, but not longer."[23]

Just as coldly, he assayed some other popular ways of gilding power politics. The glittery argument that white men were merely trying to get entrenched against the rising hordes of Asia drew no warmer response from him than, "The Real Yellow Peril: Gold."[24] More and more he suspected that whatever the rallying cry for a push into the primitive areas some of the loudest pushers had a cash return in mind. Especially skeptical when they invoked Christianity, he jeered during the Boer War that God's support was being claimed by both sides as usual. Even earlier, after his world tour, he had dashed off an essay on the double life of any nationalist whose religion teaches brotherhood. Recalling that a toastmaster had once rated Twain's own Americanism as of "more than ordinarily pronounced" strength, he decided that—"soberly contemplated"—there was no reason for him to be proud "unless one would [rather] be called little than large, narrow than broad . . . a poor sort of Christian—cordial blood-brother to all Americans, but not even second cousin to the rest of the race."[25] A polished result of such musings was "The War Prayer," which spelled out the harsh realities of the success that patriotic clergymen beseech for troops going into battle.

Since that banquet many orators, and some judicious scholars as well, have also praised Twain's Americanism. They are surer about it than he was, and much less analytical. His early reading in the eighteenth-century savants had made him at least aware of the cosmopolitan spirit. Then, while spending most of the Civil War on the sidelines, he noticed that both the North and South claimed the toga of the founding fathers and so began wondering if patriotism was not sometimes a protective coloring instead of a vital gland. When the corruption of the 1870's disgusted him he suffered no trauma from finding that his love of country was gone. When he slowly moved back toward it he took along the Liberal ideal of nation-states amiably bound together by world trade. Appropriately, his first direct analysis of patriotism came after he bolted to the mugwumps in 1884.

Grated by the Republicans' howl that voting against them was treason, he had charged that their attitude was "borrowed—or stolen—from the monarchical system."[26] No matter what other points he later made against a blind allegiance to party or country, he always insisted it was a holdover from the patterns of kingcraft, which was mortally afraid of the independent mind. Brandishing a word whose modern impact he could not foresee, he bulled ahead into deciding he would have to teach "disloyalty," though Hank Morgan still spoke well of a loyalty to "one's country" if the nobility or a political machine did not misuse it. Twain had entered a maze that was further complicated by the different kinds of government and the rocky course of events. A few ideas later his essay on "The American Press" argued that newspapers should keep a people "in love with *their* country and *its* institutions, and shielded from the allurements of alien and inimical systems," and as the insecurity he felt and saw in the early 1890's continued to beat down his iconoclasm, he closed the prose hymn to Joan of Arc with the overwrought tribute that she would "stand for PATRIOTISM through all the ages until time shall end." However, he would soon go far beyond even Hank Morgan's arguments for disloyalty to the crown of England.

The recoil began as he sauntered through Asia and Africa. In his notebook for the spring of 1896 he wrote, "Talking of patriotism what humbug it is; it is a word that always commemorates a robbery." After a hard look from another angle he reported with double-edged bite, "Patriotism is being carried to insane excess. I know men who do not love God because He is a foreigner."[27] Though he was still given to backsliding, after 1900 it was seldom for long and was usually tactical instead of impulsive. He was obviously being crafty when he argued that the Boxers who hated western influence were merely good patriots or that the Filipinos harassing our troops fought "for their country's independence, the highest and noblest of all causes." When he rounded out his case against General Funston by appealing to the memory of George Washington, his tone grew perfunctory. As his notebooks and unpublished manuscripts show best, Twain was not eager to renew the pristine nationalism of '76, even as defined by himself, but to cast doubt on the broad phrases being mouthed so actively. If he thought for a while they might be refurbished to the Filipino's benefit, he eventually scribbled, "Patriot/Traitor, rebel . . . all are silly."[28] Before this signing off he had publicly invited the label of traitor if it meant he rejected the code that let General Funston wipe out a primitive tribe.

His most provocative ironies about loyalty Twain kept to himself during the heady years when Americans first tasted world power. In "As Regards Patriotism" he quietly analyzed how the majority wraps its opinions in the flag, ignoring the chance that heresies may someday become truisms guarded by holy fire. Probing from a broader viewpoint he decided that, since the average person rushes for every bandwagon because the majority's smug taunts hurt him worse than his own conscience, the "soul and substance of what customarily ranks as patriotism is moral cowardice—and always has been." An unfinished satire based on this summing up also held that pride in nationality is created by "one unthinking & incompetent idiot imitating another"; he imagined a tribe of monkeys who are fond of bowing in prayer because it shows off the unique blue ring on their buttocks.[29]

In both senses of the phrase, Twain could not have published this satire except at his own expense. While doodling with such Rabelaisian strokes he wrote "The Privilege of the Grave" to charge that—"out of fear, or out of calculated wisdom, or out of reluctance to wound friends"—the living do not dare to say what they really think.[30] Unsurprisingly, his argument ended up using political instances most of all. Whenever he wanted to prove in his closing years that men are slavish about ideas or that the mob insists on conformity, he named "politics and religion" as examples and usually as the only two.

Because he liked being petted he could still gratify a patriotic audience if the mood struck him; for the sake of a better copyright law he could even go back to orating that literature trains the "children of the Republic" in "that love of country and reverence for the flag which is Patriotism." Yet, too busy with the present to wait genially for speaking his mind from the grave, he sometimes lashed out where pleasant clichés were expected. At a banquet in the Waldorf-Astoria he rasped about the schools: "There are some which teach insane citizenship, bastard citizenship, but that is all. Patriotism! Yes; but patriotism is usually the refuge of the scoundrel. He is the man who talks the loudest." Trying to be a better schoolmaster himself, Twain grappled with the problem of what able-bodied young men should do during a war they oppose and, after much sifting and canceling, concluded they must ignore every pressure to enlist unless the republic's life is in danger.[31] However, this obviously left the chance of helping to defeat a powerful enemy who was also right; it could not stand up in the long run, and Twain suspected so without foreseeing the rigors of total war among industrial giants. He must have been relieved when he could go back to the apparently simple matter of fanning disloyalty toward Russian autocrats.

Since the early 1890's he had checked on the Czar now and then, but the Romanoff star gave no sign of falling until the Russo-Japanese war changed the picture in several ways. Avidly following the headlines, Twain ripped off a sketch—

first named "A Difficult Conundrum"—that pretended to wonder why God had created the housefly or the Russians; its serious point belabored them for foolishly wasting their courage on Japan instead of turning it against their royal "chipmunk."[32] The Treaty of Portsmouth only enraged him further because he had been hoping the war would last until enemies on the home front could swamp the Czar's thinned line of defense. Indeed, the riots that began on Red Sunday in January, 1905 had already inspired him to burst into print with "The Czar's Soliloquy." This effective bit of imposture made Nicholas II, undressed after his bath, concede that a king looks puny without the right clothes and marvel at the docility of his subjects; giving Twain's answer to the tender-minded, he even sneered at reformers who deny the "tremendous moral force" of assassination. In a candid analysis that happened to sound like Marx while echoing the Tom Paine chords of *A Connecticut Yankee*, the Czar also conceded, "All thrones have been established by violence; no regal tyranny has been overthrown except by violence." Because an old-style autocrat was involved, Twain had no qualms about the riots that, it is now clear, were leading to the momentous upheaval of 1917.

There was of course another rush to exploit his talents and valuable name. Fund-raisers for the "Jewish sufferers" in Russia roped him into one of his best nonsensical speeches, which got more publicity than Sarah Bernhardt's share of the program. This put him still higher on the list of a Nikolai Chaykovsky, who was here to raise money for buying guns. Since Twain honestly could not go he sent an open letter fit for a rally at which the Russian—wearing a bright red tie—greeted the audience as "Tovarishky," touching off a three-minute cheer that unsettled the "big squad of policemen on duty on the floor."[33] Chaykovsky had even better luck with a second purpose: to line up Twain's support for an impending tour by Maxim Gorky, who had wide prestige because of his fiction and hoped to draw a flood of American dollars.

Only an invitation was needed to land Twain among a group of eminent sponsors, and he emerged as their loudest member. At a dinner run by a socialist club of New York City he invoked our revolutionary past and thundered on, ". . . let us hope . . . the fighting may be postponed for a while yet, but when it does come let us be ready for it." Tingling with a republican fervor that made him feel years younger, he helped start a fund for Russian civil liberties and told the press he was, along with Howells, arranging a "gala literary dinner."

It has been common to smile at how prudishness routed Twain and Howells when a scandal broke over Gorky's common-law wife. But the militant talk had bothered Howells' pacifist conscience so keenly that the scandal was only a last straw, if not an excuse, and Twain's retreat was more grudging and orderly than anybody gives him credit for. When the "secret" hit the front pages he insisted Madame Gorky was a separate question and the dinner should still be held. As the wail of outraged propriety soared to a storm the next day—April 15, 1906—he ignored Howells' advice to hide from reporters and instead gave public notice of "sticking to the flag until everybody else deserts." Nor did he flinch when slyly asked if he was a socialist; though accounts vary a little, he answered in effect, "I am a revolutionist by birth, reading, and principle. I am always on the side of the revolutionists because there never was a revolution unless there were some oppressive and intolerable conditions against which to revolute."[34] Until quietly bowing off the vanishing dinner committee a few days later, he hoped Gorky would somehow recoup his "blunder."

Though Twain gave in to the storm over a lady who—Howells said—"did not look as if she were not" Gorky's legal wife, he had defied the first gusts of tabloid criticism. Indeed he stubbornly felt as late as 1908 that he was still supporting the anti-czarist movement. Gorky was right in refusing to shrug him off as a coward. He had been less short of nerve than of understanding that middle-class republicans were as old-fashioned as the volunteer fireman and that Gorky was a Bolshevik instead of a king-buster. Coldly eying the Czar, Twain did not see that Gorky's fatal mistake was to side with leftist unions here, alienating the powerful groups who hated the modern proletarian much more than the autocrat.

Out of touch in some ways but by no means doddering, Twain probably had a much clearer sense of the reasons for his honorary degree from Oxford in 1907. In spite of natural pride he must have realized it came under a Liberal cabinet as well as in the large cause of Anglo-American friendship on which British parties united because of the growing need for allies. His fresh enthusiasm for this cause had not weakened though the news since he wrote *Following the Equator* had nailed down his opinion of Rhodes as a "very great sinner" in Africa. Any such differences were ignored on both sides during his last triumphal tour of England. A member of Parliament saluted him as the "consolidator of nations," and editors raced to outdo each other on this theme while he responded gallantly, giving a lesson in geniality to our official ambassador, icy Whitelaw Reid—who also got a degree at the same time—and perceptibly raising the ocean of good will that would carry over the A.E.F. ten years later.

The Oxford ceremony added stature and a scarlet gown to Twain's role as a self-appointed, roving diplomat. Never given to collapse when he was a center of attraction, he gladly threw in his prestige wherever it might do good. During his festive weeks in England he took time for a luncheon he thought was of "political and commercial, and of international importance"—it concerned a drive for cheaper ocean mail and, he hoped, his own plan for simplified money orders.[35] In his last year of life he let it be known he was still available for service against King Leopold. When he scrawled "Letters from the Earth" during his last illness in Bermuda, weary of human cruelties but not indifferent, he tinkered with more arguments for cooling the war fever. Not that these "letters" were his unswervingly final testament; he could not have written one. Around the same time, the arms race moved him to grate that man "will always thirst for blood."

Twain's flair for emphasis does not mean that he was essentially dogmatic. Painfully changeable, he was less consistent than ever during his last years, ranging from complacent stretches all the way to days when even a game of billiards could not let him forget mankind's depravity. If he took the broadest perspective he seldom saw cause for hope, yet he kept plunging into specific battles. His anti-imperialist writings alone should kill the notion that his old age was fogged with unrelieved and unrelieving gloom. Politically at least, such gloom settled only when events bulldozed across the roads he knew and trusted, leaving him baffled with problems his favorite oracles had not expected. Like other warnings of disaster for the United States if it did not call its armies home, his own famous apostasy from the doctrine of progress —through a letter to Twichell on March 14, 1905—really signed off merely from the expansionists' version. After that he still offered advice on how to forge ahead, and when it seemed to be coming true he cheered up until the next major blow. According to his Boswell he chatted in October, 1909 about the "possibility of America following Rome's example" but "thought the vote of the people would always, or at least for a long period, prevent" the worst.

This opinion also reveals a smaller pattern that was at least stable. Instead of exploring the latest schools of history and social theory he had been rereading Lecky, Carlyle, and especially Suetonius. The pageant of Roman folly held a wry comfort: surely men had improved a little, no matter what easy chances they muffed. But it was directly engrossing because the old villains, kingcraft and priestcraft, could be hissed again. When the tiny organisms in "30,000 Years Among the Microbes"—written in 1905—glimpse the world

beneath their natural limit of vision, they find priests sending the masses off to fight for a showy king. The campaigns
of his lustiest years haunted Twain as he basked weakly in
the sun; browsing through *A Connecticut Yankee* a few
weeks before his death, he most admired the parts that ex-
coriate the nobility and the church.[36] If he looked into the
future on a dark day he could even predict the return of
monarchy (under the aegis of a new state religion unless he
did his share to stop the boom in Christian Science). Because
this may sound foolish or senile, it has seen suggested he had
something like the dictatorships of the 1930's in mind; but
he was warning that history can repeat itself closely. His late
fantasy about a Great Republic (obviously the United States)
sapped by the corruptions of empire had Inca hordes who
march north as easily as the barbarians once broke through
the sagging walls of Rome—whose fatal "imperialism" was a
favorite theme of nineteenth-century orators.[37]

These Inca hordes were not related to the yellow terror
that many Anglo-Saxon trumpeters were alarmed about.
Born to an era of rising nationalism, Twain had steadily
fought clear of its excesses and the prejudice that usually
came with them. Perhaps the brightest side of his whole intellectual career is his progress away from racism. As he kept
refining his vision of Captain Stormfield's great voyage he
made room in paradise for everybody—Negroes of course
and Chinese, Arabs, Incas, and even white men (who found
themselves an obscure minority there). Inside heaven or out
he had long since dropped his Washoe tagline that "No Irish
need apply." More slowly, the American Indians also stalked
into the circle of his sympathy as he became capable of realiz-
ing how the pioneer had pre-empted their lands and smashed
their culture. Twain's final musings decided that "Patriotism,
even at its best—& scarcest—has one blemish—it naturally
erects barriers against the B of M—makes that phrase a de-
licious sarcasm."[38] He could use initials for the brotherhood
of man because it was so heavy on his mind that he would not

forget what this note meant. Fittingly, he named his last house Stormfield, a token of his bitter struggles to establish the truth but also of an ideal he now held without reservation.

Though economics and politics outgrew Twain's frame of reference, his passion for honesty had led him well. Raised in a sleepy village that was an obsolete social form soon after he left it, he moved far beyond provinciality; mostly self-educated he arrived at better human answers than many savants. As he browsed through every continent and most islands he learned without reading Thoreau that your worst neighbor may be yourself. If he had thought of counting the cats in Zanzibar he would have done it, but if the count came late in his life it would have been uncondescending and fair; having given up dollar diplomacy he would not have twisted his figures into a pretext for a white man's coup. He ended up a true cosmopolitan and an unpaid yet energetic ambassador to any country including his own that would listen. If our spaceships find the sky-blue men with seven heads that Captain Stormfield saw in heaven, we can do much worse than to meet them the way Twain would have done.

I am a moralist in disguise; it gets me into heaps of trouble when I go thrashing around in political questions.

NINE

The White Knight

TWAIN'S HOME thoughts, as the United States plunged toward and into the twentieth century, were as unflagging as his analysis of global politics. Irrepressibly a guardian of the public conscience in spite of his suspicion that life is a pointless nightmare, he would keep lifting his hand to guide the course of American society. In the daylight it looked real and the chance of improving it still looked worth taking when editors and chairmen of banquets, memorial meetings, unveilings, or ribbon-cuttings literally begged him to say something, anything. To keep his standing as a pampered oracle he sometimes obliged with the cheerful platitudes they wanted to hear, unaware that bankruptcy had killed his illusion of having the golden touch and that the general economic stumbling had bruised his faith in dynamic capitalism. Though his outlook was often more hopeful than *The Mysterious Stranger*, which suggests that material progress does not matter after all because human nature stays morally in-ert, he could not swing back to the swashbuckling confidence of the late 1880's. If the master of Stormfield started to talk about change, his retainers more and more expected a savage lament for the simple years when there were no rich or poor in a contented village like Hannibal.

His nostalgia came much more from baffled protest than the retreat of old age. He had always faced up to current problems and gave signs of revising the Liberalism of his Nook Farm years as it proved inadequate. In his report on Queen Victoria's Jubilee of 1897 he got around at last to openly supporting the eight-hour day because it had "made labor a means of extending life instead of a means of committing salaried suicide"; and the angel in *The Mysterious Stranger* coldly exhibited a French factory where men and women and children drudged fourteen hours six days a week for starvation wages. Yet, alert to economic injustice only in an Old World locale, Twain still found it hard to think that free enterprise could go seriously wrong in the wide open spaces of the United States. Traveling across North Dakota in 1895, he was too easy to convince that there were "no poor" on this edge of the Populist whirlwind, that "want is unknown . . . all have enough to eat and wear."[1]

Whatever his searing pessimism from a personal or cosmic viewpoint, he likewise found it confusingly easy to believe still that—"taken by and large"—success in business is proof of a man's honesty. *Following the Equator* cited a forgotten speech in which, sounding even more like a self-satisfied tycoon, he had deplored the "injuries inflicted by the high school in making handicrafts distasteful to boys who would have been willing to make a living at trades and agriculture if they had but had the good luck to stop with the common school." Unaware that the heyday of the lonewolf tinkerer was passing, Twain also warned that higher education was luring future inventors away from their mechanic's bench. Unaware that the lonewolf investor was outdated too, as the wounds left by his typesetter started healing he yearned to re-emerge as a promoter of steely miracles. Before H. H. Rogers waved him off he was soon scheming to corner the latest carpet-weaving patents with the "grip of a single giant Company."

Especially pleased by the cheer the London dockers raised when he was arriving in 1907, he liked to remember it as coming from men of his own class. This bit of make-believe shows his freedom from rigid snobbery as well as his uneasy guilt at accepting the hospitality of the British upperclass he had belabored so often. But—if he ever held it—he had long since dropped the idea that he was a Huck Finn wriggling under the burden of acting "sivilized." For many years he had thought himself a man of substance and station; indeed he had learned to enjoy a reasonable deference, as he proved by imitating the genteel vigilante of "Travelling with a Reformer." In Vienna he handed a cabdriver over to the police and promised to appear in court; he did the same thing in New York City before long and later harried a streetcar company about the attitude of its conductors. Each of these incidents started with an overcharge on the fare but he listed rudeness in each bill of particulars and, grumbling at Americans as the Impolite Nation and raging at a conductor who had bawled at him to hurry up, worked his spleen into one of his ever more frequent speeches.[2] Actually, as the editorials on his side reveal, he was only airing a starched-collar resentment at the "insolence of menials" that nobody else here dared to admit frankly.

This dying rattle from the days of powdered wigs and silver snuff boxes is especially strange in the mouth of a man sometimes featured as a cracker-barrel democrat. Yet the harsh truth is that Twain, like his father, usually felt a gap between himself and the average clerk or waiter: there should be no surprise at "The Quarrel in a Strong-Box" when it is eventually printed. Written in 1897 and loosely related to the running debate about the gold standard, it imagined a brawl over "right & privilege" among pieces of money because each

—starting with the penny—had claimed first rank by giving its own gloss on democratic catchwords. Hauled into court, the coins and bills are told by the judge that they are "free & equal," but he goes on:

. . . the meaning of that phrase is curiously misunderstood. It does not propose to set aside the law of Nature—which is, that her children are created *un*equal & of necessity *must* be. . . . The Constitution cannot alter that & has not tried to. It only makes all equal in one way; it gives each an equal right with his neighbor to exercise his talent, whatever it may be, thus making free to all, many roads to profit & honor which were once arbitrarily restricted to the few.[3]

To clinch his decision the judge assures each piece of money that it brings in five percent and therefore enjoys its full "market value," neither more nor less, all pedigrees aside. Over-anxiously, Twain ended up with an explicit warning that the "character of the Equality established by our laws is commonly misunderstood on both sides of the water; & not oftener by the ignorant than by the ostensibly wise."

Perhaps he never sold "The Quarrel in a Strong-Box" because he thought it went too far. Even in his most conservative mood he stopped well short of the railroad president who earned a sour immortality by telling strikers they should trust the "Christian men to whom God in His infinite wisdom has given control of the property interests." Yet Twain's parable said nothing he had not said as clearly elsewhere out of attitudes that left room for chumming around with H. H. Rogers, who did his share of the dirty work so ruthlessly that apologists for Standard Oil have to insist he was acting on his own hook. Appropriately, they first met on a luxurious yacht. When they met again in 1893 Rogers took over so fast as a financial godfather that Twain scornfully refused a few months later even to consider publishing an exposé of Standard Oil. Sure that they had much in common, a typical letter from Rogers—after McKinley defeated Bryan the first time

—commented that it was good to know that "business sense" would be "exercised" in Washington against the "politicians"; it also noted that Twain wanted to keep him company on a business trip.[4] Twain had growing reason to admire these trips and in 1899, with a happy sigh, would thank his new crony for turning "steel and copper and Brooklyn gas into gold." Always eloquent about the ingratitude of others, he carefully avoided the same mistake. Mostly to please Rogers he spoke at least twice to the junior Rockefeller's Bible class in the Fifth Avenue Baptist Church.

Hobnobbing weekdays and Sundays with Rogers's circle, Twain was more often in earshot of Republican preaching than he had been for years. Seemingly it came just in time on fiscal policy, because he had started to backslide in the late 1890's and at his shakiest point had drafted a prediction that the free coinage of silver would be celebrated with a "Second Independence Day" if it ever got a chance to make the United States a giant in world trade. This may be another item that second thoughts barred from print; his final attitude toward free silver was indecisive, and he kept debating with himself after the issue was dead. Yet he did not support Bryan in 1900 even as a protest against McKinley's foreign policy. After working up a hot interest he stayed away from the polls because "some pretty shrewd financiers" convinced him that Bryan "wasn't safe on the financial question."[5]

If Rogers helped pull Twain back to the gold standard, it was probably during casual give and take over a hot toddy. He sincerely liked Twain and had not, at least not deliberately, been using him as a tool. But, the first of the Standard Oil clique to worry about public opinion, Rogers bluntly asked for help in late 1901 when Ida Tarbell was writing her muckrake history. By dutifully warning her publisher against being party to an unfair attack, Twain cleared the way for a series of conferences between Miss Tarbell and the Standard Oil tycoons—who bowed out when they felt that she was not hearing their side with proper faith.[6] He also dashed off a character reference that thanked Rogers for earning him a quick one-third profit on a $100,000 investment—perhaps with money put up by Rogers in his name, as was sometimes the case. Though the subject of this testimonial decided against letting it go into print, he surely did not mind when, a few weeks after Miss Tarbell's first installment came out, Twain said at a birthday dinner staged by Rogers and other wealthy admirers, ". . . all you men have won your places, not by heredities, and not by family influences or extraneous help, but only by the natural gifts God gave you at your birth, made effective by your own energies."[7]

Taken on his own terms Rogers was the practical proof of axioms every Liberal trusted. It is impossible to draw the line between Twain's sincere respect and a defiant gratitude to the pilot who steered him out of bankruptcy. When a Boston court was looking into some much less generous feats of finance, he coolly described himself as Rogers' "principal intimate" who often relaxed on a sofa in his office to savor his "reasonings with the captains of industry." Part of these reasonings must have covered the reckless and brutal raids that got Rogers into more courtrooms, but he offered Twain no apologies and his continuing letters expected a loyal eye and tongue—which is credited with parrying when somebody questioned the odor of Rogers' money, "It's twice tainted—tain't yours, and tain't mine."

As Standard Oil itself bobbed in a rising storm, which got dangerous when a judge levied a $29,000,000 fine in 1907, Twain obviously yearned to throw out some lifelines. His "ABC Lesson" argued that Standard's sixty per cent profit was due not to its monopoly prices but to the high protective tariff set by the Republicans. "Something about Standard Oil" grumbled that federal attorneys were harassing "my corporation" for political reasons and that unfriendly editors would change their tune if they held a wad of its stock. Though neither of these efforts reached print, comments to his private entourage show that Twain did not waver. Indeed, after the Hepburn Bill and other moves to stop Standard's practice of forcing kickbacks on its freight costs he exploded, "I would like to know what kind of a goddam govment this is that discriminates between two common carriers & makes a goddam railroad charge everybody equal & lets a goddam man charge any goddam price he wants to for his goddam opera box."[8] When Twain said he would publish this squib over Howells' name he was kidding that soft-spoken reformer but not Rogers' partners. While unable to get enthusiastic about Rockefeller senior, he insisted that muckrakers were handling the king of oil too roughly. Seemingly as total as Twain's exemplary affection for his wife, this loyalty to Rogers stepped up his dislike of Theodore Roosevelt, who had chosen Standard Oil as the prize target for federal discipline. From then on he would often ease himself on a restless day by dictating about Roosevelt's mistakes or mulling over publishable slander.

Finding fault with the most impetuous president in our history was common, however. Any notion that Rogers had a hypnotic influence here or elsewhere would go too far. For that matter Twain had shoals of friends, including many other stalwarts of high finance. Since 1890 he had become a steady guest in circles that also suited Chauncey Depew or Joseph Choate, long a model for corporation lawyers. If he was invited to Andrew Carnegie's house too often for sheer pleasure, his grumbling must not be misread; while despising the little millionaire's glee over being consulted on policy by Roosevelt, he believed that Carnegie was "thoroughly competent" to give advice of the "highest value and importance" and only wished Carnegie would "brag about his real achievements" instead of about rubbing shoulders with presidents and kings.[9] This passion for self-respect was a strong rein on Twain's own pride at mixing with the rich and on the natural pull toward thinking like the company he kept. In spite of following Rogers into some dark alleys, he broke away on a major issue like imperialism; and in spite of spending much time with men who underwrote the Republican party, he resisted every pressure to join their caucus again.

When Twain got home in 1900 he announced from the wharf, "I am a Mugwump now. I shall be a Mugwump until I die." Finding most of his former cohorts already dead or nestled in McKinley's corner, he next insisted he was a "Grand Old Party" all by himself. The New York *Evening Post*, a rallying point in the 1880's, was still his favorite newspaper, and an irrelevant "Conclusion" to his book on Christian Science lashed at party machines in terms that sounded like an old attack on James G. Blaine. However, being the last mugwump was lonely and ineffective. After joking about an Anti-Doughnut label he drew up a "Skeleton Plan for a Proposed Casting Vote Party," another scheme to force the Republicans and Democrats into picking their best men for "good and clean government" at all levels. Serious about building up mass support, he called a reporter in for a long interview during the voting season of 1905.[10]

For once he was ahead of his time politically. Today most experts think the independent vote is pivotal and many kinds of hands are groping for ways to manipulate it. While his gadfly buzzings obviously did not discover a way, they aroused some startling gestures. A worshipful recruit who was all for naming the task-force after Twain had to be reminded that it must avoid creating popular heroes of its own because they might eventually try to get elected instead of exploiting the balance of power to make the major parties behave. When one newspaper asked him to run for president, he rightly had no public comment; to the less grandiose notion of booming him for the Senate he answered soberly that he was neither qualified nor available. Though he always had to watch out for tinhorn plays to hoax the master himself, at least two of these flattering gestures looked sincere.

His personal experience still told him often that they also looked too hopeful about how elections work. Declaiming that he had served as a "statesman without salary for many years," he again turned his restless eyes on politics in New York City soon after camping there in 1900. When a Fusion ticket challenged Tammany Hall a year later, he churned up publicity, climbed to the platform at mass meetings, and—defying his doctor—marched along Broadway in a parade. As an independent he put special effort into helping plant the Order of Acorns and for its organizing dinner at the Waldorf-Astoria wrote "Edmund Burke on Croker & Tammany," which was rushed into print by *Harper's Weekly* and also bound as a pamphlet for immediate use.[11] When the Fusion crusade pried Tammany out of city hall he dusted off a routine he had used in 1880 and gave a jubilant mock-elegy for the heirs of Boss Tweed—unsuspecting that the Order of Acorns would fail to grow and the antimachine coalition would crumble as usual before the next election. Busy then taking his family abroad, Twain nevertheless scribbled a public letter giving a "shout for the clean ticket from the Acorn platform" with all his "little might"; and Tammany's return to power touched off more of his dark mutterings.[12] He was not, however, too discouraged to endorse the anti-boodle ticket once more in 1905 and at the last minute send an open telegram announcing he was on his way to vote for virtue—"once as Clemens and twice as Twain."[13] Off the record Tammany comment about such a showy and persistent heckler must have been racy.

These maneuvers in New York City were his most concrete efforts toward improving the twentieth century. But he offered advice on so wide a sweep of matters that he sometimes felt a need for apologetic irony about "my natural trade —which is teaching"; and—on a pledge to support phonetic spelling—he put down "Professional Moralist" as his occupation. The label of moralist covers Twain well only if it means that civic right and wrong made up a substantial part of his sermonizing. His anonymous essay on "Christian Citizenship" obviously cared as much about political as private ethics and more about this world than the next.[14] Published just before

the elections of 1905, it listed the cities and states where corrupt machines were entrenched and accused Americans of
parking their religion outside when they entered the polling
booths. While dwindling by then into a mild bromide, the
concept of citizenship once had a vigorous rationale as the
middle class proudly took over the control of public life from
the aristocrat; usually with a purely secular emphasis, Twain
futilely did his share in a movement to make it vital again and
sounded appeals from any handy forum during his last ten
years. When he was supposed to praise the City College of
New York at a banquet, he instead complained because there
was no chair of citizenship in even our biggest universities
and, with fine impartiality, went on, "You can place it above
mathematics and literature, and that is where it belongs."

Without a sense of paradox Twain felt as civic moralist
that he could not relax his old vigilance against letting any
religion get temporal powers. Though still fretting about the
Roman Catholic hierarchy, he was wildly projecting the
latest trends and fretting much more about Christian Science
mushrooming into our state church, complete with another
Inquisition. In the area of present danger the drive to put "In
God We Trust" back on our coins moved him to open ridicule as well as a sly flash of that motto on a government spit-
toon in one of his short stories. Favorable to a less popular
drive, he drafted a petition demanding that New York give
equal status to all "sabbaths" or else take away the special
position of Sunday. The first angina pangs in his chest did
not affect his nerve. In his very late "Letters from the Earth"
his rationalism searched for fresh ways of proving that
clergymen stifle intellectual freedom and creativeness. After
his death a Mark Twain Association of freethinkers would
meet for a while in Montclair, New Jersey.

Critics who see Twain as a mental butterfly are misled by
the variety of his interests, which made for sudden darts back
to any spot that showed life. As long as popular opinion kept
pushing Negroes down to their lowest status since the days

of slavery, he quietly compromised on a minstrel-show version of the "shiftless, worthless, lovable black darling." But when lynching earned dark headlines again he wrote his trenchant essay on "The United States of Lyncherdom" (1901) and started amassing a study meant to be grimly "effective" whether it took "one volume or six," with or without help from George Kennan—historian of czarist cruelties. Twain insisted to a hesitant publisher that the project was haunting him.[15] Though he did not get very far with it or release his essay he made his anger public, growling to the press that the South would soon need a law against lynchings on Christmas day and describing a fast yacht as having a "reach like a Christian mob with a nigger in sight." One of the times that Booker T. Washington—who considered Rogers a good friend—cast down his bucket for northern money to educate Alabama Negroes, Twain introduced him to an audience at Carnegie Hall.

The energy with which he poked his white head into such matters caused spreading comment and—forty years late—the Louisville *Courier-Journal* found he was "developing into a modern knight-errant." Ignoring Howells' word that Twain had always looked after the "public conscience," editorials in other newspapers puzzled over the change. They at least helped readers get used to seeing, for example, that he had turned up in Brooklyn at the Hebrew Technical School for Girls and had spoken out for female suffrage again. Everybody was slower now to suspect a joke when he joined a campaign to make osteopathy legal in New York. Temporarily sure of its unique powers, he bustled to Albany and gave a Liberal sermon before a flattered committee of the legislature: the "State should not fetter a man's freedom" of treating his own body as he likes to his "peril or to the peril of any one else."[16] However, when asked to add pressure for a law fettering vivisection he obliged with "A Dog's Tale" —and ended up by also writing "A Horse's Tale" to protest against the cruelty to animals that bullfighting involved.

Famous men who show any thirst for worthy causes are of course flooded with invitations. To the last, Twain honored a surprising share and variety of them. Helen Keller, who had no trouble getting him to pitch in wholeheartedly at an affair for helping the blind earn their own way, wrote out of her luminous inner vision, "You once told me you were a pessimist. . . . You are an optimist. If you were not, you would not preside at the meeting." While still bothered by the danger of pampering able-bodied loafers he obviously was more available than ever for the right kind of charity work. In 1901 he made his first visit to a settlement house, coming away convinced that its on the spot advice and example is more helpful than moral exhortation and perhaps moved to write his sparkling dialogue between an evangelist and a stunted child of the slums who thinks the chief of police created him and knows for sure his pants came from Mike the Ragman, not God.[17] Twain was "very glad indeed" to let the Anti Child Slavery League use his name. Yet he did not get far into even the middle-class efforts to clean up the slums and left no trace of interest in tenement reform, a step beyond the settlement-house oases. Essentially, he kept looking for and never found a safe way of tiding the poor over until the largess of technology filtered down to their level, though he never talked politics with Rogers more cordially than with Howells, who had been leaning toward a utopian socialism since the 1890's.

Even Howells was not flexible enough anymore to move with the rising Progressive movement or the muckrakers who cleared the road. Though Twain knew of their exposés, his only overt support was a tiny blast at the reputable men who —for a price—endorsed quack doctors and nostrums.[18] Upton Sinclair was dismayed by the limits that made him stop half-way through *The Jungle* in bewildered "anguish." While Sinclair later found ideas to admire within those limits, not a single Progressive was to list Twain as a shaping influence or inspiration. For his biographer he chose Albert

Bigelow Paine after liking his woodenly conservative book on Thomas Nast.

In the years when young Progressives were proving the need for federal action against monopolies that could set prices almost where they liked, Twain's economic judgments usually drifted back into personal ethics, as his notebook for January, 1904 shows. For the "offspring of riches" he listed pride, ostentation, and tyranny; the matching list for poverty was greed, sordidness, cruelty, cheating, and murder.[19] If a social code was implied here it was the middle-class norm that shaped "The $30,000 Bequest," published the same year. This novelette, though its irony was too cross-hatched in places or just careless, chided the appetite for speculative profits very much as *The Gilded Age* had done thirty years ago. A dying victim of stock-market dreams is made to warn, "Vast wealth, acquired by sudden and unwholesome means, is a snare. It did us no good, transient were its feverish pleasures; yet for its sake we threw away our sweet and simple and happy life." Nor will "The Man That Corrupted Hadleyburg" stand reading as a radical attack on the banker or robber baron. While not starving, its old couple are poor enough to have some excuse for grabbing at a stray bonanza, and the prediction that the town of Hadleyburg will behave better in the future kills any argument that the portrait of its leaders obliquely lampoons the new millionaires who were choking off competition in steel, oil, or cigarettes. With ironic timing the story was published in December, 1899, joining the century to which its attitudes deeply belong.

The more Twain's well-known complaints in his final years about the "lust for money" are examined, the less they show relevance to the current economic pattern. Lumping together the "butcher, landowner, corporation, shoemaker," he still thought their right to the pursuit of property had a higher sanction than any law devised by a legislature. If one set of nearly cryptic notes accused a few big bankers of lately hunting down so much property that their power was unhealthily deep and broad, he still cursed Jay Gould as the arch-fiend. At last—if only now and then—he was seriously liable to nostalgic romancing that the America nested in dewy villages like Hannibal had not hungered for quick profits or put up with the shady big-dealer. Honestly disturbed when the House of Morgan controlled our national solvency in the panic of 1907, he could only waste time regretting that Gould had ever lived.

Until the very end he kept clouding new issues with the grievances from his great years at Nook Farm. Still nursing a mugwump touchiness about the "stupendous evil of an unrestricted suffrage," he even jotted down more ideas for a "wisely limited ballot" that by now had no more chance of going over than the unicycle.[20] This tenacity, rooted in his habit of intense commitment, had its positive side too. Forlornly but loyally he still insisted that Grover Cleveland was the "greatest and purest American citizen" whose closest rival as a "statesman" ranked two-hundred and twenty-fifth. When the pension system for Civil War veterans ripened into staggering harvests, how he ached for the vetoes with which Cleveland had cut off its first shoots—and for new champions in his mold to rout the many forces that were stripping power away from the states faster than ever and centralizing it at Washington.

This is mostly what Twain had in mind after 1905, whenever he grumbled that the framework for an American monarchy was up and some form of hereditary succession to the White House would come next. Just as free corn and oil had corrupted the Roman masses, the cynical generosity with pensions was buying support for a ruling clique in the United States, he thought; centralism made it simpler for this clique to control the almost invincible Republican party, whose presidents were packing the Supreme Court with sympathetic justices. His grumblings rose to a howl when Roosevelt, blocked by a pledge not to run again, seemed to pick the Republican candidate in 1908. Yet he voted for Taft—not from a sardonic impulse to hurry up the final disaster but from eagerness to scotch the immediate threat of a William Jennings Bryan, who had once flirted with the Populists and given other cause for suspecting he might not guard the purity of laissez faire against every pressure. For all Twain's talk about a quasi-monarchy he even admitted to being "glad" that Taft won.[21]

Obviously there was more show than solidity to the gloom of his sunset years. Cast less often by private troubles than by a conviction that public affairs had gone wrong, it thinned away whenever the voters went right for a change. When it thickened politically it marked how much he cared and how unendingly he was driven by his outraged ideals. The snow-topped oracle of Stormfield was not so different after all from the sarcastic reporter in Washoe who first signed himself Mark Twain. Even the closing upsurge of pessimism was merely a heavier wave of the outrage long shored up by a stronger confidence that rational man, generating the thunderbolts of technology, would demolish his errors and redeem his shabby past. At other times, even less willingly and culpably, Twain was finally betrayed into despair by some of his richest habits of mind.

Next to the elusive workings of humor itself his impact depended most on the use of fresh and startling perspectives, from Huck Finn's mudcat heresies to the cosmic irony of an archangel named Satan. But the relativism that cut through fatuous dogmas carried Twain to the brink of suspecting that his own values were lopsided and that impartial truth in politics or religion did not exist. The astronomical time and distance he imagined so keenly could make life on this earth look hopelessly trivial. His abnormally high sense of mankind's talents could likewise betray him. When the masses fell short of it he reacted by charging that they are always wrong, that only one in a thousand—"inventors, explorers, usurpers . . . giants of finance, giants of Commerce"—rises above the despicable average to drive the world ahead while the rest scramble to conform and to worship their leaders.[22] Even Liberalism could turn into a dark trap. If extended rigidly Bentham's theory that self-interest gears a calculating machine in man's soul led straight to the conclusion that there is no free will.

Yet, trying to keep the Liberal ethic facing bright side out, the saturnine determinist of *What Is Man?* left an opening for self-interest to guide itself toward society's welfare, and in soft counterpoint to its own tirades *The Mysterious Stranger* reasserted a faith in the masses as "kind-hearted," just as a partly relieving warmth had flowed from the good-natured crowd in "The Man That Corrupted Hadleyburg." And no matter how often Twain's very last stories and sketches pitted supermen against the gullible majority, the battered sage of Stormfield could show a new breadth of sympathy instead, as when burglars forced a test of his bitter determinism.[23] Looking back a few days later he held loftily that they had followed the laws of their heredity and child-hood training and that moral judgment was useless. However, he had first rushed down to the police station and—mistakenly—scolded one of the burglars for blunting the point of his half-finished rebuttal to a charge that the Jew is criminally inclined. More kindly, he had gone on to ask whether the recession of 1907 had forced them to create their own jobs.

He could not help believing that social forces matter or that politics make a difference. He could even suspend his matured racial tolerance when, enraged by the latest victories of Tammany Hall, he wrote a campaign anthem for it that needed a rising emphasis on the lines:

Ho, burghers of Dutch Albany, ho, buggers of New York, Ho, sons of bitches from the slums and painted whores from Cork.[24]

Unsurprisingly, there is no record that either side used his anthem; but in 1908 the New York *Evening Post* published his letter praising Charles Evans Hughes, who was running for re-election as governor. One of Twain's very last speeches —in the spring of 1909—came when the friends of William T. Jerome, the district attorney in Manhattan, launched a drive to make him mayor. Because too many voters suspected Jerome of nabbing petty racketeers and ward bosses while letting the big game slip around the corner, Twain only succeeded in adding to his gallery of lost causes. Yet, between painful cruises to Bermuda, he still thought it worth his energy to scrawl a gibe at the protective tariff that he knew would get quoted somewhere and then reprinted all over the country.

Practice overrode dark theory to the last and made his famous white suits appropriate even in winter. To one of the young girls to whom he wrote surprisingly solemn letters he confessed, "Yes, you are right—I am a moralist in disguise; it gets me into heaps of trouble when I go thrashing around in political questions."[25] But he kept inviting trouble. On the surface he looked like the White Knight of Alice's adventures—cheerfully grave, kind, eager to cope with stray problems, and ready to remount no matter how often he was dumped to the ground. There was no telling where he might turn up next. One of his final manuscripts, "The International Lightning Trust," was a restless melange of new and old causes; loosely tied to the late insurance scandals, it commented firmly on the Mafia, unfair rumors about "bloated" trusts, the buying of titled husbands by rich Americans, and immigrants who voted within two weeks and supposedly drew a federal pension within a month.[26] In the area of purely modern problems his essay on "Overspeeding" had already demanded a law putting extra-large license plates on automobiles whose owners were caught going too fast for the general welfare.[27]

Just getting used to Twain as a crusader, the public had little idea of his nihilistic moods. In all impulsive sincerity he kept adding to the confusion with occasional statements of faith, as when—helping to toast the centennial of the steamboat—he unreservedly praised "that stupendous prodigy, the globe's modern commerce, and . . . the equally stupendous moral and intellectual civilization" of the west.[28] Perhaps more from pity on the public than any other motive he generally hid the leapings of black doubt that reached even his darling technology when he wondered if mass production had not made life harder for as many as it helped. When denying that mankind had fulfilled its social or intellectual promise, he at least included himself and his chief talent. The archangel in *The Mysterious Stranger* revealed that human wit had failed as yet to perceive the "ten thousand high-grade comicalities which exist in the world." Yet, proving once again that Twain's sweeping contempt could merely be intended to open up smug and self-defeating minds, he also pointed out the way toward final victory: "Power, money, persuasion, supplication, persecution—these can lift at a colossal humbug—push it a little—weaken it a little, century by century, but only laughter can blow it to rags and atoms at a blast. Against the assault of laughter nothing can stand."

If I were to start over again I would be a Reformer . . . There would be an increasing interest in it that would pay handsomely for all the hostilities I should raise.

March 12, 1910[1]

TEN

Conclusion

WHEN we review Twain's career and add up the many specific cases when he was involved with political and social questions, it may seem strange that the substantial total has for so long been largely overlooked. The fault lies primarily in our own time. The twentieth-century writer has typically become an alienated intellectual, more and more engrossed in problems of deepest selfhood and unrelentingly suspicious or else cynical about the public world manipulated by press agents, lobbyists, and—lately—cold-war maneuvers. Today the writer who displays a political label is taken as an oddity; yet his nineteenth-century counterpart naturally lined himself up as a Democrat or Whig or Republican, or at least a mugwump.

From the first Twain always wore one or another of these labels and never doubted that he should. He assumed that what happened on election day did matter greatly, and, moreover, that sporting a Hayes or Cleveland button for a few weeks was not enough. Between elections he kept up with day-to-day events as anxiously as a modern tycoon watches his tax deductions. In Twain's own time, this surprised no one who knew any of his writing beyond his newspaper and magazine clowning, most of which he abandoned as soon as he could afford to. While the label of "politician" had already acquired much of the derogatory connotation that it still has, Twain's circle did not despair of America's ability to produce statesmen of the caliber of the founding fathers, if the majority could be taught to think and vote right. Faulkner or Hemingway or O'Neill or Wallace Stevens have been nowhere near so hopeful, but Twain was, and he acted on that hope.

That he acted so heavily on it has been overlooked also because his political preferences and the reasons for them were different from what his later admirers would expect. Only with a regretful wrench can most of these admirers come to think of him as cleaving to the middle class, the upper middle class, in fact. Thinking of Twain in this way has sounder bases, however, than a crude Marxist determinism. As the temper of his social mind is studied from his Hannibal days onward, it becomes clear that he would have sided with the claims of property even if his own bank account had not been sizable after 1870. Seldom in his long life did he doubt that almost everybody makes as much money in the end as he deserves, that property rights are the foundations of the happiest society, that the amount of property a man has largely determines the extent of his right to help guide society, and that political rights are secondary to the need to safeguard the health of private property. Learning early to believe that the main business of America is business, as Calvin Coolidge would say, he was always concerned about how a bruising political campaign or a new law would affect Wall Street or the captains of industry. He felt painful sympathy for the down and out and could get friendly in a minute with a butler or bartender, but he believed unshakably in the free enterprise system even though it might pinch quite a few plain folk on its way to making everybody comfortable.

In part Twain perhaps took this stern yet hopeful outlook because it was the easiest stance as he found himself surrounded more and more by friends who were comfortably fixed and convinced that things were working out nicely. And Twain too liked to get along, to stand in well with his social peers. Yet, especially after 1884, he looked deep into the mental gymnastics of conformity and came up with sardonic insights that are very much worth reading. Whether or not his opinions on politics and economics are convincing now, they were in the final analysis sincerely held, and backed by more cold reason than those of the average modern intellectual who turns his back on public affairs. Twain agreed with the wide majority of Americans who believed that democracy of the Hayes or Cleveland variety and economic free enterprise were inevitably working for each other in a grand harmony, that the demagogue was more dangerous to this harmony than the monopolist, that the natural rights of the elective process were not meant to hamstring the glorious system of profit and loss and free competition.

Twain read much history all of his life. He would not have seriously contended that society had reached a state of near-perfection marred only by political machines in the biggest cities. Still, for most of his life, when he looked at the total picture he saw a splendid upward curve over the centuries, with applied reason and Liberal democracy and laissez-faire merging to a climax in titans like Thomas A. Edison, Grover Cleveland, and Andrew Carnegie. This may seem like one of Twain's worst anticlimaxes, but he would have seen no satire in such a statement. The inventor, the statesman who guarded the public treasury from reformers as well as grafters, and the successful entrepreneur topped his list of heroes—the iconoclast, whom he praised more and more, was as a rule only working to clear their path. As the late nineteenth century felt the stresses and strains of major social and economic shifts, Twain was more inclined to worriment than to humor as he tried to account for apparent cracks in the foundations of society. He found it hard to adjust himself to many changes which he abstractly cheered as progress, but which he often disliked or could not understand.

The worst way to get an overall picture of Twain's politics is to work from the epigrams he more and more amused himself with like a reincarnated Alexander Pope. He could boil down an argument that reformers liked to use, "The radical invents the views. When he has worn them out the conservative adopts them." But he also came up with his version of a dully standpat attitude, "If all men were rich, all men would be poor." Obviously both conservatives and radicals can claim him if they merely look for what they want to find.

Perhaps the central, essentially consistent Twain cannot be drawn with sharp lines. Though swayed at the moment by cheerful memories of the river rather than by his subconscious, he chose a pen name that is emblematic of the deep divisions that ran through his mind and heart; the faculty of humor, for that matter, usually seems to be correlated with inner tensions. Still, politically at least, the contradictions in Twain's ideas are not as serious as they may look; they often clear up if he is taken on his own terms instead of being used to prove a sweeping theory about the American mind or psyche, if he is put in his milieu and allowed to change his stand from year to year or from decade to decade as fresh problems emerge. Defining the concrete issues his abstractions were meant to cover shows, for instance, that Hank Morgan's fighting defense of the duty to overthrow a bad government was directed only at monarchy; even so, Twain could not have written it ten years earlier and no longer applied it to England ten years later. Sometimes the speed with which he reacted to the news made him reverse his stand as dazzlingly as a syndicated columnist of today. However, anybody who is tempted to brush Twain off as hopelessly-erratic should be sure his own snap judgments make a neater pattern.

Whether doctrinaire or mercurial, Twain kept close tab on current affairs during what Bernard DeVoto has described as "forty years of tireless castigation of American society, government, morals and manners."[2] This rich stream of commentary must be sounded more carefully than has been done by those who design panoramas of our culture in which he serves as a pivotal figure, usually in the role of a frontiersman who got lost on an east-running trail but later wore political linsey-woolsey under his broadcloth. Other designers, who play up a New World motif, should measure how deeply he was committed to Liberal ideas from abroad. We do have a special fondness for Twain, but that does not entitle us to read into him our own mid-twentieth-century notions.

Late in life Twain refurbished an old fable to conclude: "You can find in a text whatever you bring, if you will stand between it and the mirror of your imagination. You may not see your ears, but they will be there." This should warn everybody against mulishly dominating the view. Though a rigorous aesthetic approach is on solid ground when it insists that Twain is finally important for his ability to stir the imagination, it is also true that he very seldom thought in modern terms of art for art's sake. Of course if he had cared only about writing for money's sake, posterity would already care much less about his work. In his dedicated moods he was guided by the long-honored ideal that literature judges the social as well as the personal aspect of man's condition.

Not that he neglected either aspect. Briefed by a father who left him more principles than cash, he set out as a partisan of the moribund American Whigs and of a social theory that applied best to the eighteenth century. He never got beyond a Liberal faith in the powers of technology if it was free from the shackles of otherworldly dogma and hereditary privileges. By the time he fully embraced this faith, events were outmoding it, putting him more and more often on the defensive. Most instances of what seems like confused flipflopping were in fact quite logical shifts, as the situation demanded, between attacking the vestiges of a closed system and opposing the moves to put safety limits on laissez-faire. The greed of the steel industry did not enrage him like the tyranny of kings, and the damage caused by the cycle of economic boom and bust was less important to him than keeping the road open for progress—a line that most Republicans take today. The real inconsistency came when he vacillated between his basic theoretical beliefs and an impulsive sympathy for the underdog, which Twain professed to get from his mother. This imbalance between a stern social mind and warm heart might be added to the conflicts that intrigue his psychoanalysts.

But any attempt to account for his politics as the product of his neuroses will have to explain the fact that his friends felt the same indecisions, which were a natural result of the problems forced on their era. Despite his outrageous irony and his impulses toward nonconformity he was usually, at heart, in tune with his times. When an American newspaper started a fund to ease the strain of his bankruptcy in the mid-1890's, many of the donations were tagged with superlatives proving how sure of him the public felt. Instead of denouncing him as eccentric or radical, newspaper pundits thought that his social criticism fell mostly within the allowable range of dissent and that he did not mean to interfere with business as usual. Basically they were right, though he later harassed the imperialist armada and though his passion for honesty always sought to challenge the platitudes that can cover up obvious injustice if nobody questions them.

Besides clearing the way to his greatest achievement—a prose style grounded on the common idiom—his contempt for hollow pretense enabled him to use the catch phrases of the natural rights school with a sincerity that often makes his own version memorable. When his personal democracy, middle-class Liberalism, and excitement over the headlines meshed for awhile, the result was some of his finest passages, such as the Sherburn-Boggs episode in *Huckleberry Finn*, or a compelling book such as *A Connecticut Yankee*. To be sure, his power had other sources too: *Roughing It*, *Tom Sawyer*, and the early chapters of *Life on the Mississippi* drew heavily on his daydreams and memories; a few pages in *A Tramp Abroad* and elsewhere will last for their pure clowning; other bits like the jumping-frog yarn will last because they are warm with native American humor; many of his most coldly brilliant pages scintillate because he would put ethics in a cosmic perspective. But no list of his achievements is complete unless it includes his crusade against the policemen who blandly watched San Franciscans stone a coolie, his making Huck go and humble himself before Jim without regretting it later, Hank Morgan's appeal to renounce humility before aristocrats, the searching inventory of the white man's burden, and Captain Stormfield's truly universal tolerance. Lifelong concern with society and its politics is vital to the Twain that will endure.

Bibliographical Note

As a way of referring workably to Twain's widely reprinted books, I cite not the page but the chapter, which is usually brief. The reprintings of short pieces that I mention can be located through Merle Johnson, *A Bibliography of Mark Twain* (rev. ed.; N. Y., 1935) and Jacob Blanck, *Bibliography of American Literature*, II (New Haven, 1957); Charles Neider, ed., *The Complete Short Stories of Mark Twain* (N. Y., 1957) is broad in scope and includes many sketches, as does his later collection of Twainiana, *Life As I Find It* (N. Y., 1962). The best biography remains J. DeLancey Ferguson's *Mark Twain: Man and Legend* (Indianapolis, 1943), though the best general discussion is perhaps Edward Wagenknecht's rewritten *Mark Twain: The Man and His Work* (Norman, Okla., 1961).

The mass of writing about Twain is huge. E. Hudson Long's *A Mark Twain Handbook* (N. Y., 1958) summarizes the major trends; Roger Asselineau's *The Literary Reputation of Mark Twain from 1910 to 1950* (Paris, 1954) is indispensable for its listing of articles in periodicals. Generally I cite only the material that is off the beaten track or is especially helpful or bears on a disputable point.

Long works that come closest to my subject are Paul J. Carter, Jr., *The Social and Political Ideas of Mark Twain* (Univ. of Cincinnati diss., 1939)–which takes a non-genetic approach–and Philip S. Foner, *Mark Twain: Social Critic* (N. Y., 1958)–which tries to prove that Twain's practical impact was leftist. Kenneth S. Lynn's *Mark Twain and Southwestern Humor* (Boston, 1959) makes good use of Twain's Whig background, but as Lynn goes along he shows less interest in Twain's politics as well as leaning more toward psychobiography. Svend Petersen, ed., *Mark Twain and the Government* (Caldwell, Idaho, 1960) is limited to excerpts from Twain's published work, arranged under helpful subheadings.

I use the following short titles for sources that appear often in my notes.

Autobiog	Albert Bigelow Paine, ed., *Mark Twain: An Autobiography* (N. Y., 1924)
autobiog dict	Unpublished passages of autobiographical dictation in Mark Twain Papers, identified further by date
Biog	Albert Bigelow Paine, *Mark Twain: A Biography* (N. Y., 1912)
Eruption	Bernard DeVoto, ed., *Mark Twain in Eruption* (N. Y., 1940)
Fairbanks	Dixon Wecter, ed., *Mark Twain to Mrs. Fairbanks* (San Marino, 1949)
Foner	Philip S. Foner, *Mark Twain: Social Critic* (N. Y., 1958)
Johnson	Merle Johnson, *A Bibliography of Mark Twain* (rev. ed.; N. Y., 1935)
Letters	Albert Bigelow Paine, ed., *Mark Twain's Letters* (N. Y., 1917)
Love Letters	Dixon Wector, ed., *The Love Letters of Mark Twain* (N. Y., 1949)
MTP	Mark Twain Papers at University of California, Berkeley
My Twain	William Dean Howells, *My Mark Twain* (N. Y., 1910)
Nbk	Unpublished notebook in Mark Twain Papers
Notebook	Albert Bigelow Paine, ed., *Mark Twain's Notebook* (N. Y., 1935)
Smith-Gibson	Henry Nash Smith and William M. Gibson, eds., *Mark Twain-Howells Letters* (Cambridge, Mass., 1960)
Speeches	Albert Bigelow Paine, ed., *Mark Twain's Speeches* (N. Y., 1923 ed.)
Webster	Samuel C. Webster, *Mark Twain, Business Man* (Boston, 1946)

In citing the unpublished notebooks I refer to the typescript copies; the dates of these notebooks (fixed by Paine from internal evidence) are conjectural at times but generally accurate. I do not give the volume or page number for a few magazine and newspaper articles because I have found them only as clippings.

Notes

ONE: POLITICAL APPRENTICE

1. Minnie M. Brashear, *Mark Twain: Son of Missouri* (Chapel Hill, N.C., 1934), 98-100, 117, 136-37, and Edgar M. Branch, *The Literary Apprenticeship of Mark Twain* (Urbana, 1950), 218-19, 273.

2. Twain's travel letters between 1853 and 1855 are reprinted in Edgar M. Branch, ed., *Mark Twain's Letters to the Muscatine "Journal"* (Chicago, 1942).

3. Bernard DeVoto, ed., *The Portable Mark Twain* (N.Y., 1946), 750.

4. Alexander E. Jones, "Mark Twain and Religion" (Univ. of Minnesota diss., 1950), 244-50; Dixon Wecter, *Sam Clemens of Hannibal* (Boston, 1952), 229-30.

5. Henry Nash Smith with the assistance of Frederick Anderson, *Mark Twain of the "Enterprise"* (Berkeley, 1957–hereafter Smith), 13-15, 156; *Letters*, 91-92; *Autobiog*, II, 308.

6. Smith, 160-61.

7. Smith, 86-88, 104-05.

8. Smith, 113, 122; Webster, 79-80.

9. Effie M. Mack, *Mark Twain in Nevada* (N.Y., 1947), 279, regards the watch as essentially a political gift.

10. Smith, 134, 164, 182.

11. Smith, 60-61, 127-28.

12. Mack, 262. To agree with DeVoto–*Mark Twain's America* (Boston, 1932), 155–that Twain was "rebuking the practices of California speculators" misses the exact point, which is made clear in Twain's own comments in "My Bloody Massacre."

13. William A. Corey, "Memories of Mark Twain," *Overland Mon.*,

N.S. LXVI (Sept., 1915), 264, insists that the *Enterprise—Daily Union* rivalry was partly political.

14. Smith, 19.

15. "Another Traitor"–reprinted in the Virginia (City) *Evening Bulletin*, April 2, 1864. Twain had promised his family to have the Nevada money sent to the St. Louis Sanitary Fair, and the decision to send at least some of it to New York City may have stimulated his unwise quip.

16. Paul Schmidt, "Mark Twain's Satire on Republicanism," *Amer. Quar.*, V (Winter, 1953), 344-49, challengingly analyzes this sketch, which has the innocent title of "An Unbiased Criticism."

17. *Eruption*, 256-58; Smith-Gibson, 326; letter to *Territorial Enterprise* on Jan. 24, 1866.

18. See letters dated Dec. 20, 22, 1865, and Feb. 15, 1866.

19. Franklin Walker, ed., *The Washoe Giant in San Francisco* (San Francisco, 1938), 57, 97; Ivan Benson, *Mark Twain's Western Years* (Palo Alto, 1938), 208; Twain's letter to *Enterprise* on Jan. 24, 1866.

20. Scrap book in Yale Coll. of Amer. Lit. The sketch is reprinted in Henry Smith and Frederick Anderson, eds., *Mark Twain: San Francisco Correspondent* (San Francisco, 1957).

21. *Biog*, 264-65. Paine's account, which depends probably on a story by "G. E. B." in the San Francisco *Call* of April 17, 1887, does not mesh in many places with the actual sequence of Twain's remarks and jobs.

TWO: ACQUIRING REPORTER

1. Walter F. Frear, *Mark Twain and Hawaii* (Chicago, 1947), 323-24, 349.

2. Reprinted in Benson, *Twain's Western Years*, 212.

3. Twain's letters appeared in the St. Louis *Democract* for March 12, 13, and 15, 1867.

4. Corrective analysis is supplied in John C. McCloskey, "Mark Twain as Critic in *The Innocents Abroad*," *Amer. Lit.*, XXV (May, 1953), 144 and Arthur L. Scott, "*The Innocents Abroad* Revaluated," *West. Humanities Rev.*, VII (Summer, 1953), 220.

5. Daniel M. McKeithan, ed., *Traveling with the Innocents Abroad* (Norman, Okla., 1958), 72, 110, 212, 250, 308.

6. *Ibid.*, 14, 84, 210-11, 233. That Twain teased the old beggar woman is confirmed by a fellow passenger—Fred W. Lorch, "Julia Newell and Mark Twain on the *Quaker City* Holy Land Excursion," *Rock County Chronicle*, II (June, 1956).

7. MTP, letter of Aug. 9, 1867, from Naples, Italy, and letter to Frank Fuller on Nov. 24, 1867, from Washington, D.C. Copyright by the Mark Twain Company, 1962.

8. See especially the three letters in *Territorial Enterprise* of Dec. 22, 1867, and Feb. 18 and March 7, 1868.

9. George R. Brown, ed., *Reminiscences of Senator William M. Stewart* (N.Y., 1908), 219-24; Twain to Laurence Hutton (letter in Princeton Univ. Lib.), Feb. 4, 1884; New York *Herald*, May 19, 1889.

10. *Letters*, 148-50; Webster, 96, 98; *Love Letters*, 60-62.

11. *Love Letters*, 60-62; *Fairbanks*, 31; Cyril Clemens, *Mark Twain The Letter Writer* (Boston, 1932), 18; MTP, Nbk *14* (1879), 10; letter to *Alta California* of Jan. 21, 1868.

12. *Fairbanks*, 11-12; *Biog*, 1601; MTP, Nbks *4-5*, II (1866), 9; letters reprinted in *Twainian*, VI (July-Aug., 1947), 4-5, and VII (Jan.-Feb., 1948), 5.

13. "Around the World," *Buffalo Express*, Jan. 22 and Feb. 12, 1870; Dixon Wecter, ed., *Mark Twain in Three Moods* (San Marino, Calif., 1948), 26.

14. Letter in *Alta California* of Jan. 21, 1868; "Information Wanted" in *Mark Twain's Sketches, New and Old* (Hartford, 1875—hereafter *Sketches*) and a second item with the same title and some of the same ideas, in New York *Tribune* of Jan. 22, 1868.

15. New York *Tribune*, Feb. 13, 1868—reprinted in *Twainian*, V (May-June, 1946), 1-3.

16. Reprinted in *Sketches* with an interesting footnote; the comment in *Autobiog*, I, 324-25, applies to this sketch rather than the one Twain named there.

17. The revealing passage in *Autobiog*, II, 14, needs two corrections: the date was probably 1868 and George Hearst was a habitual Democrat.

18. The range of Twain's comments on reconstruction and impeachment can be sampled in two small collections by Cyril Clemens, *Washington in 1868* (Webster Groves, Mo., 1943) and *Republican Letters* (Webster Groves, Mo., 1941).

19. Reprinted in *Twainian*, III (Nov., 1943), 6.

20. Letters to *Territorial Enterprise* of Feb. 19 and 27, 1868.

21. Reprinted in *Sketches*; Twain gave its history in "Memoranda," *Galaxy*, X (Sept., 1870), 432.

THREE: A CURIOUS REPUBLICAN

1. *Packard's Mon.*, I (March, 1869), 89-91; *Fairbanks*, 86-87.

2. MTP, autobiog dict of Feb. 16, 1906; *Autobiog*, II, 135; New York *Tribune*, June 15, 1869, p. 4; MTP, copies of letters from Twain to Whitelaw Reid, dated [June] 15 and June 26, 1869.

3. *Love Letters*, 68-69, 108-09; Buffalo *Express*, Aug. 20, 1869. There is a core of *Express* items that can be assigned clearly to Twain; I use those assembled in MTP (HNS).

4. "People and Things," Aug. 18, 31, Sept. 1, 1869; "Inspired Humor," Aug. 19; "Which?" Aug. 24; "The Democratic Varieties," Aug. 31; "The Legend of the Sharks," Sept. 11; Franklin R. Rogers, *Mark Twain's Burlesque Patterns* (Dallas, 1960), 114-16.

5. In MTP, a letter dated Dec. 31, 1870, from Isaac E. Sheldon, publisher of the *Burlesque Autobiography*, shows Twain was a moving spirit behind the cartoons.

6. Webster, 115; Smith, *Twain of "Enterprise,"* 100; MTP, DV 79A—notes for Senator Bonanza story; Kenneth R. Andrews, *Nook Farm: Mark Twain's Hartford Circle* (Cambridge, Mass., 1950), 238.

7. "The Noble Red Man," X (Sept., 1870), 427-28.

8. *Letters*, 188; "The New Crime" and "Our Precious Lunatic," *Express*, April 16, May 14, 1870; "Unburlesquable Things," *Galaxy*, X (July, 1870), 137-38.

9. "A Ballotd. Owed phor the Tymz; Not the Knusepaper" (copy in Yale Univ. Lib.); it was signed "Twark Main." Blanck, *Bibliography of American Literature*, II, item 3596, doubts Twain's authorship but offers no evidence. Andrews, 111, notes how closely Nook Farm followed this election.

10. MTP, Nbk 36 (1903), 8.

11. July 20, 1872, p. 2; the *Courant* announced for Grant of course. As a *Tribune* contributor Twain had good reason not to sign this attack, but his authorship is established by a letter from C. D. Warner, dated July 19, 1872 (MTP), as well as by obvious similarities with Twain's speech before the Whitefriars Club—reported in New York *Sun*, Aug. 7, 1872.

12. MTP, DV 306—apparently unpublished.

13. Arthur L. Vogelback has written three excellent articles that are relevant: "Mark Twain: Newspaper Contributor," *Amer. Lit.*, XX (May, 1948), 111-28; "Mark Twain and the Tammany Ring," *Pub. Mod. Lang. Assoc.*, LXX (March, 1955), 69-77; "Mark Twain and the Fight for Control of the *Tribune*," *Amer. Lit.*, XXVI (Nov., 1954), 374-83.

14. Vogelback, "Twain: Newspaper Contributor," 119-24, shrewdly analyzes his position, which is confirmed in a letter to Reid on Jan. 3, 1873. Foner, 242, goes too far in stating the anti-annexation tendency of Twain's *Tribune* letters.

15. Letter on March 7, 1873, copy in MTP. The "Public Virtue" original, dated March 8, is in the New York Pub. Lib. Reid wrote on it, "Letter Editor/must."

16. *Love Letters*, 153-54. This volume omits Twain's earlier and more revealing letter from Washington on July 6, 1870 (MTP).

17. "Thoughts Suggested by Mr. Froude's 'Progress,'" *The Complete Writings of Charles Dudley Warner* (Hartford, 1904), XV.

18. Invaluable for reading *The Gilded Age* is a broadside reprint of newspaper reviews—seen in MTP.

19. Twain's comments on sculptress Vinnie Ream are reprinted in Johnson, 182-83, and *Mark Twain Quar.*, V (Sum., 1942), 10-11. Twain's scrapbook for 1872 (MTP) included a clipping on abuses in commissioning statues of Civil War heroes.

20. *Twainian*, N.S. II (May, 1943), 6; *American Publisher*, July, 1871, p. 4; MTP, letter to Frank Bliss, dated June [1871].

21. *Fairbanks*, 175; *My Twain*, 12, 77; *Love Letters*, 177; Howard G. Baetzhold, "Mark Twain: England's Advocate," *Amer. Lit.*, XXVIII (Nov., 1956), 334-35.

22. Hartford *Courant*, May 14, 1879, p. 1.

23. *Autobiog*, II, 231-32; Stephen Gwynn, *Life of Sir Charles Dilke* (London, 1918), I, 160; Lillian Whiting, *Kate Field* (Boston, 1899), 289; *Love Letters*, 188; MTP, Olivia Clemens' letters to her mother, Aug. 10-11 and Aug. 31, 1873, and Twain to one Fitzgibbon in 1873-74.

24. MTP, DV 69 and Tichborne scrapbook; in *Following the Equator* Twain referred in detail to attending one of the claimant's "showy evenings." Twain kept a copy of *The Anti-Game Law Circular* for Oct. 12, 1872.

25. H. R. Fox Bourne, *English Newspapers* (London, 1887), II, 286, 308, describes as uncompromisingly Tory the London *Morning Post*, to which Twain's letter was addressed. The letter was reprinted in the *Northern Whig* of Dec. 13, 1873.

26. Hartford *Courant*, July 25, 1876.

27. Undated AMS in Webster letters, MTP; *Biog*, 541-42; M. A. D. Howe, *Memories of a Hostess* (Boston, 1922), 251-56.

28. MTP, letter from Marvin L. Bovee, dated Feb. 10.

29. MTP, Paine 249 (dated Sept. 18, 1905).

FOUR: SOLID CITIZEN

1. MTP, DV 311.
2. MTP, Nbk *13* (1878-79), 50-51, and Nbk *14* (1879), 10; *Fairbanks*, 208-09; *Letters*, 342.
3. Foner, 94; Smith-Gibson, 156.
4. Smith-Gibson, 162-63; *Eruption*, 287.
5. Smith-Gibson, 187.
6. Webster, 114-15.
7. *Report from Paradise* (N.Y., 1952), 73; MTP, autobiog dict of Nov. 21, 1906; Andrews, *Nook Farm*, 128-34, attributes such attitudes to his neighbors while mistakenly excluding Twain.
8. Smith-Gibson, 320; MTP, letters from R. M. Griswold, Jr., July 29, 1880, and from E. H. Walcott, July 15, 1880.
9. Letter to Hartford *Courant*, Sept. 29, 1875.
10. MTP, Nbk *12*, 43; *Fairbanks*, 208; *Letters*, 346.
11. Smith-Gibson, 237; MTP, Nbk *14*, 11, 38; Warner, " 'Equality,' " *Atlantic Mon.*, XLV (Jan., 1880), 19-32.
12. MTP, Nbk, *12*, 4, 11, 23.
13. MTP, DV 67.
14. MTP, Nbk *14*, 23; *My Twain*, 133.
15. *Twainian*, IX (Nov.-Dec., 1950), 2; New York *Tribune*, Oct. 25, 1881, p. 6; *Academy*, XX (Dec. 24, 1881), 469.
16. Albert E. Stone, Jr., *The Innocent Eye: Childhood in Mark Twain's Imagination* (New Haven, 1961), 111-112, nicely points up its general ambivalence toward England; Foner, 102-03, states best the argument for its antimonarchical impact.
17. Robert M. Rodney, "Mark Twain in England" (Univ. of Wisconsin diss., 1945), 45-57, 88-89. The British antimonarchist *Republican*, IX (Dec., 1883), 546-47, reprinted the satirical passage from *Roughing It*. That there was a political element in Twain's British reception is suggested by Rodney's conclusion that the *Saturday Review* displayed an "antipathy" in all of its commentaries on Twain; on March 3, 1882, Twain wrote to his British publisher that neither the *Review* nor the *Athenaeum* "would compliment the holy scriptures, if an American had written them"—original in Yale Coll. of Amer. Lit.
18. Smith-Gibson, 274; *Biog*, 708-09.
19. Edmund H. Yates, *Celebrities at Home* (London, 1879— Third Ser.), 141.
20. MTP, Nbk *15* (1880), 10; Smith-Gibson, 316.
21. MTP, telegram from E. H. House, dated Oct. 16, 1880; *Biog*, 691-93; *Autobiog*, I, 28-29; MTP, Nbk *15*, 11-13, 55; New York *Tribune*, Oct. 17, 1880.

22. "Mark Twain on the Gold-Springs," New York *Evening Post*, Sept. 16, 1880; reprinted in many newspapers, as in Hartford *Courant*, Sept. 20; now available in *Twainian*, N.S. I (April, 1942), 6. Though it is hard to see how, Warner implied that this same item also commented properly on the currency question—letter from Warner to Twain, Sept. 20, 1880 (MTP).

23. Reprinted in Cyril Clemens, *Twain The Letter Writer*, 53, from an unidentified clipping; the longer victory speech is reprinted in *Twainian*, VI (Jan.-Feb., 1947), 203. Twain's pre-election speech is covered in Smith-Gibson, 871-72.

24. *Fairbanks*, 241-42; *Autobiog*, I, 20-22; MTP, letter dated Feb. 26, 1881, from John Hay, two letters dated April 1, 1881, from Grant, letter dated April 9 from Yung Wing, letters from John Russell Young in 1881-82 and 1890.

25. MTP, Nbk *16* (1882), 43-47, 49-50, and letter to E. H. House, dated Dec. 20, 1882.

26. MTP, Nbk *12*, 7i, and AMS dated Jan. [1881 or possibly 1882]; E. McClung Fleming, *R. R. Bowker: Militant Liberal* (Norman, Okla., 1952), 121-22, 129.

27. MTP, letters in Jan., 1882, from John Russell Young and Nbk *15*, 52-55, Nbk *16*, 2-6, Nbk *17* (1883-84), 13. The relevant material from Nbk *15* was clearly written in late 1881 or after; Twain occasionally picked up an old notebook and added new entries.

28. Three letters in Aug., 1882 from R. U. Johnson, editor of the *Century Magazine*, are in MTP.

FIVE: THE SCALAWAG

1. Smith-Gibson, 198.

2. Foner, 218; "People and Things," Buffalo *Express*, Sept. 23, 1869; "The 'Tournament' in A.D. 1870," *Galaxy*, X (July, 1870), 135-36.

3. MTP, Nbk *15* (1880), 7, copyright by the Mark Twain Company, 1962; *Twainian*, VI (Jan.-Feb., 1947), 2-3.

4. Fuller proof on this point and others appears in my article, "The Southward Currents Under Huck Finn's Raft," *Miss. Val. Hist. Rev.*, XLVI (Sept., 1959), 222-37.

5. See the reply to Howells in "Scott's Latest Critics," *Saturday Rev.* (London), LXVII (May 4, 1889), 521-23. Henry Watterson, "The 'Solid South,'" *North Amer. Rev.*, CXXVIII (Jan., 1879), 51-53,

anticipates Twain's point, though he puts it much less disapprovingly. Roger B. Salomon, *Twain and the Image of History* (New Haven, 1961), 83-84, sums up the question usefully.

6. *Notebook*, 164-65; MTP, Nbk *16* (1882), 34-37.

7. Caroline Ticknor, " 'Mark Twain's' Missing Chapter," *Bookman*, XXXIX (May, 1914), 300-02; Arthur L. Vogelback, "Mark Twain: Newspaper Contributor," *Amer. Lit.*, XX (May, 1948), 128. Willis Wager's edition of *Life on the Mississippi* in 1944 reprinted the missing passages.

8. MTP, typescript copy of letter (held by Buffalo Hist. Soc.) to Mr. and Mrs. Karl Gerhardt on May 1, 1883; *My Twain*, 35.

9. Guy A. Cardwell, *Twins of Genius* (East Lansing, 1953), 71-76. Arlin Turner's definitive biography of Cable (Durham, N.C., 1956) documents this interesting friendship; Turner has also edited a relevant collection of Cable's essays, *The Negro Question: A Selection of Writings on Civil Rights in the South* (Garden City, 1958).

10. Jay B. Hubbell, *The South in American Literature* (Durham, N.C., 1954), 822, 833. The main findings of Walter Blair's impressive study—"When Was *Huckleberry Finn* Written?" *Amer. Lit.*, XXX (March, 1958), 1-25—do not clash with this conclusion; the Southern debate had started by 1876 and had reached clear intensity by 1880, before its climax in 1883-84. Also, Twain revised his earlier chapters in 1880 and again in 1883.

11. "American Authors and British Pirates," *New Princeton Rev.*, V (Jan., 1888), 50-51. Twain's comment in his copy of Harriet Martineau's *Retrospect of Western Travel* that slavery "brutalizes" the master was probably written in 1881-82.

12. *My Twain*, 36.

13. C. Vann Woodward, *Origins of the New South, 1877-1913* (Baton Rouge, 1951), 65.

14. The key phrase of Twain's letter to James R. Osgood on Jan. 15, 1883, is quoted in Blair, "When Was *Huckleberry Finn* Written?"

15. Allan Nevins, *The Evening Post: A Century of Journalism* (N.Y., 1922), 540; Henry Watterson, *"Marse Henry," an Autobiography* (N.Y., 1919), II, 195-96; Frederic Bancroft, ed., *Speeches, Correspondence and Political Papers of Carl Schurz* (N.Y., 1913), IV, 157-58, 167; Walter Blair, *Mark Twain & Huck Finn* (Berkeley, 1960), 220-21.

16. MTP, letter from J. C. Fuller dated Aug. 10, 1885, at Cincinnati, Ohio; Blair, *Mark Twain & Huck Finn*, 224, 234.

17. Bernard DeVoto, *Mark Twain at Work* (Cambridge, Mass., 1942), 66.

18. *Life on the Mississippi*—hereafter *LOM* (Heritage Press, 1944),

415. In this same decade, Charles Dudley Warner deplored Southern apathy toward killing and commented: "The most personally courageous become bullies and the terror of the community"—*Studies in the South and West* (N.Y., 1889), 398-401.

19. *Notebook*, 166. In 1866, under the heading of "Superstition," Twain recorded beliefs like Huck-Jim ideas about getting rid of warts —MTP, Nbks *4-5 (III)*, 40-41.

20. Webster, 260.

21. Quoted in Alfred E. Stone, Jr., "The Twichell Papers and Mark Twain's *A Tramp Abroad*," *Yale Univ. Lib. Gaz.*, XXIX (April, 1955), 158. Warner commented (*Studies in the South and West*, 315), "There is a popular notion that Arkansas is a 'bowie-knife' State, a lawless and ignorant State."

22. "The Second Advent," MTP, DV 76; the manuscript seems to belong to the early 1880's and the date of 1881 given in the story may be correct. Henry Nash Smith, "Mark Twain's Images of Hannibal," *Texas Stud. in Eng.*, XXXVII (1958), 12, shows that Bricksville was in some ways a redrawn Hannibal, but the fact Twain had insisted on using the name of Arkansas remains.

23. "An Appreciation," reprinted in *Europe and Elsewhere*. Lynn Altenbernd, "Huck Finn, Emancipator," *Criticism*, I (Fall, 1959), 298-307, goes far toward seeing the topical point of the novel.

24. DeVoto, *Mark Twain at Work*, 98.

25. See *LOM*, chap. 42. Twain praised cremation and spoke caustically about conventional funerals in MTP, Nbk *14* (1879), 9 and Nbk *16* (1882), 47.

26. From letter dated Dec. 12, 1881; quoted in Thomas H. English, ed., *Mark Twain to Uncle Remus* (Atlanta, 1953), 14. Leo Marx, "Mr. Eliot, Mr. Trilling, and *Huckleberry Finn*," *Amer. Scholar*, XXII (Autumn, 1953), 423-40, capably discusses the weakness in the handling of Jim.

27. In "A Little Note to M. Paul Bourget," 219-20, *How to Tell a Story and Other Essays* (N.Y., 1897), Twain needled Bourget about "playfully" warning the "public against taking one of your books seriously" and said: "I used to do that cunning thing myself in earlier days"; however, the total effect of the passage is a little confused.

28. MTP, Nbk *18* (1884-85), 19 and Nbk *22-II* (1887-88), 46.

29. MTP, DV 303; *Speeches*, 117; Webster, 264-65; Foner, 237; Robert McElroy, *Grover Cleveland* (N.Y., 1923), I, 226-30; *Publisher's Weekly*, LXXIX (Feb. 11, 1911), 900.

30. Foner, 95; Smith-Gibson, 501-03; Henry S. Canby, *Turn West, Turn East* (Boston, 1951), 134.

31. MTP, letter to E. H. House on Oct. 31, 1884. The Hartford

Times, Oct. 21, p. 1, carried a full account of the mugwump meeting.

32. It has been a commonplace that Twain badly overstated the resentment of his Republican friends and the related pressure on Twichell. However, the Hartford *Times* of Oct. 20, 1884, p. 4, ran a letter (signed "Independent Republican") that protested against the "insulting attempt to browbeat and annoy Mr. Twichell because he will not vote for Mr. Blaine and has the manliness and courage to say so." Significantly, the Hartford *Courant* did not report on the gathering Twain presided over, though it did so for regular Democratic meetings and jeered on Oct. 21 (p. 2) that "Mr. Clemens cannot have read the Buffalo newspapers . . . *since* the national conventions."

33. *Love Letters*, 221; *Puck*, XVIII (Dec. 16, 1885), 242.

34. *Masterpieces of American Eloquence* (N.Y., 1900), 439-40.

35. *Love Letters*, 245; *Notebook*, 189.

SIX: UNCLE SAM

1. Letter from Hartford—Grover Cleveland papers, Library of Congress.

2. Samuel E. Moffett, "Mark Twain: Humorist, Man of Letters and Champion of the Right," *Pilgrim*, VII (Sept., 1903), 7. The review of the *Yankee* in the *Standard*, VII (Jan., 1890), 8-10, gave greatest praise to the illustrations; any single-tax glint in Twain's eye was meant for England, where "feudal" holdovers of land were being criticized.

3. MTP, Nbk *18* (1884-85), 18; New York *Times*, Dec. 10, 1889, p. 5.

4. Foner, 168, believes that Twain's account was a defense of the closed-shop union, but it shows no sense of economic class; Foner forgets it first appeared in the *Atlantic Mon.* for June, 1875.

5. Reprinted in Paul J. Carter, Jr., "Mark Twain and the American Labor Movement," *New Eng. Quar.*, XXX (Sept., 1957), 382-88. Twain contributed some of his books to the Knights of Labor library at Spring Valley, Illinois—MTP, letters from Charles Devlin, Dec. 1 and 12, 1887.

6. "A Defense of the Eighth Commandment," *Cosmopolitan*, IV (Feb., 1888), 489.

7. *Speeches*, 132; New York *Times*, Dec. 10, 1889, p. 5; New York *World*, Jan. 12, 1890.

8. *Notebook*, 209; *Letters*, 520; MTP, Nbk *23-1* (1888), 21 and Nbk *24* (1889-90), 29-30. In *A Hazard of New Fortunes* (1890) Howells punished Christine Dryfoos with marriage to an unsavory aristocrat.

9. Quoted in Salomon, *Twain and the Image of History*, 127. Salomon has much to say about the *Yankee* that is worthwhile.

10. MTP, Nbk *23-I*, 8, copyright by the Mark Twain Company, 1962; John Higham, *Strangers in the Land* (New Brunswick, 1955), 59-60.

11. MTP, DV 16 and Paine 91A; internal evidence dates these items fairly well.

12. Lionel Trilling, *Matthew Arnold* (N.Y., 1939), 393.

13. Paine should have dated this talk as 1887 instead of 1886. Howard Baetzhold, "The Course of Composition of *A Connecticut Yankee:* A Reinterpretation," *Amer. Lit.*, XXXIII (May, 1961), 195-214, traces the book's progress.

14. MTP, Nbk *22-II* (1887-88), 64-69; Nbk *23-I*, 9; Nbk *24*, 39; Nbk *25* (1890-91), 23; DV 15 and DV 75. John B. Hoben, "Mark Twain's *A Connecticut Yankee:* A Genetic Study," *Amer. Lit.*, XVIII (Nov., 1946), 204, puts DV 14 ("On Foreign Critics") in 1883 but Paine's date of 1889 is much closer to the truth.

15. Twain once mentioned most of the Liberals' achievements or goals in a single passage—MTP, Paine 102B (early draft of a preface for the *Yankee*).

16. Allen Thorndike Rice, "The Race for Primacy," *North Amer. Rev.*, CXLV (Oct., 1887), 435-40, is especially interesting because Rice was highly responsible and normally pro-British.

17. MTP, Nbks *23-II*, 34 and *23-I*, 11. Copyright by the Mark Twain Company, 1962.

18. Reprinted in *Public Opinion*, VII (1889), 165-66; *My Twain*, 145.

19. "Editor's Study," *Harper's Mon.*, LXXIII (Sept., 1886), 643; MTP, letter from Stedman, dated July 7, 1889.

20. Yale Univ. Lib.—report of Walter R. Pforzheimer and A. M. Vietor on their visit with Beard in 1934. There are hostile references to Tennyson in the holograph manuscript of the "Yankee" (Berg Coll., New York Pub. Lib.).

21. MTP, Paine 102B.

22. *Yankee*, chap. 13; Smith-Gibson, 595-96, 613; MTP, Paine 91.

23. Letters to Twain dated from Aug. 12, 1886, to Dec. 8, 1905; Twain to Fred Hall on Nov. 24, 1889, and Paine 92; Nbk *21* (1885-87), 49 and Nbk *23-II*, 54-55—all in MTP. An autobiographical sketch appeared in the *Republican*, XI (May, 1885), 9-10.

24. Algar L. Thorold, *The Life of Henry Labouchere* (N.Y., 1913), 239.

25. MTP, Nbk *23-I*, 4 and Nbk *25* (1890-91), 47; Beard's own penciled identification of the top head in the drawing on p. 297 of the *Yankee*—copy in Yale Coll. of Amer. Lit.

26. MTP, Nbk *22-II*, 64. Copyright by the Mark Twain Company, 1962. Hartford *Courant*, June 29, 1888.

27. MTP, Paine 277 and also Paine 102A, "The American Press"; New York *Times*, Dec. 10, 1889, p. 5.

28. Suggestive comments occur in W.E.H. Lecky, *History of European Morals* (N.Y., 1877), I, 140-47; J. L. Spalding, "The Basis of Popular Government," *North Amer. Rev.*, CXXXIX (Sept., 1884), 205-06; Howells, "Editor's Study," *Harper's Mon.*, LXXIII (Sept., 1886), 643. Tennyson's remark in 1886 on the reverential purpose of "my *Idylls*" is instructive—Robert F. Horton, *Alfred Tennyson* (London, 1900), 272.

29. MTP, Nbk *24*, 3.

30. MTP, Nbk *23-I*, 17. In his 1889 letter to Whitman he remarked that monarchy was "reduced" to a "machine which makes an imposing show of diligence and attention to business, but isn't connected with the works."

31. Interesting comment on hermits, besides the obvious passages in Lecky, occurs in John W. Draper, *History of the Intellectual Development of Europe* (N.Y., 1876), I, 434-38, and David Swing, "The Failure of the Southern Pulpit," *North Amer. Rev.*, CXXX (April, 1880), 367.

32. On advowsons see Act I of the Colonel Sellers play written in 1883 (Yale Univ. Lib.) and MTP, Nbk *23-II*, 60 and the clippings pasted in Nbk *24*. On taxes see DV 24 and Nbk *23-I*, 18 (MTP) and *Notebook*, 223. On tithing see *Notebook*, 190-91 and the long clipping dated "Post. Aug. 16, 1889" in Twain's scrapbooks.

33. Laura Stedman and G. M. Gould, *Life and Letters of Edmund Clarence Stedman* (N.Y., 1910), II, 371.

34. *Pall Mall Gazette*, Dec. 23, 1889, p. 2. Beard insisted he was boycotted for ten years after these drawings, principally because of religious objections.

35. *Biog*, Appendix S; MTP, DV 23; Stedman and Gould, II, 371. That Hank was from Connecticut clearly bore on the Blue Laws controversy.

36. *Pall Mall Gazette*, Dec. 23, 1889, p. 2. Twain said much the same thing to the New York *Times*—Dec. 10, 1889, p. 5. The character of the Stuart kings was still a warm subject politically.

37. MTP, Nbk *24*, 13-15. Seemingly, this differed from the appendix Twain planned earlier.

38. *Athenaeum*, No. 3251 (Feb. 15, 1890), 211; Reginald B. Brett, "Mark Twain on Tennyson," *Pall Mall Gazette*, Feb. 28, 1890, p. 1; *Truth*, XXVII (Jan. 2, 1890), 25; Robert M. Rodney, "Mark Twain in England" (Univ. of Wisconsin diss., 1945), 142-50.

39. *Review of Reviews*, I (Feb., 1890), 144-56.

40. Thorold, *Labouchere*, 41-42; Frank Thistlewaite, "The Citadel and the Caravan: Anglo-American Relations in the Twentieth Century," *Amer. Quar.*, IX (Spring, 1957), 27-29.

41. Burton J. Hendrick, *Life of Andrew Carnegie* (N.Y., 1932), I, 258-60, 267-70; *An American Four-in-Hand in Britain* (N.Y., 1883), 103, 211, 333; *Scots Observer*, Jan. 18, 1890.

42. Burton J. Hendrick and Daniel Henderson, *Louise Whitfield Carnegie* (N.Y., 1950), 93; Hendrick, *Carnegie*, I, 274; James Howard Bridge, *Millionaires and Grub Street* (N.Y., 1931), 45.

43. Letter dated March 17—in New York Pub. Lib. Copyright by the Mark Twain Company, 1962. Carnegie claimed that Twain told him the idea for the *Yankee* came from reading his book—"Tributes to Mark Twain," *North Amer. Rev.*, CXCI (June, 1910), 827.

44. Walter F. Frear, *Mark Twain and Hawaii*, 501. John M. Ward, *Baseball* (Philadelphia, 1888), 9-33, spent much time denying that the game was derived from cricket.

45. MTP, Paine 102B.

46. Reprinted in Foner, 165, from Nbk for Feb., 1890.

47. *Notebook*, 210; *Letters*, 525-28; Smith-Gibson, 610.

48. MTP, Paine 102B (on the same kind of paper as the last part of "Yankee" MS) and DV 128 (6)—clearly to be ascribed by internal evidence to the late 1880's. (copyright by the Mark Twain Company, 1962) *My Twain*, 80-81.

49. *Notebook*, 199; MTP, DV 24—a passage omitted from the *Yankee*. Walter F. Taylor, *The Economic Novel in America* (Chapel Hill, 1942), 146, has an xcellent analysis of Twain's attitude toward the machine. "Yankee" MS, I, 153, includes: "I shall have considerable to say about my patent office by & by, in its proper place."

50. *Letters*, 520; Percy Douglas, "Iconoclasm Necessary to Progress," *North Amer. Rev.*, CXLVIII (June, 1889), 768-69; Thomas P. Neill, *The Rise and Decline of Liberalism* (Milwaukee, 1953), 36-37.

51. "On Foreign Critics," *Speeches*, 150-51.

52. Letter to Charles Webster on June 20, 1887—Berg Coll.; Webster, 347.

53. New York *Sun*, Nov. 12, 1886.

54. Margaret Duckett, "The 'Crusade' of a Nineteenth-Century Liberal," *Tenn. Stud. in Lit.*, IV (1959), 109-20.

55. Besides Howells', American reviews that especially saw the anti-British point were in the Boston *Herald*, Dec. 15, 1889, p. 17; "Literary Gossip," *American Standard* (San Francisco), May 17, 1890; *National* (Quincy, Calif.), July 5, 1890.

56. Foner, 176; letter to Twain from George H. Warner, dated Nov. 17, 1891—Berg Coll.

SEVEN: THE BANKRUPT

1. *Free Russia* [I], Sept., 1890, p. 12. Fuller detail on this and related points appears in my article, "Twain, Howells, and the Boston Nihilists," *New Eng. Quar.*, XXXII (Sept., 1959), 351-71.

2. *Biog*, 1656-57; *Free Russia*, [I], Oct., 1890, p. 11.

3. *Biog*, 1639; *Letters*, 535-38. "The Answer" is in MTP.

4. Letter from Stepniak to Howells, April 18, 1891—in the Howells Coll. at Harvard.

5. MTP, Boxed MS #14. Copyright by the Mark Twain Company, 1962.

6. Sherwood Cummings, "Mark Twain's Social Darwinism," *Huntington Lib. Quar.*, XX (Feb., 1957), 169-73.

7. *Spectator*, LXIX (Nov. 19, 1892), 714.

8. MTP, Nbk *25*, 45.

9. *A Connecticut Yankee*, chap. 30 and drawings on pp. 297 and 365; MTP, Nbk *23-l* (1888), 5; New York *Times*, Dec. 10, 1889, p. 5.

10. MTP, Paine 73—an unpublished travel letter dated Jan. 18, 1892; *Notebook*, 224; MTP, Nbk *27* (1893-94), 20; Jervis Langdon, *Samuel Langhorne Clemens: Some Reminiscences*, 13.

11. MTP, DV 316, written around 1892.

12. Anne P. Wigger, "The Composition of Mark Twain's *Pudd'nhead Wilson and Those Extraordinary Twins*: Chronology and Development," *Mod. Philology*, LV (Nov., 1957), 94.

13. Martha M. Williams, "In Re *Pudd'nhead Wilson*," *Southern Mag.*, IV (Feb., 1894), 99-102; Foner, 215-16.

14. Quoted in Arlin Turner, *Cable*, 269.

15. J. Alexander Karlin, "New Orleans Lynchings of 1891 and the American Press," *Louisiana Hist. Quar.*, XXIV (Jan., 1941), 187-201.

16. *Love Letters*, 277-78.

17. MTP, Nbk *21* (1885-87), 44, Nbk *23-l* (1888), 7, Nbk *24*, 9, copyright by the Mark Twain Company, 1962; *Notebook*, 210, 213.

18. *Tom Sawyer Abroad*, chap. 11; *Letters*, 565; Foner, 97. Jim's trouble (chap. 12) fits our exchange with Chile (1891-92) over the mobbing of some American sailors.

19. MTP, Nbk *22-ll* (1887-88), 40.

20. MTP, Paine 79—written on the back of the MS of *Tom Sawyer, Detective*.

21. MTP, Nbk *25*, 26; in this passage Twain wrote "money" for "work" the last time he intended the latter word. Copyright by the Mark Twain Company, 1962.

22. "Does the Race of Man Love a Lord?" 326, in *The $30,000 Bequest and Other Stories*. "The Esquimau Maiden's Romance" appeared

in Nov., 1893; it is anticipated in Nbk *25*, 34 (MTP)—an entry close after the defense of American millionaires.

23. The Major was modeled partly after a wealthy friend described in Charles Neider, ed., *The Autobiography of Mark Twain* (N.Y., 1959), 311. However, see the New York *Sun*, Nov. 9, 1890, and New York *World* of Nov. 13 for Twain's role in getting a rude horsecar conductor laid off. A later speech on citizenship—New York *Journal*, March 5, 1906—indicated that perhaps the Major imitated some of Twain's own actions.

24. MTP, Nbk *26*, 45. Copyright by the Mark Twain Company, 1962.

25. "Aix, The Paradise of the Rheumatics," 96-98 in *Europe and Elsewhere*.

26. Letter to Annie Trumbull, undated but clearly written in Aug., 1895—Yale Coll. of Amer. Lit.

27. MTP, letter to Samuel E. Moffett on April 9, 1895.

28. MTP, Nbk *27*, 37, 46, and autobiog dict of Sept. 7, 1906, pp. 1263-64; *Biog*, 933.

29. MTP, DV 72, "Labouchere's 'Legal Pillory,' " copyright by the Mark Twain Company, 1962, and also (for 1895) Nbk *28*, 25 and Nbk *28a-ll*, 57-58; *Notebook*, 252.

30. *Notebook*, 236; Wayne McVeagh was our ambassador to Italy from 1893 to 1895.

31. Foner, 317.

32. Letter to Annie Trumbull from Paris, Jan. 18, 1895—Yale Coll. of Amer. Lit.; MTP, Nbk *26*, 3.

33. Letter to [Lloyd S.] Bryce on Oct. 13, 1894—Yale Coll. of Amer. Lit.; *Notebook*, 340.

34. Foner, 90; Samuel E. Moffett, "Mark Twain: Humorist, Man of Letters and Champion of the Right," *Pilgrim*, VII (Sept., 1903), 7.

35. An unpublished essay summarized in St. Louis *Post-Dispatch*, Dec. 9, 1928. In "Mark Twain and Woman's Suffrage," *Missouri Mag.*, March, 1935, Clara Clemens Gabrilowitsch testified to her father's strong support.

36. *Following the Equator*, chap. 32; *Notebook*, 256; *Joan of Arc Mag.*, April-May, 1910. Though rich in insights, Albert E. Stone's *The Innocent Eye* overstresses the extent to which Twain saw Joan as a child; her sex is always relevant, and she is far more mature than Tom Sawyer or Huck Finn.

37. *Letters*, 616; *St. Louis Post-Dispatch*, Dec. 9, 1928. Twain's marginalia in Sarah Grand, *The Heavenly Twins* (1893) commented impatiently that the "American woman is and has always been a coward and a slave, like her sex everywhere." Before and after *Joan*, of course, he often sketched the weepy, impractical female.

EIGHT: DOLLARLESS DIPLOMACY

1. MTP, letter to Albert Sonnichsen on March 18, 1901.
2. Clippings in MTP of an interview Twain gave in Oct., 1900.
3. MTP, Nbk *32a-l* (1897), 17. Copyright by the Mark Twain Company, 1962.
4. MTP, letter on June 8, 1896. Copyright by the Mark Twain Company, 1962.
5. Smith-Gibson, 665. "Queen Victoria's Jubilee" is reprinted in *Europe and Elsewhere*.
6. MTP, Nbk *32a-l*, 30.
7. Smith-Gibson, 665; "Letters to Satan," *Europe and Elsewhere*.
8. MTP, Paine 46, "The New War Scare"—written in 1899.
9. MTP, Nbk *28b* (1895-96), 39, and letters to H. F. Gordon-Forbes and to Chatto and Windus, both in the fall of 1899; Foner, 229.
10. Letter on Feb. 8, 1898—copy in MTP.
11. MTP, DW 22; Foner, 221-38.
12. *Letters*, 647; MTP, Paine 58; *Speeches*, 168-77.
13. *Letters*, 672-74; MTP, letter to Twichell around May, 1899 and letters to Baronin Bertha Suttner, Feb. 17 and May 7, 1899; *Critic*, N.S. XXX (Nov., 1898), 325.
14. *Kipling Note Book*, VIII, 115-16; *Biog*, 1064; MTP, Documents File for 1899-1900—clippings of many interviews.
15. My account depends finally on the often differing newspaper reports—MTP, Documents File for 1900; a longer speech than the one Twain gave perhaps, but identical in all sentiments, is in MTP, DV 101.
16. Letter in Library of Congress.
17. MTP, DV 359; *Speeches*, 200.
18. MTP, MS addressed to "Mr. Bell"—Moberley Bell of London *Times*.
19. Foner, 285-88, gives generous excerpts from the unpublished MS in MTP.
20. MTP, Documents File for 1902—clipping from New York *Times* of June 6 or 7; Foner, 33-34.
21. Foner, 295-303. Twain's unnoticed dealings with the State Department can be traced through letters to him in late 1905 and through his letter of Feb. 10, 1906, to Thomas L. Barbour—all in MTP.
22. "Brief Biography of the Government"—MS in Berg Coll. See also *Eruption*, 8 and 48.
23. MTP, Paine 27, "M. T. Interviewed"—from 1903 or 1904. Copyright by the Mark Twain Company, 1962.
24. MTP, Nbk 37 (1904), 18; *More Maxims of Mark* (1927), 12.
25. MTP, Nbk *32a-ll* (1897), copyright by the Mark Twain Company, 1962; excerpts from this essay are given in *Notebook*, 332-33.

26. *Speeches*, 126; *Autobiog*, II, 17; *Notebook*, 199, 394-95; *Eruption*, 382.

27. *Notebook*, 295-96; MTP, Nbk *29-II* (1896), 47, and Nbk *32b-II* (1897-99), 54; Foner, 183.

28. MTP, DV 359 and (HNS) Misc MS from Harper's; Foner, 305-07.

29. MTP, "Moral Cowardice," DV 128 (13), and *Notebook*, 332-33. "As Regards Patriotism" appears in *Europe and Elsewhere*.

30. MTP, "The Privilege of the Grave," Paine 249—dated Sept. 18, 1905; also chap. 9 of *The Mysterious Stranger*.

31. MTP, DV 25 and 359 and "Passage from 'Glances at History'" in "Letters from the Earth," 152-55; Winston Churchill, *My Early Life: A Roving Commission* (London, 1930), 375; Foner, 267.

32. MTP, "Flies and the Russians," Paine 28.

33. New York *Herald*, March 30, 1906, p. 7. For fuller detail on the Gorky episode see my article on "Twain, Howells, and the Boston Nihilists," *New Eng. Quar.*, XXXII (Sept., 1959), 365-70.

34. New York *World* and *Sun* and *Tribune* for April 15, 1906.

35. MTP, autobiog dict of Aug. 22, 1907, and DV 109—copy of a letter on Oct. 1, 1908; John D. Carr, *The Life of Sir Arthur Conan Doyle* (N.Y., 1949), 199.

36. Elizabth Wallace, *Mark Twain and the Happy Island* (Chicago, 1913), 139.

37. "Passage from 'Outlines of History' (Supressed paper)," *Sat. Rev. of Lit.*, XIX (Dec. 10, 1938), 4.

38. MTP, "Moral Cowardice," DV 128 (13). Copyright by the Mark Twain Company, 1962.

NINE: THE WHITE KNIGHT

1. MTP, Nbk *28a-I* (1895), 15.

2. *Letters*, 643, 647; *Speeches*, 281-82, 301; *Notebook*, 298; John S. Mayfield, *Mark Twain vs. The Street Railway Co.*; editorials in *Outlook*, LVII (Sept. 1, 1897), 145 and *Harper's Weekly*, XLIV (Dec. 1, 1900), 1,128.

3. MTP, Paine 52 (copyright by the Mark Twain Company, 1962) dated by the paper used and by comments in Nbk *32a-II* (1897), 44 and Nbk *32b-I* (1897), 34-35.

4. Letter dated Nov. 10, 1896 (MTP); *Letters*, 612, 638-39.

5. *Speeches*, 221. The sketch favoring free silver is in MTP, DV 341; Foner, 98-99, summarizes it.

6. Letter to Twain from Rogers on Dec. 26, 1901—Columbia Univ. Lib.; Ida M. Tarbell, *All in the Day's Work* (N.Y., 1939), 211-12; Allan Nevins, *Study in Power: John D. Rockefeller* (N.Y., 1953), II, 339-40.

7. *Speeches*, 251-52. On Twain's investments see letters in MTP from Katharine Harrison, Rogers' secretary, on March 3 and May 20, 1902. When Twain died he owned $87,000 worth of stock in Utah Consolidated Mining Company; Thomas Lawson, *Frenzied Finance* (N.Y., 1906), 261-80, gives the grisly details on how Rogers raided this corporation.

8. Dated Oct. 4, 1907—printed in Smith-Gibson, 827; "ABC Lesson," *Eruption*, 105-06; "Something about Standard Oil," MTP, DV 257.

9. *Eruption*, 41-42; MTP, autobiog dict of Dec. 12, 1907.

10. New York *Herald*, Nov. 12, 1905. There was much editorial response, as in "Crumbling of Party Lines," *Literary Digest*, XXXI (Dec. 2, 1905), 816-17. The "Skeleton Plan" was written around 1901.

11. *Biog*, 1146; Foner, 100; Johnson, 74; MTP, Nbk *34* (1901), 12-15; Paul Fatout, *Mark Twain on the Lecture Circuit* (Bloomington, Ind., 1960), 277.

12. *Acorn*, Oct. 31, 1903; MTP, Nbk *36* (1903), 27; MTP, DV 345, "The Stupendous Procession." The *Acorn* noted that Twain also spoke at a meeting in 1902.

13. *Harper's Weekly*, XLIX (Aug. 26, 1905), 1238; MTP, HNS—photostat of letter to R. W. Gilder on Aug. 15 and of telegram on Nov. 3, 1905. Twain's rebuke to Twichell (*Letters*, 762-63) only damns machine politics.

14. *Collier's*, XXXV (Sept. 2, 1905), 17. Twain's authorship is indicated in Willis F. Johnson, *George Harvey* (Boston, 1929), 81. For similar ideas see *Speeches*, 276-80.

15. Foner, 220-21; MTP, copies of letters to Frank Bliss on Aug. 29 and Sept. 8, 1901.

16. F. Severance Johnson, *Capitol Jokes of the Legislative Session of 1901* (Albany, 1901), 49-56; *Speeches*, 232-34; *Letters*, 691.

17. MTP, DW 17—an undated typescript copy of the manuscript, which I have not seen; also *What Is Man?*, chap. 3, and *Speeches* (1910 ed.), 225-27.

18. Upton Sinclair, *Mammonart* (Pasadena, 1925), 328; *Collier's*, XXXVII (Sept. 22, 1906), 16-17.

19. *Biog*, 1194. Old-style Liberals who survived past 1890, like R. R. Bowker or Edward Atkinson, supported most of the same reforms that Twain did; Atkinson became an anti-imperialist and favored female suffrage while protesting against lynching and the patent medi-

cine rackets. By the time Twain signed a petition favoring the initiative and referendum, good Republicans such as Charles Evans Hughes were openly favorable too.

20. MTP, Paine 136 ("An Imaginary Interview").

21. MTP, letters on Dec. 29, 1908, and March 2, 1909.

22. Nbk *38* (1905), 4; DV 128 (11); Paine 249, "The Privilege of the Grave"—all in MTP.

23. MTP, autobiog dict of Nov. 12, 1908; *Twainian*, XVI (Jan.-Feb., 1957), 2—reminiscences by one of the burglars, who was obviously a glib spirit but was writing fairly soon after the event; Caroline Harnsperger, *Mark Twain, Family Man* (N.Y., 1960), 247.

24. In Berg Coll. and recopied by Twain in a letter to Twichell on Jan. 26, 1907 (Yale Coll. of Amer. Lit.).

25. *Letters*, 719.

26. MTP, DV 374—Paine firmly ascribes this typescript of forty-eight pages to 1909.

27. *Harper's Weekly*, XLIX (Nov. 4, 1905), 1606.

28. *Extracts from the Minutes and Report of the Robert Fulton Monument Association*, 75; *Speeches*, 360; *Eruption*, 52.

TEN: CONCLUSION

[1] From letter printed in Elizabeth Wallace, *Mark Twain and the Happy Island*, 138.

[2] *Mark Twain's America*, 267-68, and "Introduction," *Portable Mark Twain*, 13. Fifty years plus, instead of forty, is closer to the truth.

Index

This index is centered on Twain. A heading such as "labor unions" or "nationalism" refers primarily to his opinions on that subject. Books, stories, and essays by Twain also are integrated with the main alphabetical listing.